INLABORATUS ET FACILIS

MNEMOSYNE

BIBLIOTHECA CLASSICA BATAVA

COLLEGERUNT

W. DEN BOER · W.J. VERDENIUS · R.E.H. WESTENDORP BOERMA

BIBLIOTHECAE FASCICULOS EDENDOS CURAVIT

W.J. VERDENIUS, HOMERUSLAAN 53, ZEIST

SUPPLEMENTUM TRICESIMUM OCTAVUM

B.L. HIJMANS Jr.

INLABORATUS ET FACILIS

ASPECTS OF STRUCTURE IN SOME LETTERS OF SENECA

LUGDUNI BATAVORUM E.J. BRILL MCMLXXVI

INLABORATUS ET FACILIS

ASPECTS OF STRUCTURE IN SOME LETTERS OF SENECA

BY

B. L. HIJMANS Jr.

LUGDUNI BATAVORUM E.J. BRILL MCMLXXVI

Published with financial support from the Netherlands Organization
for the Advencement of Pure Research (Z.W.O.)

ISBN 90 04 04474 4

PRINTED IN BELGIUM

MARION VAN ASSENDELFT
UXORI DILECTAE
LITTERIS
DEDITAE ET IPSI
HUNC LIBELLUM DO DICO

CONTENTS

This little book represents a side track: while working on Seneca's dialogues I found I knew too little about various aspects of Seneca's style, and the information I sought was not easily obtainable from the work of others. I do not pretend to have treated those aspects exhaustively, however. I wish to express my gratitude to the editors of Mnemosyne for accepting the resulting manuscript as volume 38 in their series of Supplements. Thanks, too, are due to Professor R.E.H. Westendorp Boerma for his criticism and suggestions.

SYMBOLS USED (see also p. 107):

$$1 \qquad \overset{\alpha \ \beta \ \gamma \ \delta \ \epsilon}{- \ \cup \ - \ - \ \sim}$$

$$11 \qquad - \ - \ - \ - \ \sim$$

$$1^{\text{tr}} \qquad - \ \cup\cup \ - \ - \ \sim$$

$$1^{1} \qquad \cup\cup\cup \ - \ - \ \sim$$

$$1^{2} \qquad - \ \cup \ \cup\cup \ - \ \sim$$

$$1^{3} \qquad - \ \cup \ - \ \cup\cup \ \sim$$

$$2 \qquad \overset{\alpha \ \beta \ \gamma \ \delta \ \epsilon \ \zeta}{- \ \cup \ - \ - \ \cup \ \sim}$$

resolutions etc. as with 1

$$3 \qquad \overset{\alpha \ \beta \ \gamma \ \delta \ \epsilon \ \zeta \ \eta}{. \ . \ . \ - \ \cup \ - \ \sim}$$

resolutions etc. as with 1

$$4 \ | \qquad \overset{\alpha \ \beta \ \gamma \ \delta \ \epsilon}{- \ \cup \ - \ \cup \ \sim}$$

resolutions etc. as with 1

The *anceps* has not been marked.

<u>44αδ</u> strength of pause level 5			
<u>44 αδ</u>	–	– –	– 4
<u>44 αδ</u>	–	– –	– 3
<u>44 αδ</u>	–	– –	– 2
44 αδ	–	– –	– 1

Certain brief commata have rhythms denoted by letters a, b, c etc. A complete list occurs on p. 113.

Cl: single colon or comma
G: Group
P: Period
S: Complex Sentence

For the critical apparatus Reynolds' (OCT) symbols have been adopted.

INTRODUCTION

> Veneror itaque inventa sapientiae inventoresque; adire tamquam multorum hereditatem iuvat. Mihi ista adquisita, mihi laborata sunt. Sed agamus bonum patrem familiae, *faciamus ampliora* quae accepimus; *maior* ista hereditas a me ad posteros transeat. Multum adhuc restat operis multumque restabit, nec ulli nato post mille saecula praecludetur occasio *aliquid* adhuc *adiciendi*. Sed etiam si omnia a veteribus inventa sunt, hoc semper novum erit, *usus* et inventorum ab aliis *scientia* ac *dispositio*. Puta relicta nobis medicamenta quibus sanarentur oculi: non opus est mihi alia quaerere, sed haec tamen morbis et temporibus *aptanda* sunt.

Seneca's claim in *ep.* 64.7 f. is unmistakable. His work is to be seen under the two aspects of amplification and disposition. In letter 80 he repeats the claim that he adds to received doctrine if he is so inclined (1: *permitto mihi et invenire aliquid et mutare et relinquere*). It should be noted that the terminology used for adding in both cases also has its well-known rhetorical connotation; and though it is reasonably obvious that Seneca is thinking of amplification in a slightly wider sense than the strictly technical tools described by Quintilian (*Inst.* 8.4.3), it is hardly likely that he excludes the results of an application of these techniques from his thought. Similarly *invenire* is certainly used of *res novae*, but these *res* may refer as well to new examples and applications as to new doctrine, indeed are more likely to do so.[1] This question however, fascinating as it is, will not engage us in the present little book, but rather the *dispositio* as it appears to be intended in the quotation: the proper application of the precepts of philosophy to people and circumstances. There is no doubt whatever that here, too, content and form are intertwined inextricably and that for instance the sequence of the arguments used would be felt to be part of the *dispositio*: the medical metaphor should not cause us to forget that arguments *are* the moralist's medicine.[2]

---

[1] For *res novae* cf. *N.Q.* 7.25.4. and L. Edelstein, *The Idea of Progress in Classical Antiquity*, Baltimore, Johns Hopkins Press 1967, p. 168 ff. The notion of the progressive elucidation of the unknown is hardly the only content referred to in the remarks on addition of our passage.

[2] See also Maurach's discussion of *dispositio* (Der Bau, p. 131).

The *recte disponendi scientia* figures large in rhetorical education (see e.g. Quint. *Inst.* 8 pr. 1) and Seneca so obviously has made use of it that in recent years much attention has been paid to the structure of his letters. Not only is it, today, obvious to all that Seneca composed his letters with great care, it has also been claimed with considerable force that the structure of the *corpus* was far from haphazard.[3] The present study is not meant to oppose or contradict those valuable observations. It claims, however, that the examination of all structural elements of Seneca's prose has not yet been completed. In support of this claim I shall try to show that a number of structural and formal aspects occur in close interplay with the subject matter treated in seven letters.[4] The letters have been chosen from various parts of the corpus: the phenomena observed are not confined to a small interconnected group. Each of the letters was chosen originally to see whether the pattern observed in letter 41 was accidental. The fact that similar concentric arrangements occur elsewhere (and not only in five of the seven letters treated here) argues careful composition. More curious than the Chinese Box arrangement is the integration of one type of clausula with the main subject matter of the letter in which it occurs. The use made of the colometric tool is less startling, but sufficiently marked to be worthy of note.

In order to put the materials in a convenient form, a text has been prepared in which each colon is numbered and printed separately, is provided with scansion marks, in which the clausula is marked by a symbol, the syllables are counted, and the groups of cola are marked as period (P), non-periodic sentence (S) and loose grouping (G) or combinations of these. In presenting a text it is not my intention to do any textual criticism in the strict sense of the word. Reynolds' text is perfectly satisfactory for the purposes I have in mind.[5] I have, however, noted all variants that might, by any stretch of the imagination, be of interest in our context of structure. Finally, the text section

---

[3] See the Bibliography, in particular the works of Cancik and Maurach.

[4] The search for structural elements has not been exhaustive. Numerous other structural principles will doubtless be found. An excellent example of detection of several such principles in a small letter is found in M. v. Albrecht, *Horazens Brief an Albius. Versuch einer metrischen Analyse und Interpretation.* RhM. 114, 1971 pp. 193-209. (One cannot follow him in every detail: e.g. to speak of percentages when dealing with so small a piece of material (p. 199 and n. 12) is useless).

[5] I do not think it necessary to change punctuation (as Thraede does, *Grundzüge*, p. 65 note 90), nor am I prepared to give paragraphing quite as important a place as

may be used as an index: I have attempted to add full references to the various chapters of the discussion. These references have not been repeated in the general index at the end of the book.

Neither of the two main aspects of this study have received much attention in the past. Most work on Seneca's prose rhythm was intended to establish the fact that his prose is rhythmical, but once that fact had been established the only use made of it has been in the area of textual criticism. One exception is Zander's huge work in which he attempts to show that in Seneca, too, a system of rhythmic responsions may be found. E. Norden's[6] important remark concerning punctuation (ich..interpungiere in den Proben aus Seneca und Plinius nicht in unserer Manier, sondern in antiker, d.h. nach dem Rhythmus) has been elaborated and superseded in recent colometric studies, an area in which E. Fraenkel is our chief guide. However, another remark by Norden, to the effect that the rhythms have a descriptive quality, has remained without elaboration. The present study indeed suggests a descriptive quality for some closing rhythms, but this is almost certainly not the type that Norden had in mind.[7] Nor have I been able to discover any ancient theoretical statements that might be applicable to the descriptive aspect I have in mind, and thus mine must remain a suggestion based on a statistical argument.

Geometric patterns in Seneca's prose have, to my knowledge, not been studied as such. Karlhans Abel refers to frames in *Dial.* 2 (p. 143), *Dial.* 11 (pp. 75, 83), *Tableautechnik* in *Dial.* 12 (p. 68). He also notes a case of 'Omphaloskomposition' in *Dial.* 11 (p. 85) and in general speaks of Seneca's 'Vorliebe für rahmende Komposition' in the dialogues (p. 83). M. Lausberg, *Untersuchungen zu Senecas Fragmenten*, Berlin, W. de Gruyter, 1970, p. 61, speaks of ring composition in connection with Seneca's *Exhortationes*.

The present study is in neither area intended to be exhaustive: it attempts no more than to suggest a fruitful field of study. I am fully aware, however, of the hypothetical character of part of the very

---

Maurach does (*Bau* p. 11 ff.). The important thing is to try to re-create the total impact of structure/content that presumably enabled the ancient reader to interpret his much less explicit text correctly. More is to be expected from an awareness of rhythm and other elements of structure than of the always somewhat vague distinctions between . : ; and , ! The necessary indications of what Maurach calls *Gliederung* should — as admittedly he tries to do, often successfully — be found in the text.

[6] E. Norden, *Die Antike Kunstprosa*, 310ff.; 941f.

[7] Cf. e.g. Cic. *Orator* 212: *cursum contentiones magis requirunt, expositiones rerum tarditatem.*

material on which my conclusions are based: the margin of uncertainty of necessity remains rather large in matters colometric (possibly as much as 10%). For that reason I present this little book not so much as the result of completed research, but rather as the starting point for a discussion—which indeed I hope it will engender.

TEXT

LETTER 1

§1	1	GS	7	⌣⌣ − − − −− Ita fac, mi Lucili	11 αβγ
	2		8	− ⌣ − − ⌣ − vindica te tibi, et tempus	1 βδ
	3		9	⌣ ⌣ − − −⌣− − quod adhuc aut auferebatur	1 α
	4		7	− − ⌣⌣− − aut subripiebatur	1ᵗʳ α
	5		5	− − ⌣ − aut excidebat	3 γδ
	6		5	−⌣ — − collige et serva.	1 αδ
	7	G	10	− − − ⌣ — − − − — − Persuade tibi hoc sic esse ut scribo:	11 βδ
	8		11	— − − ⌣ —⌣⌣ − − − quaedam tempora eripiuntur nobis,	33 αζ
	9		6	− − − − quaedam subducuntur,	33 βδ
	10		4	− — ⌣ quaedam effluunt.	m
	11	P	10	− − ⌣ ⌣ ⌣ ⌣ − − − Turpissima tamen est iactura,	33 βδε
	12		8	− − ⌣ ⌣ − ⌣− quae per neglegentiam fit.	3 βη
	13	G	10	− − ⌣⌣⌣ − − − ⌣ Et si volueris adtendere	2¹ γ
	14		13	− ⌣ − − —⌣ − ⌣⌣ − ⌣ magna pars vitae elabitur male agentibus	4ᵗʳ β
	15		8	−⌣ ⌣ ⌣⌣ ⌣ − ⌣ maxima nihil agentibus,	4¹ β

---

14 magna ς, maxima ω.
15 maxima ς, magna ω.

---

§1 groups of cola: 6 (2+3+1), 4 (1+3), 2, 4 (1+3).

	16		10	tota vita aliud agentibus.	4^1 β
§2	17	S	5	Quem mihi dabis	4 αβδ
	18		11	qui aliquod pretium tempori ponat,	1 αδ
	19		5	qui diem aestimet	4 β
	20		11	qui intellegat se cotidie mori?	4 δ
	21	PG	7	In hoc enim fallimur	2 αβδ
	22		7	quod mortem prospicimus:	33^2 βδ
	23		9	magna pars eius iam praeterit;	22 αγδ
	24		10	quidquid aetatis retro est mors tenet.	2 βδε
	25	PG	7	Fac ergo mi Lucili	11 βγ
	26		7	quod facere te scribis,	1^1 αβγ
	27		8	omnes horas complectere;	22 αγ
	28	P	13	sic fiet ut minus ex crastino pendeas,	2 αδ
	29		9	si hodierno manum inieceris.	2 β
	30	P	9	Dum differtur vita transcurrit.	1 αγ

---

§2 groups of cola: 4 (1+3), 4 (2+2), 3 (2+1), 3.
30: a *sententia* in which *vita* serves to link the two verbs, hence no incision after *differtur*[1].

16: p. 126
17-20: p. 98
17: p. 112; 118
18: p. 109; 117; 135, n. 20
19: p. 127; 135, n. 20
29: p. 127
21: p. 92, n. 19

24: p. 128; 135, n. 20
25-27: p. 92, n. 19
26: p. 134
27: p. 134; 135, n. 20
28: p. 128
29: p. 109; 128; 135; 135, n. 20
30: p. 118

---

[1] There is a parallelism between cola 21-24 and 25-29, the second set topping off the first by replacing the factual statement of 24 by the advice in 28-29. Their content is repeated in chiastic order in the sententious statement of colon 30.

§3 31 GS 10 $\quad\overline{\quad}\ \underset{\smile}{\overline{\smile\smile}}\ \underline{\quad\quad}\ \smile\ \smile\underline{\smile}$
Omnia, Lucili, aliena sunt, $\qquad$ 4^{tr} ε

32 $\quad$ 6 $\quad$ $\overline{\quad}\ \overline{\quad}\ \overline{\quad}\ \overline{\quad}\ \overline{\quad}\ \overline{\quad}$
tempus tantum nostrum est; $\qquad$ 33 βδζ

33 $\quad$ 25 $\quad$ $\smile\ \overline{\smile\smile}\ \underline{\quad\quad}\ \smile\smile\ \smile\ \smile\underline{\smile}\ \overline{\quad}\ \overline{\quad}\ \smile\ \overline{\quad}$
in huius rei unius fugacis ac lubricae

$\overline{\quad}\ \overline{\quad}\ \overline{\smile}\underline{\smile}\ \overline{\quad}\ \overline{\quad}\smile\smile\ \overline{\quad}\ \overline{\quad}$
possessionem natura nos misit, $\qquad$ 1 γδ

34 $\quad$ 8 $\quad$ $\overline{\quad}\ \overline{\quad}\ \overline{\smile}\underline{\quad}\ \overline{\quad}\ \overline{\quad}\ \smile$
ex qua expellit quicumque vult. $\qquad$ 2² γζ

35 P 11 $\quad$ $\overline{\quad}\ \overline{\quad}\ \overline{\quad}\ \overline{\quad}\underset{\smile\smile\smile}{}\ \overline{\quad}\ \overline{\smile\smile}$
Et tanta stultitia mortalium est $\qquad$ 2¹ γ

36 $\quad$ 10 $\quad$ $\overline{\quad}\ \overline{\quad}\ \smile\smile\ \overline{\quad\quad}\ \underline{\quad}\smile\smile\ \smile$
ut quae minima et vilissima sunt, $\qquad$ 11³ βε

37 $\quad$ 8 $\quad$ $\overline{\quad}\ \overline{\quad}\ \smile\ \smile\ \smile\underset{\smile\smile}{\overline{\quad}}$
certe reparabilia, $\qquad$ 1^{tr+3} β

38 $\quad$ 6 $\quad$ $\overline{\quad}\ \smile\underline{\quad}\ \smile$
imputari sibi $\qquad$ 2 αε

39 $\quad$ 5 $\quad$ $\overline{\quad\quad}\ \smile\ \overline{\quad}\ \overline{\quad}$
cum impetravere $\qquad$ 1 s¹

40 $\quad$ 4 $\quad$ $\underset{\smile\smile\smile}{\overline{\quad}}$
patiantur, $\qquad$ 1

41 $\quad$ 11 $\quad$ $\overline{\quad}\ \smile\ \overline{\quad}\smile\ \overline{\quad}\ \overline{\quad}\ \overline{\quad}\ \overline{\quad}\ \overline{\quad}$
nemo se iudicet quicquam debere $\qquad$ 11 αγ

42 $\quad$ 6 $\quad$ $\overline{\quad}\ \overline{\quad}\ \smile\ \overline{\quad}\ \overline{\quad}$
qui tempus accepit, $\qquad$ 1 αγ

43 $\quad$ 5 $\quad$ $\overline{\quad\quad}\ \smile\ \overline{\quad\quad}\ \overline{\quad}$
cum interim hoc unum est $\qquad$ 1 αδ

44 $\quad$ 11 $\quad$ $\overline{\quad}\ \overline{\quad}\ \overline{\quad}\ \smile\ \overline{\quad}\ \smile\smile\ \overline{\quad}\ \smile$
quod ne gratus quidem potest reddere. $\qquad$ 2 βδ

---

32 tantum] tamen p

---

§3 groups of cola: 2, 2, 10 (1+2+3+2+2).

31: p. 127
32: p. 135, n. 20; 136
33: p. 89; 118
35-40: p. 96, n. 27
36: p. 170
38: p. 112

39: p. 112
41: p. 135, n. 20
41-44: p. 98
42: p. 118; 35, n. 20
43: p. 118
44: p. 135, n. 20

---

[1] It is also possible to read colon 39 with hiatus. Cf. K. Müller, *Curtius* p. 769.
Cf. however *HF* 1259 $\smile\overline{\quad}\ \smile\ \smile\smile\ \overline{\quad}\ \overline{\quad}\ \smile\ \overline{\quad\quad}\ \underline{\quad}\smile\smile$ *morerque nihil est: cuncta iam amisi bona.*

§4   45   ?S   8   Interrogabis fortasse   11 γ

     46   6   quid ego faciam 3^{1+2} δδ^{1}εζ

     47   8   qui tibi ista praecipio. 1^3 γ

     48   G   7   Fatebor ingenue: 1^3 γ

     49   15   quod apud luxuriosum sed diligentem evenit,   2α

     50   10   ratio mihi constat inpensae.   1 αγ

     51   G   10   Non possum dicere nihil perdere, 2^2 γδ

     52   12   sed quid perdam et quare et quemadmodum

              dicam;   1 δ

     53   10   causas paupertatis meae reddam.   1 βδ

     54   G   23   Sed evenit mihi quod plerisque non suo

              vitio ad inopiam redactis: 3 αε

     55   5   omnes ignoscunt,   11 αγ

     56   5   nemo succurrit.   1 αγ

§5   57   GS   3   Quid ergo est?   f.

---

51 dicere ω] <me> dicere Hense, dicere <me> L²

---

§4 groups of cola: 3, 3, 3, 3.

§5 groups of cola: 1, 4 (2+2), 3.

54: One may think of an expanded dative in *plerisque...redactis* and thus read two cola; on the other hand those two are so closely linked by *evenit* that I am not convinced we need to separate them.

45-47: p. 91; 92, n. 1; 98

48-50: p. 98

49: p. 137

50: p. 118; 135, n. 20

51: p. 135, n. 20; 136

51-53: p. 92, n. 19; 98

52: p. 118

53: p. 117; 136

54: p. 89; 92; 136

55-56: p. 89; 90; 92, n. 19; 137

56: p. 112

57-59: p. 96, n. 26

58		6	— ᴗ — _ ᴗ Non puto pauperem	2 αβδ
59		11	— _ ᴗ — _ ᴗ ᴗ ᴗ — ᴗ cui quantulumcumque superest sat est;	2² βεζ
60	G	9	— ᴗ — _ — _ _ ᴗ tu tamen malo serves tua, et	22 αγε ¹
61		8	ᴗ _ — — ᴗ — ᴗ ᴗ bono tempore incipies.	1³ α
62		9	— _ — _ _ᴗ — _ Nam ut visum est maioribus nostris,	1 δ
63		9	— ᴗ — ᴗ —ᴗ— _ — _ «sera parsimonia in fundo est»;	1 δ
64		17	— ᴗ — _ — ᴗ ᴗ ᴗ — _ — _ non enim tantum minimum in imo sed	
			— ᴗ — ᴗ ᴗ pessimum remanet.	1³ δ
65	Cl	2	ᴗ— Vale.	a

60-64: There may be disagreement over the question whether or not these cola are to
be counted as one or two G. If the latter, one still has to notice the effect of four
cola of equal length that cross over the dividing line.

58: p. 112   63: p. 118
60-63: p. 92, n. 19; 94f.   64: p. 85, n. 8; 95
62-64: p. 95

---

¹ For suspended *et* see the note on 41.24 ff.

LETTER 26

§1	1	P	7	Modo dicebam tibi	44 αδ
	2		10	in conspectu esse me senectutis:	1 αβ
	3		4	iam vereor	k
	4		11	ne senectutem post me reliquerim.	4 αβ
	5	P	6	Aliud iam his annis,	1 βγδ [1]
	6		5	certe huic corpori	44 αγ
	7		7	vocabulum convenit,	2 δ
	8		11	quoniam quidem senectus lassae aetatis,	33 αδ
	9		6	non fractae nomen est:	44 αγε
	10	Cl	16	inter decrepitos me numera et extrema	
				tangentis.	1 γ
§2	11	GS	10	Gratias tamen mihi apud te ago:	1[tr] βδ
	12		13	non sentio in animo aetatis iniuriam,	4[tr] γ

---

2 me L²γ, meae pα, me meae *Beltrami*

---

§1 groups of cola: 4 (2+2), 6 (3+2)+1
§2 groups of cola: 3 (1+2), 5 (1, 4 (2+2)), 2
10: One may think here of two cola with a suspended et (below p. 86), but the rhythm
$\_\cup\cup\_\_\cup\cup\_$ militates against the division.

1-4: p. 92, n. 19   8: p. 118; p. 141; p. 142
1: p. 127   9: p. 127; 141; 142
2: p. 118   10: p. 118
4: p. 118; 127   11: p. 109
6: p. 127   12: p. 127

---

[1] Cf. p. 9 n. 1.

13   7   ‾ ‿ ‾ ‿ ‾ ‿
              cum sentiam_in corpore.   2 αδ

14 G   18   ‾ ᴗᴗ ‿ ‿ ‾ ᴗ ‾ ᴗᴗ
              Tantum vitia_et vitiorum ministeria

                   ᴗ ᴗ‾
                   senuerunt: 1¹⁺² γ

15   18   ᴗᴗ ᴗᴗ ᴗ ‾ ‾ ‾ ‾ ‾ ‾ ‾ ᴗ‾ ᴗ
              viget animus et gaudet non multum sibi_esse

                   ‾ ‾ ᴗ
                   cum corpore;   2 γδ

16   11   ‾ ‾ ‾ ᴗ ᴗ‾ ᴗ‾ ᴗ ᴗ
              magnam partem_oneris sui posuit.   1³ βδ

17   18   ‾ ‾ ᴗ ‾ ‾ᴗ ᴗ‾ ‾ ‾ ‾ ᴗ‾ ‾
              Exultat et mihi facit controversiam de

                   ᴗ ‾ ‾
                   senectute: 1 αβ

18   9   ‾ ‾ ᴗᴗ ‾ ‾ ‾ ‾ ᴗ
              hunc ait esse florem suum.   22 αγε

19 G   5   ‾ ‾ ᴗ ‾
              Credamus illi: 3 γζ

20   6   ᴗ ‾ ᴗ‾ ‾
              bono suo_utatur.   1 β

§3 21 S 10 ‾ ‾ ‾ᴗ ‾ᴗ‾ ‾ ᴗ
              Ire_in cogitationem iubet   2 ε

22   5   ‾ ‾ ᴗ ᴗ
              et dispicere   n

23   22   ᴗ ‾ ‾ ‾ ‾ ‾ᴗ‾ ‾ ᴗ ‾ ᴗ‾
              quid ex hac tranquillitate_ac modestia

                   ‾ ‾ ᴗᴗ‾ᴗ ‾ ‾ ᴗ
                   morum sapientiae debeam,   2 δ

24   4   ᴗ ‾ ‾
              quid aetati,   j

25   9   ‾ ‾ᴗ ‾ ᴗ ‾ ᴗᴗ
              et diligenter excutere   1³ γ

26   7   ‾ ‾ ‾ ‾ ‾ ᴗ ᴗ
              quae non possim facere,   33² αβδ

---

21 iubet p²L¹M², iubeat Q, iubat p¹v¹M¹, iuvat L²v² vulg.

---

§3 groups of cola: 9 (2+2+1+2+2), 3 (2+1)

13: p. 112   20: p. 119; 141
14: p. 118; 167   21-32: p. 129; 140
15: p. 119; 128; 141   21-24: p. 92, n. 19
15-11: p. 92, n. 19   23: p. 89
17: p. 118; 141   25-27: p. 96, n. 27
19-20: p. 91; 92, n. 19

27	3	quae nolim,	e
28	11	proinde habiturus atque si nolim	1 αγδ
29	9	quidquid non posse me gaudeo:	2 αγδ
30	5	quae enim querela est,	3 γε
31	5	quod incommodum,	p
32	13	si quidquid debebat desinere defecit?	1¹ γ

§4

33 S	6	'Incommodum summum est'	1 δ
34	2	inquis	b
35	7	'minui et deperire et,	3 αδ
36	6	ut proprie dicam,	3¹ γδζ
37	4	liquescere.	i
38 G	13	Non enim subito inpulsi ac prostrati	
		sumus:	22 βε
39	3	carpimur,	d
40	14	singuli dies aliquid subtrahunt viribus.'	2 αδ

28 *Kronenberg*, prodesse habiturus adqui ω
32 debebat *Fickert*, debeat ω
35 et (*prius*) *om.* p

§4 groups of cola: 5 (1+1+3), 3, 7 (3+4), 4 (1+2+1)
33 ff.: The rationale for reading *inquis* as a separate colon (unlike 26.52) lies in the relative independence of the preceding and subsequent cola. *Minui et deperire* (parenthesis) *liquescere* certainly may be regarded as an expanded subject. Whether the parenthesis should be seen as a separate colon is a further question: the fact that we do not have the usual formula here (as at 122.12), but an emphatic *proprie*, suggests that we should answer that question in the affirmative.

27: p. 89
28: p. 119
29-31: p. 95, n. 24
30: p. 109
33: p. 119

35: p. 86
36: p. 112
38 ff.: p. 92, n. 19
39: p. 91; 128

‾ ‿ ‾‿‿ ‾ ‿‿‿
41 P   14   Ecquis exitus est melior quam in finem

‿
suum   22 βγε

‾ ‾ ‾ ‾ ‾
42   6   natura solvente   11 γ

‾ ‾
43   3   dilabi?   e̲

‾ ‿‿‿ ‾ ‿‿‾ ‿
44 P   9   non quia aliquid mali ictus <est>   4 βε

‿ ‾ ‾‾ ‿ ‾ ‾ ‿ ‾
45   11   et e vita repentinus excessus,   1 γ

‾ ‿‿ ‾‿ ‾ ‾ ‿
46   9   sed quia lenis haec est via,   2 αγδε

‾ ‾ ‾
47   3   subduci.   e̲

‿ ‾ ‾
48 S   4   Ego certe,   j̲

‿‿ ‾ ‿‾ ‿ ‾ ‿‾ ‾
49   11   velut appropinquet experimentum   1 α

‿ ‾‿ ‾‾‾ ‾ ‾ ‿‾ ‾ ‿‿
50   22   et ille laturus sententiam de omnibus

‾ ‾ ‿‾ ‿‾ ‾ ‿
annis meis dies venerit,   2 βδ

‿‿ ‾ ‾ ‾ ‿ ‾ ‿
51   8   ita me observo et adloquor: 4 γ

‿‿ ‾ ‾ ‿
§5 52 G   6   'nihil est' inquam 'adhuc   44¹ αβγ

‿ ‾ ‾‿ ‾ ‾ ‾ ‾ ‿ ‿‿
53   12   quod aut rebus aut verbis exhibuimus;   3² αβδ

‿‿ ‾ ‾ ‾ ‾ ‿‿ ‾ ‿ ‿ ‿
54   15   levia sunt ista et fallacia pignora animi 3² δ

---

43 dilabi L², delabi ω
44 <est> *add.* Beltrami, est ictus ς, sit ictus P², Préchac, *om.* ω *fort. recte.*

---

§5 groups of cola: 7 (2+3+2), 6 (1+2+1+2)
54: There is no reason to divide the colon after *ista.*

$$\underline{}\,\underline{}\quad\underline{}\quad\cup\underline{}\cup\,\underline{}\,\underline{}\cup\cup$$

55   11   multisque involuta lenociniis : $\underline{2\,\gamma(?\,^1)}$

$$\underline{}\quad\underline{}\,\underline{}\cup$$

56 (P) 5   quid profecerim   44 αβ

$$\underline{}\,\underline{}\quad\underline{}\cup\underline{}\,\underline{}$$

57   7   morti crediturus sum. $\underline{1\ \alpha\varepsilon}$

$$\underline{}\quad\cup\,\cup\quad\cup\,\cup\,\cup\quad\underline{}\quad\underline{}\cup\,\cup\,\underline{}\,\underline{}$$

58 S   14   Non timide itaque componor ad illum

$$\cup$$

              diem 2^{tr} βγε

$$\underline{}\,\cup\quad\underline{}\quad\cup\,\underline{}\,\underline{}\,\underline{}$$

59   9   quo remotis strophis ac fucis   cr.+mol.

$$\underline{}\quad\underline{}\,\underline{}\cup\underline{}\,\underline{}\,\underline{}$$

60   8   de me iudicaturus sum,   cr.+mol.

$$\cup\,\underline{}\quad\cup\,\underline{}\,\underline{}\cup\underline{}\quad\underline{}\,\cup$$

61   11   utrum loquar fortia an sentiam, $\underline{2\ \alpha\delta}$

$$\underline{}\quad\underline{}\quad\cup\quad\cup\underline{}\cup\underline{}\quad\cup\cup\cup\,\underline{}\quad\underline{}$$

62   13   numquid simulatio fuerit et mimus $1^1\ \alpha\gamma\delta$

$$\underline{}\quad\underline{}\quad\underline{}\quad\cup\,\underline{}\,\underline{}\,\underline{}\quad\underline{}\,\underline{}\underline{}$$

63   18   quidquid contra fortunam iactavi

$$\underline{}\,\underline{}\,\underline{}\quad\underline{}\,\cup\,\underline{}\cup$$

              verborum contumacium. $\underline{4\ \alpha}$

$$\cup\,\cup\,\underline{}\underline{}\,\cup\,\underline{}\cup\underline{}\quad\cup\quad\cup$$

§6 64 G 11   Remove existimationem hominum : $\underline{1^3\ s}$

$$\cup\cup\cup\quad\underline{}\quad\cup$$

65   7   dubia semper est 4^1 αγε

$$\cup\,\underline{}\quad\underline{}\quad\underline{}\quad\underline{}\quad\cup\quad\underline{}\cup\cup$$

66   10   et in partem utramque dividitur. $\underline{1^3\ \gamma}$

$$\cup\quad\cup\,\underline{}\quad\cup\cup\cup\quad\underline{}\,\underline{}\,\underline{}\,\underline{}\quad\underline{}\,\underline{}$$

67   13   Remove studia tota vita tractata :   11 αγ

$$\underline{}\quad\underline{}\,\underline{}\quad\underline{}\,\underline{}\,\cup\underline{}\underline{}$$

68   9   mors de te pronuntiatura est. $\underline{1\ s}$

$$\cup\cup\,\underline{}$$

69 G   4   Ita dico : $\underline{1}$

---

§6 groups of cola: 3 (1+3), 2, 6 (1+3+1+1), 3 (1+2), 2

55: p. 140; 171	63: p. 127
56: p. 112; 127	64ff.: p. 140
57: p. 119	64: p. 127
58: p. 119	65: p. 91
59: p. 140	66: p. 127
60: p. 109	68: p. 119

---

[1] Possibly a case of synizesis? See however W. Sidney Allen, *Accent and rhythm*, p. 146, who shows that in cases of synizesis the preceding short syllable tends to be lengthened. If this is the case here we have another instance of cr.+mol.

		— ‿ —‿— — — ‿ —‿ — ‿ ‿ ‿	
70	15	disputationes et litterata colloquia	1^3 γ
		‿ — — — — ‿‿— ‿— — ‿ — —	
71	15	et ex praeceptis sapientium verba collecta	1 αγ
		‿ — ‿ — — —	
72	6	et eruditus sermo	cr. + mol.
		— — ‿ — — — — ‿ ‿‿	
73	11	non ostendunt verum robur animi;	3^2 βδζ
		— ‿ —— —‿ ‿ ‿— ‿ —‿ —	
74	15	est enim‿oratio‿etiam timidissimis audax.	1 δ
		‿ — ‿	
75 P	4	Quid egeris	i
		— — — —	
76	5	tunc apparebit	11 αβ
		‿‿ ‿ ‿	
77	4	cum‿animam‿ages.	g
		— ‿‿— — ‿‿—	
78 P	9	Accipio condicionem,	3^{tr} δ
		— ‿ — — — —‿‿	
79	9	non reformido iudicium.	11^3 γ
§7	80 G	5	— — — ‿ Haec mecum loquor,	44 αβδ
		— — — ‿ ‿ — ‿ — — ‿	
81	11	sed tecum quoque me locutum puta.	2 αβε
		‿ ‿ ‿‿	
82 G	5	Iuvenior es:	q
		‿ —	
83	3	quid refert?	f
		— — ‿ ‿— ‿ —	
84	8	non dinumerantur anni.	3 ζ
		— —	
85 SG	3	Incertum‿est	e
		— ‿— — — — —	
86	8	quo loco te mors expectet;	11 αβγ

---

§7 groups of cola: 2, 2, 1, 3 (2+1)
76-77: If these two cola are read as one, the clausula would be of type 11^3; however, the combination of pun and symmetry argues separate commata.

70: p. 92, n. 19; 127
70-73: p. 84
71: p. 92, n. 19; 119
73: p. 141; 142
74: p. 119
75-77: p. 92, n. 19
77: p. 109
78: p. 92, n. 19; 142

79: p. 92, n. 19; 142; 170
80: p. 127; 140
80ff.: p. 91
81: p. 140
82-84: p. 95
83-84: p. 91
85-86: p. 92, n. 19

87		10	itaque tu illam omni loco expecta.	<u>1</u> β
§8	88 G	8	Desinere iam volebam	3 δε
	89	10	et manus spectabat ad clausulam,	2 γδ
	90	9	sed conficienda sunt aera et	1 γδ
	91	11	huic epistulae viaticum dandum est.	<u>1</u> δ
	92 P	7	Puta me non dicere	22 βγδ
	93	9	unde sumpturus sim mutuum:	<u>44</u> βγ
	94 Cl	6	scis cuius arca utar.	1 αβγ
	95 G	7	Expecta me pusillum	3 αγδ
	96	11	et de domo fiet numeratio;	4^{tr} β
	97	11	interim commodabit Epicurus	1² γ
	98	2	qui ait	b
	99	6	'meditare mortem',	3 βζ
	100	16	vel si commodius sic transire ad nos hic	
			potest sensus:	1 αβδ
	101	12	'egregia res est mortem condiscere'.	22 αγ

---

87 in omni p
89 spectabat α, expectabat pγ
90 confidenda p; aera *Madvig*, sacra ω
100 potest *Madvig*, patet ω (Cfr: Reyn. in app. crit.)

---

§8 groups of cola: 4 (2+2), 3 (2+1), 2, 5 (1+2+2)

87: p. 119
90: p. 86; 119; 140
91: p. 119; 140
93: p. 127
94: p. 112

96: p. 127
98: p. 109
99-107: p. 140
100: p. 119

§9	102	P	10	Supervacuum forsitan putas	4 αδ
	103		10	id discere quod semel utendum‿est.	1[tr] αβγ
	104	S	4	Hoc est ipsum	h
	105		10	quare meditari debeamus:	3 δ
	106		5	semper discendum‿est	11 αγ
	107		13	quod an sciamus experiri non possumus.	22 γδ
§10	108	GP	6	'Meditare mortem':	3 βζ
	109		3	qui‿hoc dicit	e
	110		10	meditari libertatem iubet.	22 αε
	111	GP	6	Qui mori didicit	1[3] αβδ
	112		7	servire dedidicit;	1[3] γ
	113		7	supra‿omnem potentiam‿est,	4 β
	114		4	certe‿extra‿omnem.	h
	115	G	13	Quid ad illum carcer et custodia‿et claustra?	1 δ
	116		6	liberum‿ostium‿habet.	1[3] α
	117	S	5	Una‿est catena	3 γε

112 dicit δ, corr. P[2]

§9 groups of cola: 2, 2, 2
§10 groups of cola: 3 (1+2), 4 (2+2), 2, 11 (3+2+3+3), 1

102: p. 127
104-107: p. 92, n. 19
106: p. 112
108-110: p. 95, n. 24
108-128: p. 91; 140
111: p. 84; 92, n. 19; 112; 127
112: p. 92, n. 19; 127
113: p. 127
115: p. 119
116: p. 127
117: p. 84

118	8	quae nos alligatos tenet,	$2\ \alpha\varepsilon$
119	4	amor vitae,	j
120	8	qui ut non est abiciendus,	$1^2\ \alpha\beta$
121	7	ita minuendus est,	$4^{1+tr}\ \alpha\beta\varepsilon$
122	8	ut si quando res exiget,	$22\ \gamma\delta$
123	7	nihil nos detineat	$11^3\ \beta\gamma$
124	5	nec impediat	o
125	8	quominus parati simus	cr.+mol.
126	8	quod quandoque faciendum est	$1^2\ \gamma$
127	5	statim facere.	o
128 Cl	2	Vale.	a

118: p. 84   121: p. 127; 140
119: p. 140   123: p. 170
120: p. 140

LETTER 41

§1	1 P	5	⏑– ⏑ ‾ ‾ ‾ ⏑ Facis rem optimam et	p
	2	6	⏑⏑ ⏑–‾‾ tibi salutarem	1 β
	3	13	‾ ‾ ‾ ‾ – ⏑ – ‾ ‾ – ‾ ⏑ – si, ut scribis, perseveras ire ad bonam	
			‾ mentem,	1 βδ
	4	6	‾ ‾ ‾ ‾ ‾ quam|stultum est optare	11 αγ
	5	8	‾ ‾ ‾ ‾ ⏑ – cum possis a te inpetrare.	3 αγδ ¹
	6 GS	10	‾ ‾ ‾ ‾ —⏑ – ‾ ‾ ⏑ Non sunt ad caelum elevandae manus	2 ε
	7	9	⏑ ‾ ‾ ‾ ⏑ —⏑⏑ nec exorandus aedituus	1³ γ
	8	9	⏑ ‾ ⏑ ‾ ‾ ⏑ ⏑– ut nos ad aurem simulacri,	3ᵗʳ αβγε
	9	11	⏑ ⏑ ⏑⏑ ‾ ‾ ‾ ‾ ‾ ‾ quasi magis exaudiri possimus,	11 γ
	10	3	‾ ‾ admittat:	e̲ ̲
	11	6	⏑ ‾ ‾ ‾ ‾ ⏑ prope est a te deus	44 βγδ
	12	5	‾ ‾ ‾ ‾ ⏑ tecum est, intus est.	44 αεγ
§2	13 G	7	⏑⏑ ‾ ‾ ‾ ‾ Ita dico, Lucili:	11 αγ

---

1 Facies p.

§1 groups of cola: 5 (2+3), 7 (2+3+2).
§2 groups of cola: 5 (1+2+2), 2, 1, 2.

12: For the colometry (doubtful) see p. 92, n. 21.

1-5: p. 95
1: p. 86
2: p. 112
3: p. 95; 120; 142
4: p. 142
6: p. 142; 143

8-10: p. 92
11: p. 112
11-12: p. 92; 92, n. 19; p. 142
12: p. 112
13-15: p. 95; p. 96, n. 26; p. 143

---

¹ It is not easy to decide whether cola 6-12 are to be classified as S or G. The paratactic element clearly outweighs the hypotactic.

14	10	‿‿ – – – –‿– – sacer intra nos spiritus sedet,	<u>1</u> αδ
15	16	‿– – ‿– – ‿ malorum bonorumque	
		– – —– –‿ – – nostrorum‿observator et custos;	<u>1</u> γδ
16 P	10	– ‿‿ – –– – –‿ hic prout a nobis tractatus est,	<u>22</u> γζ
17¹	7	‿‿ – – ‿ – ita nos ipse tractat.	<u>3</u> δζ
18 G	11	‿ – –– – ‿‿ ‿– – Bonus vero vir sine deo nemo‿est:	<u>1¹</u> βδ
19	21	– ‿– ‿‿ – ‿ – – – – ‿‿ an potest aliquis supra fortunam nisi‿ab	
		– — –‿ – – ‿ illo‿adiutus exsurgere?	<u>2</u> γ
20 G	14	– ‿ – – ‿‿‿ – ‿‿ ‿ –– Ille dat consilia magnifica‿et erecta.	<u>1¹</u> γ
21	11	‿ – – – — ‿ ‿– – ‿ – In unoquoque virorum bonorum	3 βε
22	11	"(quis deus incertum est) habitat deus".	
§3	23 P	6	– ‿ — – ‿ Si tibi‿occurrerit	<u>2</u> αβ
24	17	‿ – – – – ‿‿ ‿ – vetustis arboribus et	
		‿‿ —– ‿–‿ —– – solitam‿altitudinem‿egressis	<u>1</u> s

---

15 et *om.* p
19 an *om.* p
20 erec*ta*] recta p Q¹ P

---

§3 groups of cola: 8 (1+3+3+1), 5 (1+3+1), 4.
19: I prefer to read one colon since *potest...exsurgere* binds its elements together. Neither *nisi* nor the participle necessarily separate; cf. however, cola 8-10.
24ff.: The element *vetustis arboribus* has been expanded so heavily that its sheer weight (Fraenkel *Lesepr.* 82f. and 93 n. 18) causes a pause after *egressis*. For suspended *et* see p. 86.

14: p. 120
15: p. 95; 120
16-17: p. 95, n. 24; 100
18: p. 143
19: p. 120

21-22: p. 92, n. 19
22: p. 143, n. 30
23: p. 112
23-40: p. 91; 97; 143
24: p. 120

---

¹ Note the symmetrical arrangement of lengths of cola 13-17.

25	5	‿ – – ‿ frequens lucus et	p
26	25	– – – –– – – conspectum caeli <densitate> ramorum	
		‿ ‿– ‿ ‿– –‿ – ‿– – ‿ _aliorum_alios protegentium summovens,	2 δ
27	8	– ‿ – –‿– – illa proceritas silvae_et	1 δ
28	5	– – – ‿ secretum loci_et	44 αδ
29	17	– –‿– ‿ ‿ – – – admiratio_umbrae_in aperto tam	
		– – ‿ – ‿ ‿ densae_atque continuae	1³ γ
30	10	‿ – ‿‿ – ‿– ‿‿ fidem tibi numinis faciet.	1³ αδ
31 P	4	– – ‿ Si quis specus	m
32	8	– – ‿‿‿ – – saxis penitus exesis	1¹ γ
33	6	– – – – ‿ montem suspenderit,	22 γ
34	5	– ‿ – – non manu factus,	1 αβδ
35	18	– – – –‿ – –– – – – sed naturalibus causis in tantam	
		–‿ – –– ‿ – laxitatem_excavatus	3α
36	21	‿‿ – ‿– – – ‿‿‿–– animum tuum quadam religionis	
		– ‿‿–‿ – ‿‿ suspicione percutiet.	1³ γ

---

26 densitate *suppl. Reynolds ex* ς
30 faciet *Madvig*, facit et ω, faciet et ς

---

27 ff.: There are three subjects, all showing a similar extension (nom. + gen.) and arranged in a climax of content: the case for three distinct cola is quite strong [1].

---

[1] If one were to read these cola as one, it would be the longest in our sample and exceed the next longest by no less than seven syllables. The fact that such a colon would indeed support the general notion that Seneca uses long cola for specific purposes should not be allowed to seduce us into colometric sin.

37 G	13	Magnorum fluminum capita veneramur;	$1^{1+2}\,\alpha\gamma$
38	16	subita_ex abdito vasti_amnis eruptio_aras	
		habet;	$2\ \gamma\varepsilon$
39	12	coluntur aquarum calentium fontes,	$1\ \delta$
40	20	et stagna quaedam vel opacitas vel	
		inmensa_altitudo sacravit.	$3\ \varepsilon$
§4 41 P	6	Si_hominem videris	$2\ \alpha\delta$
42	8	interritum periculis,	$4\ \beta$
43	9	intactum cupiditatibus,	4
44	8	inter adversa felicem,	$1\ \gamma$
45	12	in mediis tempestatibus placidum,	$1^{3}\ \delta$
46	17	ex superiore loco_homines videntem, ex	
		aequo deos	$22\ \delta\zeta$
47	11	non subibit te veneratio_eius?	$3\ \alpha\beta$
48	3	non dices,	e
49	25	'ista res maior est altiorque quam_ut credi	
		similis huic in quo_est corpusculo	
		possit'?	$1\ \delta$

---

§4 groups of cola: 9 (1+4 (2+2)+1+2+1)

46: the single colon is defensible in view of the parallelism *interritum*..*intactum*..*felicem* ..*placidum*..*videntem*. The participle *videntem* ties *homines*..*deos* together.

49: None of the dividing points that might produce an acceptable clausula (..*est*/; ..*altiorque*/; ..*ut*/) produce a really satisfactory colon from the point of view of sense, a division after ..*huic*/ produces an awkward clausula.

37-40: p. 97; 143   44: p. 120
39: p. 120   47: p. 144
41-49: p. 97; 100; 121   49: p. 89; 97; 120; 143
42-44: p. 92, n. 19

§5 50 G   9   V̄i̇s ĭstŏ dīvīnă dēscēndit;   1 γ

    51   6   ănĭmŭm_ēxcēllēntem,   33 s

    52   4   mŏdĕrātum,   1

    53   12   ōmnĭă tāmquăm mīnōră trānsēūntem,   3 αδ

    54   12   quīdquīd tĭmēmŭs ōptāmūsquĕ rīdēntem,   1 γ

    55   9   cāēlēstĭs pŏtēntĭă_ăgĭtat.   3² γ

    56 G   17 Nōn pŏtēst rĕs tāntă sĭnĕ_ădmĭnĭcŭlō

                nūmĭnĭs stāre;   1 αδ

    57   17 ĭtăquĕ māiŏrĕ sŭĭ pārtĕ_īllĭc ēst ūndĕ

                dēscēndit.   1 γ

    58 PG 16 Quĕmādmŏdūm rădĭī sōlĭs cōntīngūnt

                quĭdēm tērrām   1 δ

    59   9   sēd ĭbĭ sūnt ūndĕ mīttūntur,   1 γ

    60   10   sīc ănĭmūs māgnŭs ăc săcĕr ĕt   1³ αγδε

    61   5   ĭn hōc dēmīssŭs   33 γδε

    62   10(12) ŭt prŏpĭŭs [quĭdem] dīvīnă nōssēmŭs   1 γ

    63   9   cōnvērsātŭr quĭdēm nōbīscŭm   cr.+ mol.

---

62 quidem *om.* ς

---

§5 groups of cola (1+4+1), 2, 10 (2+3+2+2+1).
60: One may hesitate on the colometry; I felt the pause after *et* was a stronger one
than after *demissus*.

64	9	— ‿ ‿–‿– ‿ sed haeret origini suae;	4 δ	
65	4	— — — illinc pendet,	h	
66	8	— — — ‿ — —‿ illuc spectat ac nititur,	2 αγδ	
67	10	— — — — ‿‿ ‿– ‿ nostris tamquam melior interest.	4¹ αγ	
§6	68 G	7	‿ — — — ‿‿ Quis est ergo hic animus?	3² βγδζ
69	11	— — — ‿ — ‿‿ ‿– ‿ qui nullo bono nisi suo nitet.	4¹ αβδ	
70 G	6	‿ ‿ — — ‿ Quid enim est stultius	44¹ α'γ	
71	10	‿‿ ‿ ‿ ‿ ‿– ‿ — quam in homine aliena laudare?	1 γ	
72	7	‿‿ ‿– — — ‿ quid eo dementius	44 β	
73	17	‿‿ — — — ‿‿ ‿‿ — — — — qui ea miratur quae ad alium transferri		
		—‿ — — protinus possunt.	1 δ	
74 Cl	13	— ‿‿– ‿‿– ‿ — — ‿– — Non faciunt meliorem equum aurei freni.	1 δ	
75 S	12	‿‿‿ ‿– — — ‿ — ‿ Aliter leo aurata iuba mittitur	2 βδ	
76	5	— — — dum contractatur	33 γδ	
77	22	‿ — ‿‿– ‿– ‿‿‿ ‿– — — — — — et ad patientiam recipiendi ornamenti		
		—‿ — ‿– — cogitur fatigatus,	1 β	
78	6	‿‿‿ — — — aliter incultus	1¹ γ	
79	6	— ‿ — —‿ integri spiritus:	2 βδ	
80 S	8	— —‿‿ — ‿ — hic scilicet impetu acer	3 δ	
81	10	— — — — ‿ ‿‿ qualem illum natura esse voluit,	3² βζ	

§6 groups of cola: 2, 4 (2+2), 1, 5 5 (3+2), 6 (1+2+2+1).

65-67: p. 92, n. 19
68: p. 143
69: p. 109; 143
71: p. 109; 120
73: p. 109; 120

74: p. 120; 144
75ff.: p. 128; 144
77: p. 89f.; 120
78-79: p. 92, n. 19
79: p. 112

	82	8	‿‿–‿ – – ‿ speciosus ex horrido,	2 γδ
	83	6	–‿ – ‿‿ cuius hic decor est,	1³ αγδε
	84	8	– ‿‿ – –⏜ ‿ non sine timore‿aspici	44 α ¹
	85	12	– – ‿ – – – ‿ ⏜ – ‿– praefertur illi languido‿et bratteato	¦3 αδ
§7	86 Cl	12	– ‿ –⏜– ‿‿ ⏝ – Nemo gloriari nisi suo debet.	1¹ αβδ
	87 P	5	– – – – Vitem laudamus	11 γ
	88	9	– – – – ‿– ‿ ‿ si fructu palmites onerat,	1³ αδ
	89	7	– – ‿ – ‿ – †si‿ipsa pondere‿ad terram	1 δ
	90	14	‿– – ⏝ – ‿‿ ‿‿ – – eorum quae tulit adminicula deducit :	1¹ γ
	91 P	10	– – ‿ – – – – num quis huic illam praeferret vitem	33 αγζ
	92	12	– – ‿ – – ⏝ ⏝‿ – cui‿aureae‿uvae,‿aurea folia dependent?	1¹ γ
	93 G	13	‿ ⏝ – – – – –‿ – ‿‿ Propria virtus est in vite fertilitas;	1³ αγ
	94	9	‿ ‿‿ ‿ – – – – in homine quoque‿id laudandum‿est	33 γε
	95	5	‿ – –‿ quod ipsius est.	p
	96	13	‿ ‿‿ – – – ‿ ‿ – ‿ – Familiam formonsam‿habet et domum	
			– pulchram,	1 αβδ
	97	4	– – ‿ multum serit,	m

---

89 ad terram *secl. Haase, Reynolds*; the place remains unsatisfactory.

---

§7 groups of cola: 1, 6 (2+2+2), 3, 5 (3+2).

84: p. 108   96-100: p. 97
87: p. 112; 144   97-98: p. 92, n. 19; p. 97
96: p. 120

---

¹ Concerning the hard question of accent shifting under the influence of synaloephe see now W. Sidney Allen, *Accent and Rhythm* p. 159-161 who agrees with Soubiran p. 475 that the case for such a shift is not very strong.

	98	5	multum fenerat:	44
	99	6	nihil horum in ipso est	3βδ
	100	4	sed circa ipsum.	h
§8	101 G	4	Lauda in illo	3 δζ
	102	10	quod nec eripi potest nec dari,	2 βδε
	103	7	quod proprium hominis est.	?4tr+2
	104 G	4	Quaeris quid sit?	h
	105	13	Animus et ratio in animo perfecta.	11¹ γ
	106 GP	11	Rationale enim animal est homo;	4¹ γδ
	107	10	consummatur itaque bonum eius,	3¹ γε
	108	8	si id inplevit cui nascitur.	22 γδ
	109 G	4	Quid est autem	j
	110	10	quod ab illo ratio haec exigat?	2tr βδ
	111	5	rem facillimam,	4 αβ
	112	11	secundum|naturam suam vivere.	2 δ
	113 G	15	Sed hanc difficilem facit communis	
			insania:	2 γ
	114	11	in vitia alter alterum trudimus.	2 αδ
	115 PG	13	Quomodo autem revocari ad salutem	
			possunt	cr.+mol.

§8 groups of cola: 3 (1+2), 2, 3 (1+2), 4 (2+2), 2, 3 (1+2).

105: p. 144	108: p. 109
106-108: p. 92, n. 19	109-112: p. 91; p. 92, n. 19
107: p. 170	112ff.: p. 128

116   6 quos nemo retinet,   3²αγδζ

117   6 populus inpellit?   1¹αγ

118 Cl 2 Vale.   a

116-117: p. 92, n. 19

LETTER 75

§1 1 Cl 17 Minus tibi accuratas a me epistulas mitti

            quereris.   33² γ

    2 P   9   Quis enim accurate loquitur   33² ε

    3   9   nisi qui vult putide loqui?   4 αδ

    4 PS 8   Qualis sermo meus esset   3ᵗʳ αγζ

    5   7   si una desideremus   1 α

    6   6   aut ambularemus,   1 α

    7   9   inlaboratus et facilis,   1³ γδ

    8   11 tales esse epistulas meas volo,   4 βδ

    9   11 quae nihil habent accersitum nec fictum.   11 γδ

§2 10 P 6   Si fieri posset,   1ᵗʳ αβδ

    11   7   quid sentiam ostendere   2 α

    12   5   quam loqui mallem.   1 αβδ

    13 PS 8   Etiam si disputarem,   3 γδ

---

5 desideremus Q, sederemus γ

---

§1 groups of cola: 1, 2, 6 (3+1+2).
§2 groups of cola: 3 (1+2), 7 (1+3+1+2).
5-6: Thraede p. 70 prints these cola as one. The parallelism of the repeated clausula seems to be sufficient reason for accepting two cola.
11-12: Thraede p. 70 prints these cola as one. He may be right, but there is a perfectly acceptable resting point after *ostendere*. See, however, 41.49.

1: p. 129
2: p. 92, n. 19; 129
3: p. 92, n. 19
4-6: p. 92, n. 19; 96, n. 27
5: p. 121

6: p. 112; 121
8-9: p. 92, n. 19
10: p. 112
12: p. 112; p. 121
13-16; p. 92, n. 19

$$- \quad - \quad -\cup- \quad \cup$$
14   7   nec supploderem pedem $4\ \delta$

$$- \quad \cup- \quad - \quad -$$
15   6   nec manum iactarem   cr.+mol.

$$\cup \quad - \quad -\cup- \quad -$$
16   7   nec attollerem vocem, $1\ \delta$

$$\cup \quad - \quad - \quad -\cup \quad - \quad \cup- \quad -$$
17   11   sed ista oratoribus reliquissem, $1\ \beta$

$$- \quad - \quad - \quad - \quad - \quad \cup- \quad - \quad - \quad - \quad \cup-$$
18   13   contentus sensus meos ad te pertulisse, $3\ \beta\gamma\delta$

$$- \quad \cup \quad - \quad - \quad - \quad \cup \quad \cup \quad - -$$
19   10   quos nec ornassem nec abiecissem. $1^{tr}\ \beta\beta'$

$$- \quad - \quad -\cup- \quad \cup \quad -\cup \quad -$$
§3   20 PS   12   Hoc unum plane tibi approbare vellem, $3\ \alpha\zeta$

$$- \quad \cup \quad -\cup \quad - \quad -\cup \quad - \quad -\cup$$
21   12   omnia me illa sentire quae dicerem $2\ \delta$

$$- \quad - \quad - \quad -\cup \quad \cup \quad \cup \quad -$$
22   10   nec tantum sentire sed amare. $1^{2}\ \gamma\delta'$

$$\cup\cup \quad \cup \quad \cup \quad - \quad \cup \quad -$$
23 G   9   Aliter homines amicam, $3\ \beta\varepsilon$

$$\cup\cup- \quad - \quad \cup \quad - \quad - \quad \cup-$$
24   10   aliter liberos osculantur; $3\ \alpha\delta$

$$\cup \quad \cup \quad \cup \quad - \quad - \quad - \quad - \quad -$$
25   15   tamen in hoc quoque amplexu tam

$$- \quad - \quad \cup \quad \cup \quad -$$
     sancto et moderato $3^{tr}\ \beta\gamma\varepsilon$

$$\cup \quad - \quad -\cup \quad - \quad -$$
26   8   satis apparet adfectus. 1γ

$$- \quad \cup- \quad \cup- \quad -- \quad - \quad \cup \quad -\cup \quad \cup \quad \cup$$
27 G   14   Non mehercules ieiuna esse et arida volo $2^{3}\ \gamma\varepsilon$

$$- \quad - \quad - \quad - \quad - \quad -$$
28   10   quae de rebus tam magnis dicentur $11\ \alpha\gamma$

$$\cup \quad \cup \quad - \quad \cup\cup \quad \cup \quad \cup- \quad \cup \quad - \quad \cup$$
29   15   (neque enim philosophia ingenio renuntiat), $4\ \beta$

---

§3 groups of cola: 3 (1+2), 3 (2+1), 4 (3+1).

21-22: the colometry remains doubtful; in both cases it may be possible to divide after *sentire*, but in the second case the terse *nec..sed* seems to tie together rather than divide (see also p. 85 and n. 9) and if colon 22 is one, the likelihood that colon 21 also should remain undivided is slightly increased.

14-16: p. 92, n. 19; 93   22: p. 85
16: p. 121   23-26: p. 96, n. 26
17: p. 121   26: p. 121
20-21: p. 92, n. 19   28: p. 84, n. 6
21: p. 84, n. 6   29-30: p. 92, n. 19

30	15	‿ ‿ ‿ ‿ ‿ ‿ — — — — — — — multum tamen operae‿inpendi verbis non		
		‿ — oportet.	3 βδε
§4	31 G	10.	— — — ‿‿— — — — Haec sit propositi nostri summa:	33 δζ
	32	7	— — — — ‿ — quod sentimus loquamur,	3 αβε
	33	8	— ‿ ‿ — — ‿— quod loquimur sentiamus;	3 αδ
	34	8	— — — — — — — concordet sermo cum vita.	11 αγδ[1]
	35 P	9	_ ‿ — — — ‿ — — Ille promissum suum‿implevit	1 β
	36	12	— — ‿ ‿— — — — ‿— qui‿et cum videas illum‿et cum‿audias	
			— idem‿est.	1 αδ
	37 G	7	‿ —‿ — — — Videbimus qualis sit,	cr. + mol.
	38	3	— — quantus sit:	e
	39	3	— ‿ unus est.	d
§5	40 Cl	11	— —— — — ‿ — ‿ — — Non delectent verba nostra sed prosint.	1 αγδ
	41 P	18	— ‿ — — ‿ — ‿ — ‿ — Si tamen contingere‿eloquentia non	
			—‿‿— ‿ sollicito potest,	4ᵗʳ αδ

35 implebit Q
39 est *Madvig*, sit ω

§4 groups of cola: 4 (1+2+1), 2, 3.
§5 groups of cola: 1, 5 (1+2+2), 2.
37-39: One may hesitate on the colometry: if these three cola are to be read as one, we have a near iscolon with 36, but the argument is weak. See also Fraenkel, *Lesepr.* p. 19.

31-34: p. 102
32-34: p. 92, n. 19; p. 94
34: p. 122; 145; 146
35: p. 122; 147

36: p. 122
37: p. 109
40: p. 85, n. 9; 122; 147

---

[1] Cola 32-34 were characterised by Norden, *Kunstprosa* p. 307, as "ein pointiertes σχῆμα".

42	4	— ◡ — si aut parata est	3 ε
43	5	— — — — aut parvo constat,	33 γδζ
44	12	— ◡ — — — — ◡ — — ◡ — adsit et res pulcherrimas prosequatur:	3 δ
45	12	— —◡ — — ᴗ — — — — — sit talis ut res potius quam se ostendat.	33 αδε
46 GP	14	ᴗ — — ◡ — ◡◡ — — — — ◡ Aliae artes ad ingenium totae pertinent,	44 αγ
47	10	— ◡◡ — ◡ —◡ ◡ ◡ hic animi negotium agitur.	3² β¹
§6 48 S	12	— —◡ — — ◡◡ —◡ — Non quaerit aeger medicum eloquentem,	3 β
49	7	— ◡ᴗ◡ — ◡ sed si ita competit	4 βγ
50	23	◡ ◡ —◡ — —◡ ◡— — — ut idem ille qui sanare potest compte	
		— — ◡◡— ◡ — — ◡ de iis quae facienda sunt disserat,	2 γδ²
51	5	◡ — — ◡ boni consulet.	p
52 S	13	— ◡ ◡ ◡— — — —◡— — ◡ Non tamen erit quare gratuletur sibi	2 αε

---

48 eloquentem Q *man. rec.*, loquentem ω

---

§6 groups of cola: 4 (1+3), 3 (2+1).

48 ff.: The colometry allows a slight hesitation: if *si* were to have a heavy syntactical stress, almost of necessity a slight pause after *sed* would result as well as a weakening of the pause after *competit*. Surely the ancient reader was as free in his interpretation at such a point as is his modern contemporary![3]

50: The colon refuses a satisfactory subdivision, though we might try ..*potest*/ which results in clausula 11³ αβδ', $-- \overset{!}{-} ◡ \overset{!}{◡} -$. This clausula finds support in 1.36 (with enclitic *sunt*) but the other instances of 11³ have $\overset{!}{-} -- \overset{!}{◡} ◡ -$ (26,79; 26.123; 80.101; 100.148; 100.149; 100.162; 122.22; 122,185; 122.186).

48-51: p. 101	49-51: p. 92, n. 19
49: p. 109	50: p. 90; 109

---

[1] It is quite clear that the thought is complete only at *agitur*, that *aliae* raises an expectation which is not fulfilled until then. Yet the element of parataxis is obvious. Hence the qualification GP.

[2] The scansion is uncertain. If *iis* is to be read with two syllables we may have a case of prosodic hiatus.

[3] For various performing practices (in verse) cf. W. Sidney Allen, *Accent and Rhythm*, p. 150, 340.

	53	14	quod inciderit in medicum etiam
			disertum; 3 ε
	54	22	hoc enim tale est quale si peritus
			gubernator etiam formosus est. 44 βε
§7	55 G	7	Quid aures meas scabis? 4 βδ
	56	4	quid oblectas? j
	57	17	aliud agitur: urendus, secandus,
			abstinendus sum. 1 αε
	58 G	7	Ad haec adhibitus es; 4^2 αβε
	59	15	curare debes morbum veterem, gravem,
			publicum; 2 βδ
	60 P	7	tantum negotii habes 1^3 β
	61	10	quantum in pestilentia medicus. 1^3 δ
	62 G	8	Circa verba occupatus es? 4 ε
	63	11	iamdudum gaude si sufficis rebus. 1 αδ
	64 G	7	Quando tam multa disces? 3 αγδζ

---

57 agitur] igitur Q V¹ P

---

§7 groups of cola: 3 (2+1), 4 (1+3), 2, 3, 3 (2+1).

57: The colometry remains doubtful: *aliud agitur* would be the only comma in our sample to consist of 6 shorts, but that fact does not constitute a strong defense of its inclusion with the subsequent colon.

60-61: These cola may have to be combined; the clausulae are quantitatively equivalent, but accentually quite different from one another.

57: p. 122
58-61: p. 92, n. 19
60: p. 170f.

61: p. 170f.
63: p. 122
64-66: p. 92, n. 19; p. 98

65   20 quando quae didiceris adfiges tibi ita ut

          excidere non possint? 1^1 γδ

66   7 quando illa experieris? 3^{tr} s

67 G 17 Non enim, ut cetera, memoriae tradidisse

          satis est: 3^2 βζε

68   8 in opera temptanda sunt;   44 βε

69   13 non est beatus qui scit illa, sed <qui>

          facit.   2 αγδε

§8 70 G   3 'Quid ergo?   f

71   8 infra illum nulli gradus sunt?   3 γεη

72   10 statim a sapientia praeceps est?'   cr.+mol.

73 GP 6 Non, ut existimo;   2 αβγ

74   14 nam qui proficit in numero quidem

          stultorum est,   cr.+mol.

75   14 magno tamen intervallo ab illis diducitur.   22 αγ

76 G 18 Inter ipsos quoque proficientes sunt

          magna discrimina: 2 αγ

77   4 in tres classes,   h

---

69 <qui> ς om. ω

---

§8 groups of cola: 3, 3 (1+2), 4 (1+3).

65: p. 90; 109   71: p. 129
67-68: p. 92, n. 1   73: p. 112
69: p. 85, n. 8; 85, n. 9; 145; 147   74-75: p. 92, n. 19
70-72: p. 95, n. 24; 96, n. 26   76ff.: p. 146; 147

	78	6	ut quibusdam placet,	2 αβε
	79	4	dividuntur.	3 δ
§9	80 P	12	Primi sunt qui sapientiam nondum habent	2 δ
	81	11	sed iam in vicinia eius constiterunt;	3 δ
	82 Cl	10	tamen etiam quod prope est extra est.	1 αβδ
	83 G	5	Qui sint hi quaeris?	11 αβγδ
	84	13	qui omnes iam adfectus ac vitia	1^{1-2} αγ
			posuerunt,	
	85	10	quae erant complectenda didicerunt,	1^2 γ
	86	13	sed illis adhuc inexperta fiducia est.	2 γ
	87 G	9	Bonum suum nondum in usu habent,	4 α
	88	17	iam tamen in illa quae fugerunt decidere	
			non possunt;	1^1 γδ
	89	11	iam ibi sunt unde non est retro lapsus,	1 αβδ
	90	10	sed hoc illis de se nondum liquet:	22 αβγε
	91	14	quod in quadam epistula scripsisse me	
			memini,	1^3 γδ

---

82 extra ς; ex ora Q V, ex hora δ

---

§9 groups of cola: 3 (2+1), 4 (1+2+1), 6 (2+2+2), 2. It is also possible to see the last group of 2 as part of the previous group: 8 (2+2+2+2).

92		6	'scire se nesciunt'.	2 αγδ
93 C		12	Iam contingit illis bono suo frui,	4 γδ
94		6	nondum confidere.	22 βδ
§10 95 S		10	Quidam hoc proficientium genus	4 δ
96		6	de quo locutus sum	1 αβε
97		6	ita complectuntur	33 βδ
98		14	ut illos dicant iam effugisse morbos animi	33² δζ
99		5	adfectus nondum,	33 γζ
100		9	et adhuc in lubrico stare,	1 αδ
101		15	quia nemo sit extra periculum malitiae	3² αε
102		8	nisi qui totam eam excussit;	1 α
103 P		6	nemo autem illam excussit	33 s
104		12	nisi qui pro illa sapientiam adsumpsit.	1 s
§11 105 P		14	Quid inter morbos animi intersit et	
			adfectus	1ᵗʳ β'γ
106		5	saepe iam dixi.	1 αγδ
107 G?		7	Nunc quoque te admonebo:	3 βδ
108		13	morbi sunt inveterata vitia et dura,	3¹ δζ

§10 groups of cola: 10 (3+2+3+2).
§11 groups of cola: 2, 1, 5 (3+2), 1, 3 (1+2), 4 (1+2+1).

	109	6	ut avaritia,	u
	110	5	ut ambitio;	o
	111	13	nimio artius haec animum inplicuerunt	3ᵗʳ s ¹
	112	12	et perpetua eius mala esse coeperunt.	1 γ
	113 G	7	Ut breviter finiam,	4¹ αγ
	114	12	morbus est iudicium in pravo pertinax,	44 αγ
	115 P	8	tamquam valde expetenda sint	4 ε
	116	9	quae leviter expetenda sunt;	4 αε
	117 GS	10	vel, si mavis, ita finiamus:	3 βδ
	118	12	nimis inminere leviter petendis	3 βε
	119	8	vel ex toto non petendis,	3 αβδε
	120	19	aut in magno pretio habere in	
			aliquo habenda vel in nullo.	1ᵗʳ ββ'γ
§12	121 S	13	Adfectus sunt motus animi inprobabiles,	4 s
	122	7	subiti et concitati,	3 αδ
	123	8	qui frequentes neglectique	1 β
	124	5	fecere morbum,	3 γζ

---

111 nimio artius haec *Rossbach ex* ς, nimia actus haec γ, minia ac vetus et Q.

---

§12 *ρroups of cola*: 8 (4+4), 2.

111: p. 167	118-120: p. 95, n. 24
112: p. 121; 167	118: p. 129
113: p. 112	119: p. 129
115: p. 129	123: p. 121
116: p. 129	124: p. 112

---

¹ The words *ambitio nimio artius haec animum inplicuerunt* form a hexameter of sorts.

125	8	sicut destillatio una	3 s
126	8	nec adhuc in morem adducta	33 βγ
127	4	tussim facit,	m
128	8	adsidua et vetus pthisin.	4 βδ
129 P	15	Itaque qui plurimum profecere extra	
		morbos sunt,	11 γε
130	14	adfectus adhuc sentiunt perfecto proximi.	44 γ
§13 131 PG	9	Secundum genus est eorum	3 βδε
132	16	qui et maxima animi mala et adfectus	
		deposuerunt,	3^{tr} αδ
133	20	sed ita ut non sit illis securitatis suae	
		certa possessio;	2 αγ
134	10	possunt enim in eadem relabi.	3 βε
§14 135 G	15	Tertium illud genus extra multa et	
		magna vitia est,	3² βζ
136	6	sed non extra omnia.	22 αβγ
137 G	8	Effugit avaritiam	1^{tr-3} β'

§13 groups of cola: 4 (2+2).
§14 groups of cola: 2, 10 (2+2+2+2+2)[1].

129: p. 92, n. 19; 121
129-130: p. 146
130: p. 92, n. 19
131-133: p. 96, n. 26

132: p. 150, n. 36
133: p. 146
135-146: p. 146

[1] The most striking element of this paragraph is the list rhythm consisting of a longer clause followed by a shorter. The last pair is reversed, which apparently is enough to create, together with the clausula, the impression of a full stop. The final clause is a metrical palindrome.

138		6	sed iram adhuc sentit;	1 αδ
139		11	iam non sollicitatur libidine,	4 β
140		9	. etiamnunc ambitione;	3ᵗʳ δ
141		6	iam non concupiscit,	3 βγδ
142		5	sed adhuc timet,	Γ
143		13	et in ipso metu ad quaedam satis firmus	
			est,	2 βδζ
144		5	quibusdam cedit:	33 γζ¹
145		5	mortem contemnit,	11 αγ
146		7	dolorem reformidat.	1 β
§15 147	Cl	9	De hoc loco aliquid cogitemus:	3 δ
148	P	7	bene nobiscum agetur,	3 γ
149		9	si in hunc admittimur numerum.	1³ δ
150	G	10	Magna felicitate naturae	1 γ
151		13	magnaque et adsidua intentione studii	2 ε
152		9	secundus occupatur gradus;	2 ε

---

140 etiamnunc P: et etiamnunc Q V¹ b

---

§15 groups of cola: 1, 2, 3 (2+1), 2, 4 (1+3), 2.

---

¹ Note the identical quantity but contrasting rhythm of these two cola.

153	14	sed ne‿hic quidem contemnendus est color	
		tertius.	2 δ
154 G	3	Cogita	d
155	11	quantum circa te videas malorum;	3 αβε
156	3	aspice	d
157	10	quam nullum sit nefas sine‿exemplo,	1 β
158	14	quantum cotidie nequitia proficiat,	1¹⁺³ γ
159	12	quantum publice privatimque peccetur:	1 γ
160 P	10	intelleges satis nos consequi,	44 βγ
161	8	si‿inter pessimos non sumus.	2 δε
§16 162 Cl	20	'Ego vero'‿inquis 'spero me posse‿et	
		amplioris ordinis fieri'.	1³ αδ
163 G	13	Optaverim‿hoc nobis magis quam	
		promiserim:	22 βγ
164	7	praeoccupati sumus,	2 ε
165	16	ad virtutem contendimus inter vitia	
		districti.	1¹ γ
166 G	5	Pudet dicere:	p

163 promiserim] miserim Q

§16 groups of cola: 1, 3 (1+2), 3 (1+2), 2.

153: p. 128
154-157: p. 92, n. 19
155 ff.: p. 150
157: p. 121
159: p. 121

161: p. 128
163: p. 150
163-165: p. 92, n. 19
164: p. 112
165: p. 150

		⌣ – ⌣ ⌣⌣	
167	6	honesta colimus	3^2 γζ
		– – ⌣	
168	4	quantum vacat.	<u>m</u>
		— – – ⌣ – ⌣ — –	
169 P	9	At quam grande praemium expectat,	1 α
		— ⌣ –⌣– – – – – ⌣⌣	
170	19	si occupationes nostras et mala	
		⌣ –– ⌣ — – ⌣	
		tenacissima abrumpimus'.	<u>2 s</u>
		– ⌣⌣⌣ –	
§17 171 G	6	Non cupiditas nos,	1^2 αβε
		– ⌣ – –	
172	5	non timor pellet;	1 αβδ
		⌣ ⌣⌣ — – – –⌣	
173	9	inagitati terroribus,	22 γ
		– – – – ⌣– –⌣	
174	9	incorrupti voluptatibus,	2 β
		– – — –⌣ – – ⌣	
175	9	nec mortem horrebimus nec deos;	2 δε
		⌣– – – – ⌣– – –	
176	10	sciemus mortem malum non esse,	cr.+mol.
		⌣– ⌣– – –	
177	7	deos malo non esse.	cr.+mol.
		– – — — ⌣	
178 G	7	Tam inbecillum est quod nocet	44 δε
		— – ⌣ –	
179	5	quam cui nocetur:	3 δε
		– ⌣ ⌣ – –⌣– ⌣	
180	9	optima vi noxia carent.	4 αδ
		– – –	
§18 181 P	4	Expectant nos,	<u>h</u>

---

173 inagitati b: inagitat in Q P: inagitati in V
177 malo *Hense*, maio ω, malos Q *man. rec., vulg.*
178 est *om.* δ

---

§17 groups of cola: 2, 3 (2+1), 2, 3 (2+1).
§18 groups of cola: 3 (1+2), 5 (1+3+1).
170: It is just possible that pauses should be read on either side of *et mala tenacissima.*

167: p. 171   172: p. 112
168: p. 171   173-175: p. 92, n. 19; 94
169: p. 121   179: p. 112
169-170: p. 92, n. 19   181 ff.: p. 150
171-172: p. 92, n. 19

182   20   ‹si›_ex hac aliquando faece_in illud

       evadimus sublime_et excelsum,   1 γ

183   21   tranquillitas animi_et expulsis erroribus

       absoluta libertas.   1 γ

184 G   6   Quaeris quae sit ista?   3 βδεζ

185   10   Non homines timere, non deos;   4 γδ

186   10   nec turpia velle nec nimia;   1³ αγδ

187   12   in se_ipsum_habere maximam potestatem: 1 β

188   13   inaestimabile bonum_est suum fieri.   1³ βδ

189 Cl 2   Vale.   a

---

182 ‹si› suppl. ς

185-186: The verb linking the two objects in both cases secures a single colon.

182-183: p. 92, n. 19; 146 186: p. 146
182: p. 121   187: p. 121
183: p. 121   188: p. 145
185-186: p. 92, n. 19

LETTER 80

<table>
<tr><td>§1</td><td>1 S</td><td>25</td><td>Hodierno die non tantum meo beneficio</td><td></td></tr>
<tr><td></td><td></td><td></td><td>mihi vaco sed spectaculi,</td><td>22 βγ</td></tr>
<tr><td></td><td>2</td><td>16</td><td>quod omnes molestos ad sphaeromachian</td><td></td></tr>
<tr><td></td><td></td><td></td><td>avocavit.</td><td>3 δ</td></tr>
<tr><td></td><td>3 S</td><td>4</td><td>Nemo inrumpet,</td><td>h</td></tr>
<tr><td></td><td>4</td><td>13</td><td>nemo cogitationem meam inpediet,</td><td>1³ β</td></tr>
<tr><td></td><td>5</td><td>14</td><td>quae hac ipsa fiducia procedit audacius.</td><td>2 γ</td></tr>
<tr><td></td><td>6 GS</td><td>9</td><td>Non crepabit subinde ostium,</td><td>2 β</td></tr>
<tr><td></td><td>7</td><td>8</td><td>non adlevabitur velum :</td><td>1 δ</td></tr>
<tr><td></td><td>8</td><td>8</td><td>licebit tuto vadere,</td><td>44 αγ</td></tr>
<tr><td></td><td>9</td><td>8</td><td>quod magis necessarium est</td><td>2 β</td></tr>
<tr><td></td><td>10</td><td>11</td><td>per se eunti et suam sequenti viam.</td><td>2 βε</td></tr>
<tr><td></td><td>11 G</td><td>8</td><td>Non ergo sequor priores?</td><td>3 αγε</td></tr>
<tr><td></td><td>12</td><td>23</td><td>facio, sed permitto mihi et invenire aliquid</td><td></td></tr>
<tr><td></td><td></td><td></td><td>et mutare et relinquere;</td><td>4ᵗʳ β</td></tr>
</table>

---

3 irrumpet V¹, irrumpit ω
6 crepabit *von Jan*, crepuit ω
8 tuto *Hense*, uno ω

---

§1 groups of cola: 2, 3, 5 (2+3), 4 (2+2).
12: Whichever of the three possibilities one chooses, to link *facio* with colon 11, to separate it off, to link it with 12, some objection may be raised. Even 80.44 provides no proper parallel; see, however, 100.135 and 122.200.

1: p. 85, n. 8; 90; 152
2: p. 90; 130; 152
3-4: p. 92, n. 19
3-5: p. 96

7: p. 123
11: p. 130
12: p. 1; 90

	13	5	‾ ‿ ‾ non servio illis,	3 γδ
	14	5	‿ ‾ ‾ ‿ sed assentior.	p
§2	15 S	8	‾ ‾ ‿ ‾ ‾ ‾ ‾ Magnum tamen verbum dixi,	33 βδζ
	16	11	‾ ‿‿ ‿‾ ‾ ‿‾ ‾ ‾ ‾ qui mihi silentium promittebam	33 δ
	17	11	‾ ‿ ‾ ‾ ‾ ‾ ‾‿ ‾ ‾ et sine interpellatore secretum:	1 γ
	18 G	13	‾ ‾ ‾ ‾ ‾ ‿ ‾ ‿‿‾ ‾ ‾ ‾ ‿ ecce ingens clamor ex stadio perfertur et	44 βε
	19	7	‾ ‾ ‾ ‿‾ ‿ me non excutit mihi,	4 αδ
	20	17	‿ ‿ ‾‿ ‾ ‾ ‾ ‾ ‾ ‾‿‾ ‾ sed in huius ipsius rei contemplationem	
			‾ transfert.	cr.+ mol.
	21 S	5	‾‿ ‾ ‾ Cogito mecum	1 αδ
	22	9	‾ ‾ ‿ ‾ ‾ ‾ ‿ quam multi corpora exerceant,	2 α
	23	7	‾ ‿‿‿ ‾ ‾ ingenia quam pauci;	1¹ γδ
	24	20	‾ ‿ ‾ ‾ ‿‾ ‾ ‿ ‾ ‿ quantus ad spectaculum non fidele et	
			‾ ‾‿ ‾ ‾ ‾ ‾ lusorium fiat concursus,	11 αγ
	25	12	‾ ‿ ‾ ‾ ‾ ‿ ‾ ‾‿ ‾ quanta sit circa artes bonas solitudo;	3 βδ
	26	7	‾ ‾ ‾ ‿ ‿ ‾ quam inbecilli animo sint	3ᵗʳ η
	27	12	‾ ‾ ‿ ‾ ‿ ‿ ‾ ‿ ‾ ‾ quorum lacertos umerosque miramur.	1 γ

20 contemplationem ς, contemptionem QV, contentionem δ

§2 groups of cola: 3 (1+2), 3, 6 (2+2+2).
22-23: the chiastic structure possibly argues a single colon, but the argument is not strong.

13: p. 112; 130; 153   21-23: p. 92, n. 19
13-14: p. 91; 92, n. 19 21: p. 112
16-17: p. 92, n. 19   21-27: p. 101
17: p. 123   24: p. 90; 152
18-20: p. 92, n. 19   25: p. 152
18: p. 86   27: p. 123
19: p. 152

§3 28 Cl 10 Illud maxime revolvo mecum : cr.+mol.

29 P 20 si corpus perduci exercitatione ad hanc

patientiam potest 4 δ

30 18 qua et pugnos pariter et calces non unius

hominis ferat, 2² γε

31 21 qua solem ardentissimum in ferventissimo

pulvere sustinens aliquis 1³

32 12 et sanguine suo madens diem ducat, 1 βδ

33 16 quanto facilius animus conroborari

possit, cr.+mol.

34 12 ut fortunae ictus invictus excipiat, 1³ γ

35 12 ut proiectus, ut conculcatus exsurgat. 1 γ

36 G 14 Corpus enim multis eget rebus ut valeat: 1³ αγδ

37 7 animus ex se crescit, 33 αδεζ

38 6 se ipse alit, se exercet. cr.+mol.

39 G 14 Illis multo cibo, multa potione opus est, 1³ αε

40 4 multo oleo, k

41 7 longa denique opera : 3² βδ

42 17 tibi continget virtus sine apparatu,

sine inpensa. 1 β

---

§3 groups of cola: 8 (1+4(2+2)+3), 3 (1+2), 3 (1+2)+1,1.
38: A case may be made for dividing after *alit*.
42: A case just might be made for reading *sine inpensa* as a separate comma.

29: p. 90 35: p. 86, n. 10
31: p. 90 37-38: p. 92, n. 19
32: p. 122; 122, n. 14 39: p. 152
34-35: p. 92, n. 19 42: p. 122; 152, n. 44

43 Cl 12 ‾ ‾ ‾ ⌣⌣⌣ ‾ ⌣‾ ⌣ ‾
Quidquid facere te potest bonum

‾
tecum est.   <u>1 βδ</u>

§4 44 Cl 11 ⌣ ⌣ ⌣ ‾ ‾ ‾ ‾ ⌣ ‾ ‾
Quid tibi opus est ut sis bonus? Velle.   <u>1 αβδ</u>

45 S 10 ⌣ ‾ ‾ ⌣⌣‾ ⌣‾ ‾
Quid autem melius potes velle   1 βδ

46 9 ‾⌣ ⌣⌣ ‾ ‾ ⌣ ‾
quam eripere te huic servituti   3 βδ

47 4 ‾ ‾ ⌣
quae omnes premit,   <u>m</u>

48 15 ‾ ‾ ⌣⌣⌣ ⌣ ⌣ ‾ ⌣⌣‾⌣
quam mancipia quoque condicionis

‾ ‾
extremae   1 γ

49 8 ⌣ ⌣ ‾ ‾ ⌣ ‾ ‾
et in his sordibus nata   1 αδ

50 10 ‾ ‾ ⌣ ‾ ⌣⌣ ‾ ‾
omni modo exuere conantur?   <u>1¹ γ</u>

51 GS 6 ⌣ ‾⌣‾ ⌣
Peculium suum,   <u>4 δ</u>

52 6 ‾ ‾ ⌣ ‾ ‾
quod comparaverunt   1 αβ

53 5 ‾ ‾ ⌣ ‾
ventre fraudato,   <u>11 αγ</u>

54 7 ‾ ‾ ⌣⌣⌣ ⌣ ⌣
pro capite numerant: <u>3¹⁻² γδζ</u>

55 18 ‾ ‾ ‾ ⌣‾ ‾ ‾ ‾ ‾ ⌣
tu non concupisces quanticumque ad

‾ ‾ ‾ ‾ ‾ ⌣ ‾
libertatem pervenire,   3 δ

---

§4 groups of cola: 1, 6 (1+2+3), 6 (4+2).

44-45: The connection between the first two cola is obvious: *velle*. We must suppose that
    Seneca intended some parallelism in length and clausula. Certainly the parallel
    positions create a strong pause after the second *velle*.

43: p. 152; 153   49: p. 122
44: p. 61; 87; 122   51: p. 112
45: p. 122   51-54: p. 92, n. 19; 95
46: p. 152   52: p. 167
47: p. 152   55-56: p. 92, n. 19
48: p. 122, n. 14

	56	8	qui te_in illa putas natum?	<u>1 βδ</u>
§5	57 G	9	Quid ad arcam tuam respicis?	<u>2 βδ</u>
	58	5	emi non potest.	<u>p</u>
	59 GS	18	Itaque_in tabellas vanum coicitur nomen	
			libertatis,	11 αγ
	60	7	quam nec qui_emerunt habent	22 αβε
	61	6	nec qui vendiderunt:	<u>3 βγδ</u>
	62	13	tibi des oportet istud bonum,_a te petas.	<u>2 βδε</u>
	63 G	10	Libera te primum metu mortis	<u>1 βδ</u>
	64	8	(illa nobis iugum_inponit),	<u>1 β</u>
	65	8	deinde metu paupertatis.	<u>11 β</u>
§6	66 P	12	Si vis scire quam nihil in illa mali sit,	<u>3 βγεη</u>
	67	13	compara_inter se pauperum_et divitum	
			vultus:	<u>1 αδ</u>
	68 G	12	saepius pauper et fidelius ridet;	<u>1 δ</u>
	69	9	nulla sollicitudo_in alto_est;	<u>3 αζ</u>

---

64 illa ω, ille *Gemoll*

---

§5 groups of cola: 2, 4 (1+3), 3.
§6 groups of cola: 2, 4 (2+2), 6 (2+4(2+2))

---

	70 (P)[1]	9	‿‿– – — ‿ – – etiam si qua_incidit cura,		1 δ
	71	8	‿ – – ‿ – – velut nubes levis transit:		<u>1 βδ</u>
	72 S	11	– – — – — ‿ – – horum qui felices vocantur ficta_est		cr. + mol.
	73	12	– ‿‿ – – – –‿ – ‿‿ aut gravis et suppurata tristitia,		1³ γ
	74	7	‿– ‿ – ‿‿ eo quidem gravior		1³ βδ
	75	13	‿ – – – – ‿ – ‿ — ‿ quia_interdum non licet palam_esse ‿‿ miseros,		3² γζ
	76	12	‿ – ‿ — – – ‿ – — ‿ – sed inter aerumnas cor ipsum_exedentes		3 βγ
	77	9	‿ – — ‿‿‿ — — necesse_est agere felicem.		1¹ αγ
§7	78 S	11	—‿‿ – – — – ‿— – Saepius hoc exemplo mihi_utendum_est,		<u>1 β</u>
	79	20	‿ ‿ — — ‿ –‿‿ – ‿ ‿‿ ‿ nec enim_ullo_efficacius exprimitur hic – – — – – humanae vitae mimus,		33 αδζ
	80	13	– —— – – – – ‿‿ – ‿ qui nobis partes quas male_agamus – – adsignat.		<u>1 γ</u>
	81 G	10	– ‿ — – – – –‿ – – Ille qui_in scaena latus incedit		1 αγ
	82	8	‿ – ‿‿– – – et haec resupinus dicit,		<u>33 αβζ</u>

---

73 aut] at *Madvig*
75 palam] et palam Q

---

§7 groups of cola: 3, 7 (2+3+2).

70-71: p. 93   78-80: p. 92, n. 19
71: p. 122   79: p. 152
73-74: p. 93   80: p. 123
76: p. 130   81: p. 123
78: p. 123; 152

---

[1] The P is bracketed as a subgroup within a Group.

	83	13	«en impero Argis; regna mihi liquit	
			Pelops,	
	84	12	qua ponto ab Helles atque ab Ionio mari	
	85	5	urguetur Isthmos»,	
	86	3	‾ ᴗ servus est	<u>d</u>
	87	15	‾ ᴗ ᴗᴗ ‾ ‾ ᴗᴗ ‾ ‾ ᴗ quinque modios accipit et quinque	
			‾ ‾ᴗ denarios.	<u>2 αγ</u>
§8	88 G	10	‾ ᴗ ‾ ᴗ ‾ ᴗ ‾ ‾ ᴗ Ille qui superbus atque_inpotens	2 γ
	89	12	‾ ‾ ‾ ‾ᴗ‾ ‾ᴗ‾ ᴗ ᴗ ᴗ et fiducia virium tumidus ait,	2³ γζ
	90	14	«quod nisi quieris, Menelae, hac dextra	
			occides»,	
	91	5	ᴗ‾ ‾ ᴗ diurnum_accipit,	<u>p</u>
	92	7	‾ ‾ ‾ ᴗ ‾ ‾ in centunculo dormit.	<u>1 δ</u>
	93 S	11	‾ ‾ ‾‾ ‾ ᴗᴗ ‾ ᴗ ‾ ‾ Idem de_istis licet omnibus dicas	1 αδ
	94	23	‾ ᴗ ‾ ᴗᴗ‾‾ᴗ ᴗ ‾ ᴗ ‾ ᴗ quos supra capita_hominum supraque	
			‾ ‾ ‾ᴗ ‾ ‾ ‾ ᴗ ‾ ‾ turbam delicatos lectica suspendit:	<u>1 γ</u>

---

92 centunculo ς, centuculo ω
83-85 Trag. Rom. fr. incert. 104-106, p. 289 Ribb. 3, see also Quint. *Inst.* 9.4.140, who
    reads *sceptra* for *regna*.
90 Trag. Rom. fr. incert. 27, p. 276 Ribb. 3.

87: colon 87 may have to be divided after *accipit*, but it is not a very clear case.
88-89: it is not impossible that the two cola belong together as one.
94: One might think of dividing after *delicatos* (extended object), but the prepositional
    elements so obviously qualify the verb that such a break of necessity is very weak.

87: p. 128   92: p. 123
88ff.: p. 94   93: p. 123
89: p. 171f.   94: p. 86, n. 10; 123
91-92: p. 92, n. 19

	95		14	omnium istorum personata felicitas est.	3 γη
	96	Cl	11	Contemnes illos si spoliaveris.	4^{tr} αβ
§9	97	GP	10	Equum empturus solvi iubes stratum,	1 βδ
	98		11	detrahis vestimenta venalibus	2 γ
	99		11	ne qua vitia corporis lateant:	1^{3} δ
	100		8	hominem involutum aestimas?	2 s
	101	GP	11	Mangones quidquid est quod displiceat,	11^{3} αβγ
	102		11	id aliquo lenocinio abscondunt,	1^{tr} s [1]
	103		15	itaque ementibus ornamenta ipsa suspecta sunt:	2 γζ
	104	P	15	sive crus alligatum sive brachium aspiceres,	1^{3} α
	105		16	nudari iuberes et ipsum tibi corpus ostendi.	1 αγ

102 id Q, *om.* γ

§9 groups of cola: 4 (1+2+1), 5 (2+1+2). 104-105: Possibly these cola should have been divided respectively after *alligatum* and *iuberes*.
99: One may think of *quā*, but I prefer to read it as an adjective.

96: p. 152
97: p. 122; 123
98-99: p. 92, n. 19
101-102: p. 92, n. 19
101: p. 170
102: p. 108
103-105: p. 92, n. 19
104: p. 89, n. 10
105: p. 123; 153

[1] If we read with synizesis the accent shifts to *lenócinjo/abscóndunt*. This would change the clausula to a simple type 1, or 11 if ī results as in Vergil *Aen.* 2, 16 ābjete costas. Cf. W. Sidney Allen, *Accent and Rhythm*, p. 146.

§10 106 Cl 22 Vides illum Scythiae Sarmatiaeve
     regem_insigni capitis decorum?   3 βε

107 P 7 Si vis illum_aestimare   3 αβγ

108 8 totumque scire qualis sit,   1 αγε

109 5 fasciam solve: 1 αδ

110 9 multum mali sub illa latet.   2 βγε

111 Cl 6 Quid de_aliis loquor?   4^{tr} αβδ

112 P 8 Si perpendere te voles,   4^{tr} γδ

113 13 sepone pecuniam, domum, dignitatem   3 βδ

114 8 intus te_ipse considera: 2 αγ

115 9 nunc qualis sis aliis credis.   1^{tr} αβδ

116 Cl 2 Vale.   a

---

§10 groups of cola: 1, 4 (2+2), 1, 4 (1+2+1).

106-116: p. 104f.   111: p. 109; 172
106-107: p. 90; 130; 153   112-114: p. 92, n. 19; 98
108: p. 123   114: p. 128; 153; 156
109: p. 112; 123   115: p. 153; 156; 172
110: p. 128; 156

LETTER 100

§1	1 Sc	9	‿‿⏑‿ ‿ ‿‿‿⏑ Fabiani Papiri libros		2 βε
	2	8	‿ ‿‿‿ ‿ ‿‿⏑ qui inscribuntur civilium		22 γ
	3	11	‿‿ ⏑ ‿ ⏑⏑‿⏑ ‿ ‿ legisse te cupidissime scribis,		1 δ
	4	13	‿ ‿ ‿ ‿ ‿ ‿‿ ‿ ‿⏑‿ ⏑ et non respondisse expectationi tuae;		2 ε
A	5 P	11	⏑‿ ⏑ ‿‿ ‿ ⏑⏑⏑ ⏑ deinde oblitus de philosopho agi		4² β
	6	10	‿ ⏑⏑⏑‿ ‿‿⏑ ‿ ‿ compositionem eius accusas.		1 γ
	7 G	6	⏑‿ ⏑ ‿ ‿ Puta esse quod dicis		1 γδ
	8	9	⏑ ‿ ‿ ‿ ‿ ⏑ ‿ ‿ et effundi verba, non figi.		1 αγδ
	9 GP	11	‿ ⏑ ⏑‿⏑ ‿ ⏑‿ ‿⏑ Primum habet ista res suam gratiam		2 αβδ
	10	17	⏑ ‿ ⏑ ‿ ⏑ ⏑⏑ ‿‿⏑‿ ‿⏑‿ et est decor proprius orationis leniter		
			‿ lapsae;		1 αδ
	11	9	‿ ⏑ ‿ ⏑‿ ‿‿ ⏑ multum enim interesse existimo		44 s
	12	9	⏑ ‿ ⏑ ⏑⏑ ‿ ‿⏑ utrum exciderit an fluxerit.		2¹ γδ
	13 Cl	20	‿⏑⏑ ‿ ⏑ ⏑ ‿ ⏑ ⏑ ‿ <Adice> nunc quod in hoc quoque quod		
			‿ ‿ ‿ ‿ ‿ ‿⏑‿ ⏑ dicturus sum ingens differentia est.		4 α
§2	14 G	19	⏑‿ ‿ ⏑⏑ ‿ ‿ ‿ ⏑⏑ ⏑ ‿⏑ Fabianus mihi non effundere videtur		
			‿ ‿⏑‿ orationem		3 γ

---

13 adice *suppl.* Hense

---

§1 groups of cola: 6 (4+2), 2, 4 (2+2), 1.
§2 groups of cola: 4 (2+2), 3, 3.

3: p. 124
5ff.: p. 157
6: p. 124
7: p. 124

8: p. 86, n. 10; 87; 124
10: p. 124
11-12: p. 92, n. 19
14-15: p. 85, n. 8; 92, n. 19

	15		4	‾ ‾ ᴗ sed fundere;	__m__
	16		14	ᴗ ᴗ‾ ‾ ‾‾ ‾ ᴗ ᴗ ‾ ‾ ‾ᴗ‾ adeo larga est et sine perturbatione,	__3__ β
	17		10	‾ ᴗ ᴗ ‾ ‾ ᴗ ‾ ᴗᴗ non sine cursu tamen veniens.	1³ βδ
	18 P		10	‾ ‾ ‾‾ ᴗ‾ᴗ ‾ ‾‾ Illud plane fatetur et praefert,	1 γδ
	19		6	‾ ‾ ᴗ ‾ ‾ non esse tractatam	1 αβδ
	20		5	‾ ᴗ‾ ‾ nec diu tortam.	1 αβδ
B	21 G		9	ᴗ ᴗ ‾‾ ‾ ‾ ᴗ ‾ ‾ Sed ita, ut vis, esse credamus:	1 αγ
	22		11	‾‾ ‾ ᴗ ‾ ‾ ᴗ ‾ ᴗᴗ mores ille, non verba composuit	1³ αγ
	23		12	ᴗ ᴗᴗ ‾ ‾ ᴗ ‾ ᴗ ‾ ‾ᴗ et animis scripsit ista, non auribus.	2 αγδ
§3	24 P		4	‾ ᴗᴗ Praeterea	k
	25		5	‾ ‾ ‾ ipso dicente	11 αγ
	26		12	‾ ᴗ ‾ ‾ ᴗᴗ ‾ ‾ ‾ ᴗ‾ non vacasset tibi partes intueri,	3 βδ
	27		10	ᴗ ᴗ‾ ᴗ ‾ ‾ ᴗ ‾ adeo te summa rapuisset;	1² αγ
	28 P		8	‾ ᴗ‾ ‾‾ ᴗ ‾ ᴗ et fere quae impetu placent	4 αδ
C	29		10	ᴗ ‾ ‾ ᴗ ᴗ ‾ ᴗ‾ minus praestant ad manum relata;	3 βγε
	30 P		7	ᴗ ‾ ‾ ᴗ ᴗ ‾ sed illud quoque multum est,	3ᵗʳ βγεζ
	31		10	‾ ᴗ‾ ‾‾ ᴗ ‾ ᴗ primo aspectu oculos occupasse,	3 δ
	32		20	ᴗᴗ‾ ‾ ‾ ‾ ‾ᴗ‾ ‾ᴗ ‾ etiam si contemplatio diligens	
				‾ ‾ ‾‾ ᴗ ‾ ᴗ inventura est quod arguat.	4 βγ

---

§3 groups of cola: 4 (3+1), 2, 3.

---

§4	33	PG	5	Si me interrogas,	44 αβ
	34		11	maior ille est qui iudicium abstulit	4^tr s
	35		5	quam qui meruit;	n
	36		8	et scio hunc tutiorem esse,	1 α
	37		15	scio audacius sibi de futuro promittere.	22 γ
D	38	G	15	Oratio sollicita philosophum non decet:	44^1 γδ
	39		10	ubi tandem erit fortis et constans,	1 αγδ
	40		16	ubi periculum sui faciet qui timet verbis?	1 αβδ
§5	41	G	16	Fabianus non erat neglegens in oratione	3 βγ
	42		4	sed securus.	h
	43	G	12	Itaque nihil invenies sordidum:	44^1 γ
	44		6	electa verba sunt,	4 γε
E	45		4	non captata,	h
	46		21	nec huius saeculi more contra naturam	
				suam posita et inversa,	1^1 αγ
	47		14	splendida tamen quamvis sumantur e	
				medio.	1^3 γδ
	48	G	12	Sensus honestos et magnificos habes,	4^tr αδ

§4 groups of cola: 5 (1+2+2), 3 (1+2).
§5 groups of cola: 2, 5 (1+2+2), 3, 5 (1+3+2).
40: possibly a division should be read after *faciet*.

49	9	non coactos in sententiam	44 α
50	6	sed latius dictos.	1 αδ
51 SP	4	Videbimus	i
52	7	quid parum recisum sit,	1 βε
53	5	quid parum structum,	1 αβδ
54	11	quid non huius recentis politurae:	1 β
55	9	cum circumspexeris omnia,	4ᵗʳ δ
56	12	nullas videbis angustias inanis.	3 αε
§6 57 GP	11	Desit sane varietas marmorum	2¹ αδ¹
58	17	et concisura aquarum cubiculis	
		interfluentium	4
59	6	et pauperis cella	1 αδ²
60	22	et quidquid aliud luxuria non contenta	
		decore simplici miscet:	1 αδ
61	5	quod dici solet,	44 αβδ²

---

54 non *om.* B
58 cubiculis BD, a cuniculis cubiculis Q θψ

---

§6 groups of cola: 6 (4+2), 7 (1+1+3+2).

50: p. 124
51-54: p. 96, n. 26
52: p. 124
53: p. 112; 124
54: p. 124

59: p. 112; 124
60: p. 90; 124
61: p. 112
61-62: p. 91; 92, n. 19

---

  ¹ For the accentuation cf. K. Müller, *Curtius* p. 765 (4c) as against W. Sidney Allen, *Accent and Rhythm*, p. 188 ff.
  ² The *pauperis cella*: cf. *ep.* 17.7, Martial 3.48 and the 18th cent. vogue to have a hermit's abode in one's park.

			‿ – –	
62	4	domus recta est.		j̲

			–‿‿ – — – – – ‿‿‿– ‿ –	
63 S	15	Adice nunc quod de compositione non	

(E')   constat :   1 γδ

			– ‿– – — –‿ –	
64	12	quidam illam volunt esse ex horrido	

                              comptam,   1 αδ

			– – ‿ — ‿– —	
65	8	quidam usque eo aspera gaudent		1 δ

			‿ ‿‿– – –‿– –‿ – ‿‿	
66	14	ut etiam quae mollius casus explicuit		1³ αγ

			– – – ‿– ‿	
67	8	ex industria dissipent		2 δ

			– —‿– – –	
68	7	et clausulas abrumpant		cr.+mol.

			‿‿ – – – — – – ‿	
69	9	ne ad expectatum respondeant.		22 β

			‿ ‿ ‿ ‿ –	
§7	70 G	6	Lege Ciceronem :	v

			– ‿‿‿—‿ –	
71	8	compositio eius una est,		3 ζ

			‿– – – – — ‿– — –‿– —	
72	13	pedem curvat lenta et sine infamia mollis.		1 δ

			– – – —‿–‿ ‿‿– ‿‿ – ‿	
F	73 G	18	At contra Pollionis Asini salebrosa et	

                              –‿‿
                              exiliens   1³ γ

			‿ ‿– ‿‿ — – – ‿— –	
74	12	et ubi minime expectes relictura.		1 β

---

69 expectatum ς, spectatum ω
72 pedem curvat B, servat pedem curvat φψ, pedem servat *Haase*, servat pedem curvatur *Rossb.*

---

§7 groups of cola: 3, 2, 4 (2+2)

63: p. 124   70-72: p. 96, n. 26
64: p. 124   70: p. 170
65: p. 124   72: p. 124
69: p. 109   74: p. 124
70ff.: p. 158; 159

75	GS	13	Denique omnia apud Ciceronem desinunt,	44 γ
76		8	apud Pollionem cadunt,	2 αε
77		7	exceptis paucissimis	22 γ
78		14	quae ad certum modum et ad	
			unum exemplar adstricta sunt.	2 γζ
§8	79 G	22	Humilia praeterea tibi videri dicis	
			omnia et parum erecta:	1 β
80		11	quo vitio carere eum iudico.	2 δ
81 G		8	Non sunt enim illa humilia	3^2 αβγ
82		22	sed placida et ad animi tenorem quietum	
			compositumque formata,	1 γ
G	83	7	nec depressa sed plana.	1 γδ
84 G		10	Deest illis oratorius vigor	4 δ
85		7	stimulique quos quaeris	1 γδ
86		10	et subiti ictus sententiarum;	3 γ
87		14	sed totum corpus, videris quam sit	
			comptum, honestum est.	3 βγδ

---

§8 groups of cola: 2, 3, 4 (3+1), 1.

87: The colometric decision is hard: the elements *sed totum corpus... honestum est* form an obviously linked circle around the concessive phrase, which in my opinion should be seen as a parenthetic thought. Fraenkel, *Lesepr.* p. 54, regards a similar parenthesis as a separate colon, but treats another, longer, parenthesis as an element that interrupts (p. 64).

79: p. 90
82: p. 124
83: p. 85; p. 124
84-86: p. 92, n. 19

85: p. 84, n. 6; p. 124
86: p. 130
87-88: p. 92, n. 19
87: p. 130

	88 Cl	15	Non habet oratio eius sed dabit	
			dignitatem.	3 αβδ
§9	89 Cl	13	Adfer quem Fabiano possis praeponere.	22 αγ
	90 S	5	Dic Ciceronem,	3^{tr} δε
F₁	91	19	cuius libri ad philosophiam pertinentes	
			paene totidem sunt	1² αγε
	92	5	quot Fabiani:	3^{tr} δε
	93 P	2	cedam,	b
	94	7	sed non statim pusillum est	3 αβγε
	95	8	si quid maximo minus est.	1³ αδε
	96 G	9	Dic Asinium Pollionem:	3 δ
	97	2	cedam	b
	98	6	et respondeamus:	3 βγ
	99	12	in re tanta eminere est post duos esse.	1 αβδ
	100 GS	9	Nomina adhuc Titum Livium;	2 βδ
	101	8	scripsit enim et dialogos,	3² αγε
	102	15	quos non magis philosophiae adnumerare	
			possis	3 ζ

---

88 dabit *Lips.*, debet ω
99 eminere : enim res QDE

---

§9 groups of cola: 1, 3, 3, 4 (1+2+1), 6 (1+4+1), 3.
99 : possibly to be divided after *est*.

	103	4	quam historiae,	k
	104	16	et ex professo philosophiam continentis	
			libros:	2 αε
	105	7	huic quoque dabo locum.	4^1 αβδ
	106 GS	11	Vide tamen quam multos antecedat	3 αβδ
	107	6	qui a tribus vincitur	2 αβδ
	108	9	et tribus eloquentissimis.	2 α
§10	109 G	7	Sed non praestat omnia:	4 αγ
E_1	110	9	non est fortis oratio eius,	3 αγ
	111	6	quamvis elata sit;	22 αγζ
	112	9	non est violenta nec torrens,	1 γδ
	113	6	quamvis effusa sit;	22 αγζ
	114	6	non est perspicua	11^3 αβγ
	115	3	sed pura.	e
D_1	116 G	6	"Desideres", inquis,	1 δ
	117	12	"contra vitia aliquid aspere dici,	1 αδ
	118	9	contra pericula animose,	1^2 s
	119	8	contra fortunam superbe,	3 βε

---

105 dabo locum B, dabo dialogum φ, cedam ψ.
108 et tribus: et iis *Russell*

---

§10 groups of cola: 7 (1+2+2+2), 5 (1+4), 4 (1+3), 4 (1+3), 3.

106-115: p. 157
107-108: p. 92, n. 19
107: p. 112
109-112: p. 92, n. 19
112: p. 124

114: p. 170
115: p. 85
116: p. 124; p. 158f.
117: p. 124

120		12	— — ‿‿— — — — ‿ —‿— contra ambitionem contumeliose.	3 β
121 G		2	‿ Volo	a
122		7	— —‿ — — — — luxuriam obiurgari,	cr.+mol.
123		7	‿—‿— — — libidinem traduci,	cr.+mol.
124		7	— ‿— ‿— — impotentiam frangi.	1 δ
125 G		4	‿ ‿‿ Sit aliquid	g
126		6	— — —‿— oratorie acre,	3 β
127		5	‿‿— — tragice grande,	s
128		5	— ‿ — — comice exile".	1 α
129 G		13	— — — ‿—‿ ‿— — ‿— — Vis illum adsidere pusillae rei, verbis:	1 βδ
130		12	—‿ — — — — ‿—‿— — ille rerum se magnitudini addixit,	1 s
131		15	—‿ — ‿— ‿‿ — — — — ‿ — eloquentiam velut umbram non hoc agens	
			‿ trahit.	4 αβδ
§11	132 G	15	— ‿— ‿‿ ‿‿— — ‿‿ Non erunt sine dubio singula	33 αδ
C₁			— — — circumspecta	33 αδ
	133	6	‿ — — — — nec in se collecta	33 βγδε
	134	11	‿ — ‿ — — ‿—‿ — — nec omne verbum excitabit ac punget,	1 γδ
	135	3	‿‿ fateor;	c

---

131 non B, *om.* φψ
134 aut punget ψ

---

§11 groups of cola: 8 (4+4), 2, 3, 3 (2+1).
129: Some doubt remains whether the apposition may be treated as part of the colon;
cf. *ep.* 80, 44.

122ff.: p. 92, n. 19; 94; 125
126-128: p. 92, n. 19
128: p. 112
129: p. 125; 160
130: p. 125; 160
132ff.: p. 160
134: p. 125

	136	9	— — — — ◡ — ◡◡ exibunt multa nec ferient	1^3 αγδ
	137	16	◡ — — ——◡— ◡ —— — —◡ — —◡ et interdum otiosa praeterlabetur oratio,	2 γ
	138	10	— — ◡◡◡ — ◡ — — sed multum erit in omnibus lucis,	1 αδ
	139	11	◡ — — ◡◡ —◡— ◡◡ sed ingens sine taedio spatium.	1^3 αδ
	140 P	7	—◡ — — — — — Denique illud praestabit,	11 γ
	141	13	— ◡ ◡— ◡ — — — — ◡ — — ut liqueat tibi illum sensisse quae scripsit.	1 γδ
	142 P	7	— —◡ — — — Intelleges hoc actum	cr.+mol.
	143	10	— — —— ◡ —— ◡ — ut tu scires quid illi placeret,	3 βγε
	144	9	— ◡—◡ ◡—— ◡ non ut ille placeret tibi.	2^{tr} βε
B₁	145 G	8	— —— — — ◡◡ — Ad profectum omnia tendunt,	3^{tr} αβη
	146	5	— ◡ — — ad bonam mentem:	1 αβδ
	147	6	— —◡ — — non quaeritur plausus.	1 αδ
§12	148 S	11	—— — —— — — ◡◡ Talia esse scripta eius non dubito,	11^3 γδ
	149	14	◡◡— — ◡— ◡◡— — — ◡◡ etiam si magis reminiscor quam teneo	11^3 γδ
	150	10	—— ◡ ◡◡ ◡◡ ◡— haeretque mihi color eorum	3^1 βδε
	151	17	— — ◡ — ◡◡ — ◡◡◡ —◡◡ non ex recenti conversatione familiariter	4^1 α
A₁	152	14	— — — — ◡◡ — ◡◡◡ —◡◡ sed summatim, ut solet ex vetere notitia;	1^{1+3} αγ
	153	6	cum audirem certe illum,	11 γ

§12 groups of cola: 5 (1+2+2), 7 (1+5+1), 1, 2, 1.
152: two cola may have to be read, but the parallelism with the previous colon seems to indicate that one colon is to be preferred.

136: p. 127	148: p. 127; 170
139: p. 127	149: p. 127; 170
141: p. 125; 160	150-152: p. 160
145 ff.: p. 157	152: p. 85, n. 8
146: p. 112; 125	153 ff.: p. 157
147: p. 112; 125	

154 S	9	talia mihi videbantur,	1 αβ
155	7	non solida sed plena,	1¹ αγδ
156	12	quae adulescentem indolis	
		bonae attollerent	2 β
157	13	et ad imitationem sui evocarent	3 γ
158	11	sine desperatione vincendi,	1 γ
159	16	quae mihi adhortatio videtur efficacissima.	2 α
160 Cl	19	Deterret enim qui imitandi cupiditatem	
		fecit, spem abstulit.	22 βδ
161 G	9	Ceterum verbis abundabat,	1 β
162	23	sine commendatione partium	
		singularum in universum magnificus.	11³ γ
163 Cl	2	Vale	a

160: two, or even three, cola might be read in this sententious structure.

154: p. 125
156ff.: p. 158
159: p. 159

161-162: p. 92, n. 19
161: p. 90; p. 125
162: p. 90; 128; 170

LETTER 122

§1	1 GP	9	$\smile\!-$ $-$ — — — $\smile$— — Detrimẹntum iam dies sensit;	1 $\alpha\beta\delta$
	2	8	$\smile\smile$ $\smile\smile$ $\smile\smile$ — resiluit aliquantum,	1^{1+2} γ
	3	14	$\smile\smile$ $\smile$ $\smile$ — — — $\smile$ — $\smile$ — $\smile\smile$ — ita tamen ut liberale adhuc spatium sit	3^{tr} $\delta\zeta$
	4	12	— — — — $\smile$ $\smile\smile$ — — $\smile$— — si quis cum ipso, ut ita dicam, die surgat.	1 $\beta\delta$
	5 PG	10	— $\smile\smile$—$\smile$ — $\smile\smile$ — Officiosior meliorque	3^{tr} ϵ
	6	13	— $\smile$ — — — $\smile$ $\smile$ — — si quis illum expectat et lucem	
			— — $\smile$ primam excipit :	22 β
	7	12	— — — — — $\smile$ — $\smile$ — — $\smile$ turpis qui alto sole semisomnus iacet,	2 $\alpha\epsilon$
	8	13	— — $\smile\smile\smile$ $\smile\smile$— $\smile$— $\smile$ cuius vigilia medio die incipit;	4 β
	9	11	$\smile$ $\smile$ — — — — — $\smile$— — et adhuc multis hoc antelucanum est.	1 α
§2	10 S	14	— — $\smile\smile\smile$ — — — — $\smile$ Sunt qui officia lucis noctisque	
			— — $\smile$ perverterint	2 γ
	11	9	$\smile$ — $\smile$ — — — $\smile$ $\smile$ nec ante diducant oculos	33^2 $\alpha\gamma\zeta$
	12	8	— — — $\smile$ — — $\smile$ hesterna graves crapula	2 $\beta\delta$
	13	7	— — $\smile\smile\smile$ — — — quam adpetere nox coepit.	1^1 $\gamma\delta$

---

6 exipit *Gruter*, exuit ω
8 incipit φ, incepit Bp

---

§1 groups of cola: 2, 2, 5 (2+2+1),
§2 groups of cola: 4 (1+3), 7 (1+2+2+2).
12 and 19: examples of Fraenkel's 'erweitertes Attribut'.

1: p. 125; 126; 162   7-8: p. 92, n. 19
4: p. 125; 126; 165   9: p. 125
5f.: p. 164   10: p. 164
7: p. 163; 164   11-13: p. 92, n. 19

		‿ _ _ _ _ ‿‿_ _‿	
14	12	Qualis illorum condicio dicitur	2^{tr} αδ
15	18	— _ _ ‿ ‿_ _ ‿‿_ ‿‿_ quos natura, ut ait Vergilius, pedibus	
		_ _ _ ‿ nostris subditos	44 αγ
16	8	_ _ _‿_ ‿‿ e contrario posuit,	1³ δ
17	16	nosque ubi primus equis Oriens adflavit	
		anhelis	
18	14	illis sera rubens accendit lumina vesper	
19	10	‿_ _ _ _ _‿_ _ ‿ talis horum contraria omnibus	4s
20	7	_ ‿‿_ _ _ _ non regio sed vita est.	33 αβεζ
§3 21 S	10	_ _ ‿ ‿_ _ _ _ ‿‿ Sunt quidam in eadem urbe antipodes	11³ s
22	6	_ _ _ ‿ ‿ qui, ut Marcus Cato ait,	3² γδζ ¹
23	11	‿ ‿‿_ _ _ _ _ _ _ nec orientem umquam solem viderunt	11 αγ
24	5	‿ _ ‿ _ nec occidentem.	3 αδε
25 P	7	_ _ _ ‿ _ _ Hos tu existimas scire	1 δ
26	8	‿ _ ‿ _ _ _ _ quemadmodum vivendum sit,	11 βε
27	6	_ _ ‿_ _ qui nesciunt quando?	1 αδ

---

15 pedibus ς, sedibus ω
19 omnibus omnibus B'p'

---

§3 groups of cola: 4 (1+3), 3, 3 (2+1), 5 (3+2), 1, 1, 4 (2+2).

17: p. 163
19-20: p. 85
21-24: p. 92, n. 19
21: p. 108; 163; 164

23: p. 129; 163; 167
24: p. 112; 130; 163
25: p. 125
27: p. 112; 125

---

¹ Cf. 80.89 and the annotation on p. 171. Here *ait* produces a clausula of type 3², not an impossible one.

28 P	6	Et hi mortem timent		44 βδ
29	9	in quam se vivi condiderunt?		3 αβδ
30 Cl	11	tam infausti ominis quam nocturnae aves		
		sunt.		3 βγθ
31 P	16	Licet in vino unguentoque tenebras suas		
		exigant,		2 βδ
32	17	licet epulis et quidem in multa fericula		
		discoctis		1¹ γ
33	14	totum perversae vigiliae tempus educant,		1 αγ
34	5	non convivantur		11 αβ
35	8	sed iusta sibi faciunt.		1^{tr+3}αγδ¹
36 Cl	12	Mortuis certe interdiu parentatur.		1 β
37 Cl	15	At mehercules nullus agenti dies		
		longus est.		2 βδζ
38 G	6	Extendamus vitam:		33 βζ
39	13	huius et officium et argumentum actus		
		est.		22 αζ

---

30 ominis *Pinc.*, homines φp
32 fericula *Turnebus*, pericula ω

28f.: p. 160; 163   36: p. 125; 160
29: p. 129; 167   37: p. 162; 165
30: p. 129   38: p. 165
33: p. 125   39: p. 165
35: p. 125; 160

---

[1] If we scan sibī the clausula wil be of type 1^{tr+3}, for which there are a few parallels in our sample, if sibĭ: 1^{2+3}, for which there are none.

	40 G	6	Circumscribatur nox	$11\ \varepsilon$
	41	13	et aliquid ex illa in diem transferatur.	$3\ \beta\delta$
§4	42 P	11	Aves quae conviviis comparantur	$3\ \delta$
	43	10	ut inmotae facile pinguescant	$1^1\ \gamma$
	44	8	in obscuro continentur;	$3\ \delta$
	45 G	15	ita sine ulla exercitatione iacentibus	$4^{tr}\ \beta_1$
	46	9	tumor pigrum corpus invadit	$1\ \alpha\gamma$
	47	?12	et † superba umbra † iners sagina	
			subcrescit.	$1\ \gamma$
	48 SG	7	At istorum corpora	$44\ \gamma$
	49	9	qui se tenebris dicaverunt	$1\ \beta$
	50	5	foeda visuntur	$1\ \gamma$
	51	18	quippe suspectior illis quam morbo	
			pallentibus color est:	$1^3\ \delta\varepsilon$
	52	8	languidi et evanidi albent,	$3\ \beta\gamma\zeta$
	53	10	et in vivis caro morticina est.	$3\ \beta\delta$

---

42 conviviis T E p², convivis *rell.*
47 superba umbra B[Q]θ, superva umbra p, super membra ς, sub umbra ς, sub arta umbra *Brakman*, sub superba umbra *Wagenvoort, alii alia,* cf. p. 164, n. 57.

---

§4 groups of cola: 6 (3+3), 6 (4+2), 6 (2+3+1).

40: p. 165
41: p. 129; 165
42: p. 129
42-44: p. 92, n. 19
43 ff. : p. 163
44: p. 129

47: p. 125
49: p. 125; 167
50: p. 112; 125
52: p. 129
53: p. 129; 160

54 G	14	Hoc tamen minimum in illis malorum	
		dixerim:	$44\ \gamma$
55	10	quanto plus tenebrarum in animo est!	$3^2\ \beta\zeta$
56	5	ille in se stupet,	$44\ \gamma\delta$
57	5	ille caligat,	$1\ \gamma$
58	5	invidet caecis.	$1\ \delta$
59 Cl	13	Quis umquam oculos tenebrarum	
		causa habuit?	$11^3\ \gamma$
§5 60 P	15	Interrogas quomodo haec animo pravitas	
		fiat	$1\ \alpha\delta$
61	16	aversandi diem et totam vitam in noctem	
		transferendi.	$3\ \beta\delta$
62 G	13	Omnia vitia contra naturam pugnant,	$33\ \alpha\gamma\zeta$
63	11	omnia debitum ordinem deserunt;	$2\ \delta$
64	10	hoc est luxuriae propositum,	$1^{tr+3}\ \delta$
65	6	gaudere perversis	$1\ \gamma$
66	9	nec tantum discedere a recto	$1\ \delta$
67	8	sed quam longissime abire,	$3^{tr}\ \alpha\beta\gamma$
68	11	deinde etiam e contrario stare.	$1\ \delta$

---

§5 groups of cola: 2, 7 (2+5).

55: p. 129   62 ff.: p. 165
56-58: p. 92, n. 19   65: p. 112; 125
57: p. 112; 125   66: p. 125
58: p. 112; 125   68: p. 125
61: p. 129

§6 69 S 14 Non videntur tibi contra naturam vivere   44 γ

     70   6 \<qui\> ieiuni bibunt,   22 αε

     71   13 qui vinum recipiunt inanibus venis   1 δ

     72   9 et ad cibum ebrii transeunt?   2 δ

     73 S 14 Atqui frequens hoc adulescentium

               vitium est,   1³ δ

     74   6 qui vires excolunt   44 αγ

     75   18 \<ut\> in ipso paene balinei limine inter

               nudos bibant,   22 γε

     76   4 immo potent   h

     77   4 et sudorem   h

     78   16 quem moverunt potionibus crebris ac

               ferventibus   44 αβ

     79   6 subinde destringant.   1 γ

     80 G 12 Post prandium aut cenam bibere

               vulgare est;   1¹ γ

     81   13 hoc patres familiae rustici faciunt   1³ δ

     82   10 et verae voluptatis ignari: 1 γ

---

70 qui *add.* ς
75 ut *add.* p², balinei BC p¹, balnei *rell.*
78 moverunt: verterunt p

---

§6 groups of cola: 4 (1+3), 7 (1+3+3), 7 (1+2, 1+2, 1).
78: possibly to be read with incision after *moverunt.*

---

83 G	6	merum̲ illud delectat	11 γ
84	7	quod non innatat cibo,	4 δ
85	10	quod libere penetrat ad nervos;	1¹ γ
86	13	illa̲ ebrietas iuvat quae̲ in vacuum venit.	4ᵗʳ βδ
§7	87 P	14	Non videntur tibi contra naturam vivere	44 γ
88	10	qui commutant cum feminis vestem?	1 δ
89 P	8	Non vivunt contra naturam	11 αγ
90	18	qui spectant ut pueritia splendeat	
		tempore̲ alieno?	1² α
91 Cl	15	Quid fieri crudelius vel miserius potest?	4¹ αδ¹
92 P	5	numquam vir erit,	n
93	9	ut diu virum pati possit?	1 βδ
94 P	19	et cum̲ illum contumeliae sexus eripuisse	
		debuerat,	1³ γ
95	8	non ne̲ aetas quidem̲ eripiet?	1³ β

---

95 non ne *Hense*, none Bp, non φ

---

§7 groups of cola: 2, 2, 5 (3+2).

---

[1] For the accentuation *miserius* cf. K. Müller, *Curtius*, p. 765, 4c. There seems to be no warranty that this accentuation was still used in classical times.

§8	96 PS	8	Non vivunt contra naturam	11 αγ
	97	8	qui hieme concupiscunt rosam	2 αε
	98	10	fomentoque aquarum calentium	4 β
	99	10	et locorum apta mutatione	3 γ
	100	8 (11)	bruma lilium [florem vernum] exprimunt?	4α (22αγ)
	101 PS	8	Non vivunt contra naturam	11 αγ
	102	12	qui pomaria in summis turribus serunt?	4 αδ
	103	15	quorum silvae in tectis domuum ac	
			fastigiis nutant,	1 δ
	104	16	inde ortis radicibus quo improbe	
			cacumina egissent?	1s
	105 P	8	Non vivunt contra naturam	11 αγ
	106	13	qui fundamenta thermarum in mari	
			iaciunt	1³ βδ
	107	15	et delicate natare ipsi sibi non videntur	3 βδε

---

99 locorum *Haase*, colorum B[Q]η R¹p¹, calorum *rell.*
100 bruma lilium *Pincianus*, brumalium ω; florem vernum *secl. P. Thomas*, exprimunt η, prima int B, primu^{nt} p, exprimant [Q]θ; promunt *coni. Hense*
103 domuum [Q] domum BηR¹p domorum R²E
104 cacumina ς, cacumine ω
107 non videntur [Q], dentur B¹p¹, videntur Bᶜηθ

---

§8 groups of cola: 5 (1+4), 4 (1+3), 4 (1+3).

96: p. 161
97: p. 109; 161
99: p. 129
101-104: p. 96, n. 26; 161

103: p. 125
104: p. 125
105-108: p. 96, n. 26
107: p. 129

108	18	nisi calentia stagna fluctu ac tempestate		
		feriantur?	$1^2\ \gamma$	
§9 109 P	21	Cum instituerunt omnia contra naturae		
		consuetudinem velle	$1\ \delta$	
110	11	novissime in totum ab illa desciscunt.	$11\ \alpha\gamma$	
111 G	2	lucet:	b	
112	5	somni tempus est.	$44\ \gamma\varepsilon$	
113	3	Quies est:	f	
114	6	nunc exerceamur,	$3\ \beta\gamma$	
115	4	nunc gestemur,	h	
116	5	nunc prandeamus.	$3\ \gamma\delta$	
117 G	8	Iam lux propius accedit:	$1^1\ \alpha\gamma$	
118	5	tempus est cenae.	$1\ \alpha\gamma\delta$	
119	12	Non oportet id facere quod populus;	$1^{1+3}\ \alpha\gamma\delta$	
120	14	res sordida est trita ac vulgari via vivere.	$2\ \beta\delta$	
121	9	Dies publicus relinquatur:	$1\ \beta$	
122	15	proprium nobis ac peculiare mane fiat.	$3\ \delta\zeta$	
§10 123 Cl	13	Isti vero mihi defunctorum loco sunt;	$3\ \alpha\varepsilon\eta$	

§9 groups of cola: 2, 6 (2+4(1+3)), 6 (2+2+2).
§10 groups of cola: 4 (1+3), 6 (2+4).

109-122: p. 91
109: p. 90
111f.: p. 161
114: p. 129

116: p. 129
118: p. 112; 125
121: p. 125
123: p. 129; 160

124 P		8	quantulum enim a funere absunt	3 δ
125		5	et quidem acerbo	3ᵗʳ δε
126		9	qui ad faces et cereos vivunt?	1 αδ
127 S		16	Hanc vitam agere eodem tempore multos	
			meminimus,	3² γε
128		14	inter quos et Acilium Butam praetorium,	22 αγ
129		11	cui post patrimonium ingens consumptum	11 γ
130		4	Tiberius	g
131		8	paupertatem confitenti	3 δ
132		8	"sero" inquit "experrectus es".	44 αε
§11 133 G		12	Recitabat Montanus Iulius carmen,	1 δ
134		8	tolerabilis poeta	3 ε
135		11	et amicitia Tiberi notus	1ᵗʳ βδ ¹
136		4	et frigore.	m
137 Cl		14	Ortus et occasus libentissime inserebat;	3s

---

125 quidem ς, qui de (quide) ω; acerbo [Q]Rp, acervo *rell.*
133 Iulius ς, illius ω
134/5 poeta et B, poetae [Q]θp, poetae et η

---

§11 groups of cola; 4 (1+3), 1, 5 (2+1+2).

124: p. 129
126: p. 125
127-130: p. 96, n. 27

129: p. 164
133: p. 125
133-136: p. 92, n. 19

---

¹ If we hold to Müller's rule that no accented syllable may occur in thesi, *Tiberi* does not fit the clausula. If we read Tiberii (1¹) there is no good reason for the accentuation. Possibly the difficulty should be avoided by reading 135 and 136 as one colon.

138 S	19	itaque cum indignaretur quidam illum	
		toto die recitasse	3ᵗʳ αγε
139	16	et negaret accedendum ad recitationes	
		eius,	33 ζ
140	8	Natta Pinarius ait:	3² αβγζ ¹
141 G	12	"numquid possum liberalius agere?	3ᵗʳ⁺² βε
142	12	paratus sum illum audire ab ortu ad	
		occasum."	1 αδ ²
§12 143 S	7	Cum hos versus recitasset	3ᵗʳ βγε
144	14	incipit ardentes Phoebus producere	
		flammas	
145	16	spargere se rubicunda dies; iam tristis	
		hirundo	
146	15	argutis reditura cibos inmittere nidis	
147	14	incipit et molli partitos ore ministrat,	
148	7	Varus eques Romanus,	33 αγε

---

141 numquid ς, numquam ω
145 se *suppl.* p²

---

§12 groups of cola: 1, 4, 6 (3+1+2).
138: possibly the colon may be divided after *quidam*.

141-142: p. 92, n. 19   145: p. 164
142: p. 125   148-150: p. 92, n. 19

---

¹ Cf. 80.89 and 122.22. Ait as one syllable would produce ⏤⏤⏑⏑⏗, a derivative of the dispondaic group (Müller's D³), a very rare clausula.
² Soubiran lists various moods elisions may be used to describe; see his final chapter.

149	8	Marci Vinicii comes,	4 δ
150	9	cenarum bonarum adsectator,	11s
151	12	quas improbitate linguae merebatur,	1 β
152	4	exclamavit	h
153	8	"incipit Buta dormire".	1 αγ
§13 154 SG	11	Deinde cum subinde recitasset	1² γ
155	15	iam sua pastores stabulis armenta	
		locarunt,	
156	15	iam dare sopitis nox pigra silentia terris	
157	3	incipit,	
158	6	idem Varus inquit	3 βδζ
159	3	"quid dicis?	e
160	3	iam nox est?	e
161	8	ibo et Butam salutabo".	1 β
162 S	20	Nihil erat notius hac eius vita in	
		contrarium circumacta;	3 δ
163	12	quam, ut dixi, multi eodem	
		tempore egerunt.	1 α

---

154 cum *om.* B

---

§13 groups of cola: 8 (1+3+1+3), 2.

151: p. 125
153: p. 125; 104
159-160: p. 91, n. 17

161: p. 125
162: p. 90
163: p. 125; 167

§14 164 S 11 Causa_autem_est ita vivendi quibusdam,   3 αδ

165 18 non quia_aliquid existiment

        noctem_ipsam_habere iucundius,   2 γ

166 10 sed quia nihil iuvat solitum, 1^{1+3} αβδ

167 12 et gravis malae conscientiae lux est,   1 δ

168 13 et omnia concupiscenti_aut contemnenti   11 β [1]

169 8 prout magno_aut parvo_empta sunt   22 αγε

170 10 fastidio_est lumen gratuitum.   3 βδ

171 G 23 Praeterea luxuriosi vitam suam_esse_in

        sermonibus dum vivunt volunt;   22 βγε

172 14 nam si tacetur perdere se putant operam. 1^3 αβδ

173 G 10 Itaque_aliquotiens faciunt 33^{1+2} ζ [2]

174 6 quod excitet famam.   1 αδ

175 G 7 Multi bona comedunt, 11^{2+3}αγδ[2]

176 6 multi_amicas habent: 2 αε

177 P 11 ut inter istos nomen invenias, 1^3 γ

---

166 solitum ς, oblitum ω, obvium *Erasmus*[2]

---

§14 groups of cola: 7 (1+3+3(2+1)), 2, 2, 5 (2+2+1).
171: neither of the possible dividing points (luxuriosi/: sérmonibus/) is satisfactory.

166: p. 165   175-176: p. 92, n. 19
167: p. 126; 159, n. 50; 165f.   176: p. 112
171: p. 90; p. 165   177-179: p. 96, n. 26
174: p. 126; 165, n. 61

---

[1] If we read còntemnénti, the clausula is of type 33.
[2] A troublesome clausula that does not occur elsewhere in our sample.

178 20 opus est non tantum luxuriosam rem sed

      notabilem facere; 1^3 δ

179 Cl 23 in tam occupata civitate fabulas vulgaris

      nequitia non invenit. 2^1

§15 180 PG 14 Pedonem Albinovanum

      narrantem audieramus 3^{tr} β

181 14 (erat autem fabulator elegantissimus) 2 α

182 14 habitasse se supra domum Sexti Papini. 22 βδ ^{1}

183 Cl 12 Is erat ex hac turba lucifugarum. 3^{tr} αβδ

184 G 18 "Audio" inquit "circa horam tertiam

      noctis flagellorum sonum". 44 δ ^{1}

185 6 Quaero quid faciat: 11^3 αγδ

186 11 dicitur rationes accipere. 11^3 γ

187 G 17 Audio circa horam sextam noctis

      clamorem concitatum.   3 δ

182/3 S. Papini.is *Hense*, spapinii is p¹, spapiniis θ, spapinii qui [Q], spaniis Bη

---

§15 groups of cola: 3, 1, 9 (3+3+3).
179: possibly to be divided after *civitate*.

178: p. 90   182: p. 171
179: p. 90   184-185: p. 92, n. 19
180-182: p. 92, n. 19   187-188: p. 92, n. 19

---

[1] Both 182 and 184 have clausulae marked that offend against Müller's rule that no accentuated long may occur in thesi. Possibly the one of 184 may be regarded as an instance of Müller's F⁴ (defossae latent), a rare form in Curtius, see p. 764; 182 however remains troublesome unless we may read Sextii Papini, which, in view of the mss. seems a desperate measure.

188		4	Quaero quid sit :
189		8	dicitur vocem exercere.
190	GP	9	Quaero circa horam octavam noctis
191		11	quid sibi ille sonus rotarum velit :
192		6	gestari dicitur.
§16 193	G	8	Circa lucem discurritur,
194		6	pueri vocantur,
195		11	cellarii, coqui tumultuantur.
196		4	Quaero quid sit :
197		12	dicitur mulsum et halicam poposcisse,
198		6	a balneo exisse.
199	G	12	"Excedebat" inquit "huius diem cena".
200		3	minime ;
201		10	valde enim frugaliter vivebat ;
202		10	nihil consumebat nisi noctem".
203	P	5	Itaque Pedo
204		14	dicentibus illum quibusdam avarum et
			sordidum

Right-hand metrical column:

h

11 α

33 αζ

2 βε

44 γ

22 αγ

3 βε

3 αγ

h

1 β

1 α

1 βδ

c

cr. + mol.

3ᵗʳ εη

t

44 δ

---

191 velit ς, vellet ω
203 Pedo *Pincianus*, credo φp, credendo B, ridendo *Axelson*

---

§16 groups of cola: 3, 3, 4, 3.

197: p. 126
198: p. 126

199: p. 126
201-202: p. 92, n. 19

205	12	"vos" inquit "illum et lychnobium	
		dicetis".	11^1 γ
§17 206 PG	7	Non debes admirari	11 β
207	15	si tantas invenis vitiorum proprietates:	1^3
208	4	varia sunt,	g
209	11	innumerabiles habent facies,	1^3 βδ
210	11	conprendi eorum genera non possunt.	1^1 αγ
211 G	6	Simplex recti cura est,	33 βδζ
212	5	multiplex pravi	1 αδ
213	14	et quantumvis novas declinationes capit.	2 ε
214 G	8	Idem moribus evenit:	4^{tr} αγ
215	11	naturam sequentium faciles sunt,	3^{tr} αεη
216	4	soluti sunt,	j
217	11	exiguas differentias habent;	4 δ
218	16	[his] distorti plurimum et omnibus et	
		inter se dissident.	44 βγ
§18 219 P	17	Causa tamen praecipua mihi videtur	
		huius morbi	cr. + mol.

---

210 comprehendi φ
218 his *secl.* Haase, hi distorti ς, his distortis *Gronovius*
219 tamen p, tam Bφ

---

§17 groups of cola: 5 (2+3), 3, 7 (1+3+3).
§18 groups of cola: 2, 4 (3+1), 2, 2.

---

208 ff.: p. 166
209-216: p. 92, n. 19
212: p. 112

215-217: p. 92, n. 19
219: p. 165

220		9	vitae communis fastidium.	22 γ
221 P		12	Quomodo cultu se_a ceteris distinguunt,	cr.+mol.
222		10	quomodo_elegantia cenarum,	cr.+mol.
223		9	munditiis vehiculorum,	3¹ δ
224		18	sic volunt separari_etiam temporum	
			dispositione.	1² α
225 P		8	Nolunt solita peccare	1¹ αγ
226		11	quibus peccandi praemium_infamia_est.	2 α
227 P		7	Hanc petunt omnes isti	33 αβδζ
228		9	qui,_ut ita dicam, retro vivunt.	1 βδ
§19 229 SG		13	Ideo, Lucili, tenenda nobis via_est	2 γε
230		7	quam natura praescripsit,	1 α
231		8	nec ab illa declinandum:	11 β¹
232 S		6	illam sequentibus	4 β
233		11	omnia facilia,_expedita sunt,	4 ε
234		7	contra_illam nitentibus	22 γ

---

224 sic p², si ω; separari *Madvig*, separare ω; dispositione *Muretus*, dispositiones ω.
225 peccare *Eras.*², spectare ω

---

§19 groups of cola: 3, 5 (2+3), 1.

225: p. 165   230: p. 126
226: p. 165, n. 61   232: p. 165
228: p. 109; 126   234: p. 165

---

[1] Alternative symbol: 33 αβδ

235   6   non alia vita est 3^1 γδζ

236   9   quam contra aquam remigantibus.   4 α

237 Cl 2   Vale.   a

236: p. 165

CLAUSES, STATISTICS AND USAGE

The basis of our enquiry is colometric in a wide sense of the word. This is reasonable, in so far as according to ancient theory[1] the colon is the basic element in all sensible speech. The colon consists of a group of words when regarded from the vantage point of meaning, of syllables when seen from the angle of rhythm.[2] Counting the latter ὑποκείμενον has its own peculiar difficulties, not only of a prosodic nature but even more basic ones. Thus there is no agreement among scholars whether one should count the syllables subject to elision/synaloephe. Thraede, for instance, counts all syllables that can be seen,[3] but most appear to prefer the shorter form wherever possible. Thus e.g. Primmer (p. 157 : so wird es heute kaum jemandem einfallen zu bezweifeln, dass Cicero im allgemeinen elidierte, da sich, wenn man Elision (oder korrekter : Synaloiphe) eintreten lässt, wirklich zumeist die gebräuchlicheren Klauseln einstellen.) On the whole it would seem that if the number of syllables in a colon or comma has any importance at all it is an auditive importance. The Auctor ad Herennium (4.20.27) actually insists that one should not count the syllables but instinctively produce an isocolon if that is one's intention (cf. p. 92). But this can only be meaningful if the length of the phrases or cola may be regarded as another element in the totality of the rhythmical structure of the prose piece in question.[4] In addition there seem to be several hints in our sample of Seneca's letters that the length or brevity of a colon itself underscores an aspect of its content or, to express the matter more precisely, helps

---

[1] Arist. *Rhet.* 9,5 1409 b 13 ff. (The period consists of cola, one colon *may* form a period) does not go as far as Hermogenes does afterwards when saying that the colon contains a complete thought : κῶλον δέ ἐστιν ἡ ἀπηρτισμένη διάνοια (*Rhet. Gr.* VI p. 180, Π. εὑρ. δ ed. Rabe). For Demetrius' close link between κῶλον and διάνοια, cf. Schenkeveld, p. 24.

[2] Arist. *Met.* 1087 b 36 : ἐν δὲ ῥυθμοῖς βάσις ἢ συλλαβή.

[3] K. Thraede, *Grundzüge* p. 13 seems to imply that he admits synaloephe only in the clausulae. It would seem that there is no reasonable ground to accept it in the clausula but not in the remainder of the colon. Indeed he counts e.g. *ep.* 40.1 *nam quo uno modo potes te mihi ostendis* as 13 syllables, obviously accepting hiatus at *quo uno* (p. 73).

[4] Cf. e.g. E. Fraenkel *Leseproben* p. 21 : "jedenfalls formulieren sie immer noch mit dem Gehör, und auch wenn sie schreiben ist ihr Ohr stark beteiligt".

convey an element of meaning.[5] The length of a phrase is of necessity relative to the lengths of the surrounding phrases and it is particularly interesting to see that on several occasions Seneca appears to be at pains to achieve sameness or contrast or symmetry. The more important examples will be discussed below. Before we can do that, however, it is necessary to establish the criteria whereby a colon may be recognized.

I have neither the patience nor the capability to repeat Fraenkel's work, even in part, for Seneca. Nor is that necessary in my context. If one determines pauses by *a* requirements of meaning, *b* stylistic markers such as anaphorae, parallel constructions and the like and *c* the reinforcement of such pauses by common clausulae, there remains a series of hesitation points of an estimated 10%. Conclusions based on the length of the cola, then, rest on some 90% of the material at least. This is not to say that the 10% are beyond hope; in many cases I hope I have made the right decision, but some awkward questions remain. The most awkward, at least the least capable of solution, seems to be the question of relative clauses. There is no question in my mind that a subject clause of the type of 26.111 constitutes a colon, but ibidem 118 *quae nos alligatos tenet* would have created difficulties if it had not been for the support of the clausula of 117; indeed 117 *una est catena* introduces a sentence with a remarkably chainlike structure.[6]

I have no difficulty in marking 26,70-73 *disputationes et litterata colloquia / et ex praeceptis sapientium verba collecta / et eruditus sermo / non ostendunt verum robur animi. /* as a series of separate cola. Since even Plato's τὸ γὰρ δὴ πᾶν τόδε τὸ μὲν αὐτὸς ὁ θεὸς πορευόμενος ποδηγεῖ καὶ συγκυκλεῖ (both much more compact and shorter by some 20 syllables than Seneca's sentence) is treated as a very long one by Demetrius,[7] I feel that Thraede (p. 69) is wrong in treating those cola as one exceedingly long one.

---

[5] Cf. Demetrius Π. ἑρμ. 4-5 and Schenkeveld's discussion pp. 23 f. Demetrius finds a place for the very long colon (he quotes an example from Plato, adding "σχεδὸν γὰρ τῷ μεγέθει τοῦ κώλου συνεξῆρται καὶ ὁ λόγος". He does not approve of too many short cola, but admits (paragr. 7) τῶν δὲ μικρῶν κώλων κἂν δεινότητι χρῆσίς ἐστι. Cf. paragraph 241.

[6] 75.28 provides a good example of a relative clause that may with certainty be regarded as a colon, 75.21 one that may certainly not be so regarded, cf. e.g. 100.85. The criterion: *de rebus tam magnis* constitutes an *Erweiterung* in Fraenkel's sense.

[7] Π. ἑρμ. 5 quoting Plato, *Politicus* 269 c (slightly different from our texts: τὸ γὰρ πᾶν τόδε τοτὲ μὲν αὐτὸς ὁ θεὸς συμποδηγεῖ πορευόμενον καὶ συγκυκλεῖ, τοτὲ δὲ κτλ.).

On the other hand there is a series of doubtful cases containing the disjunctive *non....sed*. In discussing this group it is perhaps useful to start from 100.88 *non habet oratio eius sed dabit dignitatem*. It seems that the separation of verbal notions by *non..sed* is cancelled out by the common object.[8] If this is correct it provides us with a useful criterion. A little earlier on (100.83) we have a more doubtful case: *nec depressa sed plana*. If this is to be read as one colon we have a very good clausula. If it is to be read as two, we have commatia for both of which there are rhythmic parallels. On the other hand the preceding colon quite distinctly links *placida* by means of an explicative *et* with *ad...formata*, the whole of which notion is opposed to *humilia*. Both of these ideas are picked up, but in bare form, without 'Erweiterung' in *nec depressa sed plana*. It is the absence of any form of expansion that has weighted the balance in favour of a single colon for this group of words. On the other hand *non..sed* may itself serve as an expansion of the subject, as at 122.19-20: *talis horum contraria omnibus/ non regio sed vita est*. It is clear that this function serves to link the disjunctive *non..sed* within a perfectly compact colon. At 41.34-5 on the other hand *non..sed* separate the participles *factus...excavatus*, and two cola result. The colometric effect of *nec..sed* at 75.22 remains doubtful; the function is doubtless one of escalation.[9] In the case of 100.115 *sed pura* has been taken as a separate colon in view of the preceding pendulum swing negation-concession-negation-concession, which *sed pura* stops by being separate and different.

On several occasions one element serves to link two others that are in themselves contrasted with one another. Thus e.g. 80.62 *tibi des oportet istud bonum, a te petas*. It would seem that to accept a

---

[8] The verb serves as a link in a similar fashion at 1.64. Fraenkel separates at Cic. *Manil*. 30 *non terrore belli/sed consili celeritate explicavit*, but there the object (*Sicilia...*, *quam*) does not form part of either colon, whereas in our case we have a double subject (of which the second element constitutes an escalation of the first) within the colon. Cf. 80.1 though the placement of the verb may cause some further hesitation. The opposite decision has been taken at 100. 14-15 in view of the very central place of the distinction *fundere/effundere* and at 100.41-42. At 80.1 it might be possible to take *sed spectaculi* with the subsequent adjectival clause, cf. 100.152. At 75.69 I remain unreasonably unconvinced that there are two cola here.

[9] The additional question of the clausula makes the problem no easier to solve. If the colon reads "non tantum sentire sed amare" the clausula is equivalent to *esse videatur* but has an extra word division for which there is no parallel in our sample except 100.91 *paene totidem sunt* which has such a division in a different place. Escalation also at the adhortative 75.40; cf. 75.69.

pause after *istud bonum*, joint object of the two verbs, and hence hiatus, destroys a clever structure in which an a b a is intermingled with an αβ...αβ. However, there is, of course, no proof that Seneca intended no such pause.[10]

Finally : on various occasions we encounter a pause after *et*. Thus 26.35 *minui et deperire et, ut proprie dicam,..* This *et* is somehow suspended, its effect delayed until after the interruption of *ut proprie dicam*. Another example, though of a slightly different type, occurs at 1.13 *Et si volueris adtendere...* If it is possible to insert a subordinate thought after *et* in such cases, it must be because a natural pause occurs, and indeed we find an *et* before the caesura in Vergil, e.g. Aen. 2.96 *promisi ultorem et/ verbis odia aspera movi*. In this instance the synaloephe may ease the effect a little ; there is no easement at *ibidem* 2.104 *hoc Ithacus velit et/ magno mercentur Atridae*. Similar instances are to be found in Lucan, e.g. B.C. I 173 ; 197 ; 209. In view of this phenomenon I have marked 26.90 *sed conficienda sunt aera et/* ; 41.1 *facis rem optimam et* ; 41.25 *frequens lucus et* ; (a much more doubtful instance occurs at 41.60) and, a very clear instance, 80.18 *ecce ingens clamor ex stadio perfertur et/ me non excutit mihi* : the slightly unexpected character of the *non* is materially enhanced by the suspension of the *et*.

Further problems of a colometric nature have been noted under the text. But it is useful to add one more note concerning the very short cola or commatia that occur with some frequency.

On the whole I prefer to allow these short commata a life of their own, rather than attaching them to preceding or following cola. Fraenkel has gone the other way, e.g. *Leseproben* p. 38 n. 1 (Bei sehr kurzen Gliedern braucht zwischen einem Verbum dicendi oder sentiendi und der von ihm abhängigen Infinitivkonstruktion kein Einschnitt (keine Kolongrenze) stattzufinden. Das Entsprechende gilt für Relativsätze, Causal-, Condicionalsätze usw.). Similarly he has (*Lesepr.* p. 41 n. 15) collected a number of examples in which he feels that short answers belong to the colon containing the preceding question. I find it hard to follow him all the way. Thus the example from *Quinct.* 56 : *malitiosum? non negas*, when regarded within its context, seems to require a pause after *malitiosum*. *S. Rosc.* 138 ("*vellem quidem liceret :*

---

[10] Similarly the subject accusative *verba* links the infinitives at 100.8 whereas the verb constitutes a link e.g. at 80.35; 80.94; 80.104 (double link to counteract *sive ... sive*); 100.22/23 (two cola that support one another's compactness).

hoc dixissem". dicas licet. "hoc fecissem." facias licet : nemo prohibet)
does not allow Fraenkel's inclusion of the elements *dicas licet* and
facias licet with the preceding quotations, since the pause within
fecissem." facias must be stronger than the one between *licet: nemo.*
Again, *S. Rosc.* 30 (*patronos huic defuturos putaverunt : desunt ; qui
libere dicat...non deest profecto,*) should not be interrupted after *desunt*
only : the clausula rhythm of *defuturos putaverunt* should not be
overlooked, and the fact that *desunt* both picks up *defuturos* and
foreshadows *deest* warrants an emphasis marked by appreciable
pauses. On the other hand, letter 80.44 offers an example where I
am inclined to agree in view of the parallelism with the second *velle.*
The passage remains one of the ca. 10% in which I hesitate, however.
Cf. 100.8.

Fraenkel does not, of course, avoid all short cola and indeed his
listing of rhythms employed in them (*Leseproben*, Index s.v. Rhythmus)
is exceedingly useful. It is to be noted that many of those return in
Seneca. Indeed the part they play in our author is such that they
warrant a little more than a reference to however excellent a book
dealing with Cicero's and Cato's speeches. For that reason they have
been listed separately, below p. 113 at the end of the clausula statistics.

Table I below shows the frequency of each clauselength, counted
in syllables.[11] In compiling the table the lengths I used were those
that take elision into account. This table counts all clauses, including
those of the verse quotations and *vale.*

TABLE I

syll.	1	26	41	75	80	100	122	total	%
2	1	3	1	1	1	4	2	13	1.27
3	1	7	2	5	2	2	5	24	2.36
4	2	9	8	7	3	8	10	47	4.62

---

[11] H. Lausberg is very much opposed to the counting of syllables in order to
measure the length of colon or comma. Cf. *Handbuch der Literarischen Rhetorik*,
p. 360, paragr. 721 : "Die 'Gleichheit' im Isocolon meint die Gleichheit der Wortanzahl
und der syntaktische Gliederung, und zwar grundsätzlich ohne Rücksicht auf Silbenanzahl
und Silbenquantitäten". In my opinion there is no objection against using number of
syllables as the measurement of length in much the same way the Auctor ad Herennium
does (4.20). He is also opposed to counting, but requires that long practice (*usus
et exercitatio facultatis*) creates a kind of sixth sense for hitting an equal number
(*ut animi quodam sensu par membrum superiori referre possimus*). The examples he
gives are 12-12-13 and 13-12 syllables in length. Demetrius Π. ἑρμ. 25 leaves no doubt
that he counted syllables.

syll.	1	26	41	75	80	100	122	total	%
5	8	14	11	14	7	11	13	78	7.66
6	6	14	14	18	6	16	21	95	9.34
7	7	12	5	19	10	15	12	80	7.86
8	9	10	11	17	15	12	30	104	10.22
9	7	11	9	18	9	17	17	88	8.65
10	9	10	13	19	7	12	17	87	8.55
11	8	13	9	10	12	14	21	87	8.55
12	1	3	8	16	12	12	18	70	6.88
13	2	7	7	10	8	7	13	54	5.31
14		3	3	9	4	6	20	45	4.42
15	1	4	1	9	5	7	10	37	3.63
16		2	3	2	3	6	10	26	2.55
17	1		6	4	2	3	3	19	1.86
18		4	1	2	3		8	18	1.76
19			2			4	2	8	0.78
20			1	4	3	2	2	12	1.18
21			2	1	1	1	1	6	0.59
22		2	1		1	3		7	0.68
23	1			2	2	1	2	8	0.78
24									
25	1		2		1			4	0.39
+	65	128	118	189	117	163	237	1017	100

This sort of statistic, unhappily, does not show much more than the fact that Seneca in these seven letters uses certain colon lengths a certain number of times. It is, of course, possible to compute the average length (9.8 syllables) and the mean (13.5 syllables), but I find it hard to imagine what use we can make of these entities. Not only are they mythical entities in so far as there are no clauses of exactly those lengths, but neither can represent the norm with which all individual cases must be compared. Such a notion would imply that Seneca had a norm rather than a practice, something which neither the evidence of the table nor any arithmetic can prove; and if we establish that 86.8% of the clauses have between 2 and 14 syllables, 76% between 2 and 12, 60.8% between 2 and 8, and that the mode, i.e. the most common length, is 8 syllables, we shall never establish thereby that Seneca attempted to approximate an "ideal" clause length.[12]

On the other hand it is clear that a number of clauses deviate from the most usual lengths and it seems to be of some importance to

---

[12] Quintilian may refer to just such a norm *Inst.* 9.4.125: *membrum longius iusto, tardum; brevius, instabile est,* but I should not like to exclude the possibility that the *iustum* is a relative notion to be defined with reference to the subject matter at hand.

investigate whether Seneca uses clauselength for specific effect. That seems to be the case for very long clauses (20 syllables and over).

I list a number of examples (that they are mere suggestions and incapable of proof—all the more since in some cases the colometric decision is debatable—should go without saying) :

1.33 : the length of the clause *in huius rei unius fugacis ac lubricae possessionem natura nos misit* seems to perform at least two functions : it illustrates both the time-content and possibly the adjectives *fugax* and *lubricus*; it also provides a clear instance of contrast with the subsequent clause *ex qua expellit quicumque vult*, which in its relative brevity and abruptness vividly illustrates what Seneca is talking about in the letter as a whole.

1.54 : This case is less obviously illustrative in its length (though the illustrative element need not be absent : one might think of the numerous people referred to, or of the possibly rather drawn out business of *ad inopiam redigere*). The contrast with the two subsequent phrases of 5 syllables each, however, has a palpable rhythmic effect of finality, cf. below p. 91.

26.23 : The basic question is formulated in this colon, which in its length is to be contrasted with its (chiastically placed) extremely short correspondent *quae nolim* (26.27). Cf. below p. 139 for the structure of this passage.

26.50 : The length of the clause might well be illustrative of the element *de omnibus annis meis*.

41.26 : Both length and texture (with notable synaloephe) may be consciously illustrative of content. It should be noted that this paragraph, with its description of several items that cause religious awe, is studded with lengthy phrases, with the result that one suspects that the very topic is deemed worthy of wordiness. Indeed one is rather vividly reminded of Demetrius Π. ἑρμ. 5 σχεδὸν γὰρ τῷ μεγέθει τοῦ κώλου συνεξῆρται καὶ ὁ λόγος.[13]

41.49 : The length of the phrase, even without the introductory "non dices" suggests that the elements *maior* and *altior* are being illustrated, an illustration which would be the more obvious after the use of long phrases for objects of religious awe in the previous paragraph.

41.77 : One may suspect that the time consuming, drawn-out

---

[13] See also Primmer, *Cicero Numerosus*, p. 53 and note 23.

business of taming a lion is being illustrated in the length of this phrase.

75.50 : The line is suggestive of the very eloquence it treats of; so much so in fact that one is reminded of the spoof on medical eloquence in Damoxenos fr. 2 [14]; 75.54 might contain an echo.

75.65 : The colon illustrates the process of ἄσκησις, whose length and laboriousness are underscored by the very contrast with the length of the surrounding phrases. Cf. 80.29 and 31.

80.1-2 : These clauses should be taken together. Their length finds a very effective contrast in the next clause which consists of four syllables only. What it is precisely that is illustrated here is hard to catch : the relief perhaps, or the expectation, the selfsufficiency? It may be worthy of note that the next long clause in the paragraph (80.12) also deals with Seneca and his purposes, but there he states his independence, here his freedom depends on outward circumstances.

80.106-107 : The passage provides a similar contrast. The length of colon 106 may be descriptive of the outward elevation of the prince in question.

100.32 : The process of detailed literary criticism seems to be illustrated, as is the tortuous phrasing of Seneca's contemporaries in 100.46.

100.60 : The metaphor seems to provide us with an echo of that selfsame phrase in the clause which assigns most decorations to luxury. Cf. also the quotation of Lucilius' literary criticism in colon 79.

100.91 : Though its length is only 19 syllables, I include this colon here for the simple reason that the illustration of quantity through length seems obvious. Cf. also 80.24.

100.162 : Are we merely imagining that the words *verbis abundabat* (161) are being illustrated?

122. This letter has five cola over 20 syllables : 109, 162, 171, 178, 179. Surely it is hardly coincidence that all these deal directly with *luxuria*, i.e. the subject-matter of the letter as a whole?

It is much less easy to find an obvious suggestion that the very short [15] colon is similarly used for some illustrative function. Cola 1.55-56 were quoted above as being in a particular contrast with the preceding colon, but there is little more to be said than that both

---

[14] Cf. H. Dohm, Mageiros, *Die Rolle des Kochs in der griechisch-römischen Komödie.* Zetemata 32, München, Beck, 1964 p. 173 ff.

[15] The term covers cola of 5 syllables and less.

are 2 word, 5 syllable phrases that balance one another. It may be of course that brevity in itself carries an innate emphasis,[16] as seems to be the case in 26.39 (*carpimur*) and 65 (*dubia semper est*). Pungency, too, is the quality of the question *Numquam vir erit* (?) at 122.92, a quality which is further enhanced by the subsequent clause of purpose. On several occasions Seneca bunches a number of short cola together creating thereby an effect of apodictic finality as in 26.108-128, a remarkably pithy passage if compared with the much more pictorial paragraph at 41.23-40. An obvious example of the special pungency of the brief characteristic against the background of longer descriptive cola is provided by 122.109-122. This, however, remains a much more general quality than the one that could be suggested for very long cola. It should be added that the pungency is not merely enhanced if many of such short cola are placed closely together, but that tricola and isocola of this type produce the same effect. I have noted the following instances of short isocola with a strong closing effect: 1.55/6; 26.19/20; 41.11/2; 80.13/4; 100.19/20; 100.61/2.[17]

Also, there can be no doubt that Seneca is often playing with contrasting lengths as suggested above for 1.55/6 against 54. A typical example is to be found in 41.109-112, where we have a sequence of 4-10-5-11, consisting of a short question with a long qualification followed by an equally short answer with an equally long qualification.[18] In the same paragraph we find a sequence 13-6-6 (cola 115-117) whose effect is very similar to that of 1.55-56 quoted above. And no one who has read 26.41-47 (where one may regard 44-45 as a near isocolon) can doubt that *subduci* echoes *dilabi* both in absolute and in relative length (14-6-3/9+11-9-3). Counting this sort of thing is difficult and dangerous. How easily may one not succumb to the temptation of reading 26.83-84 together (with a reference to Fraenkel to lean on: *Leseproben* p. 19) in order to produce for 80ff. 5-11-5-11. Is it merely the 3-8-3-8 following that saves one from this pitfall?

Of isocola (allowing at most one syllable difference and requiring that the clauses obviously belong together) I found some 44 instances, tricola some 11, tetracola 3. Symmetrical arrangements such as e.g. 1.45-47 with 8-6-8 (lsl) syllables occur ca. 10 times, sls 9 times.

---

[16] Cf. Demetrius *Peri hermeneias* 6.
[17] This is not to say that short isocola always do this, cf. e.g. 122.159-160.
[18] Instances are collected below n. 19.

Obvious contrasts in length were as frequent as isocola: I counted some 12 instances of one long one short, 6 sl, 10 slsl, 4 lsls. Waxing and decreasing members are not frequent: 3 clear instances each. All this is based on counting only the most obvious instances:[19] what interests us is the question whether Seneca makes use of these formal elements in order to support or illustrate the meaning he wants to convey. I shall discuss a limited number of examples.

a. Isocola

An isocolon within the limits of my definition (no more than one syllable difference in length, the cola obviously belong together[20]) is found, e.g., in 41.11-12: *prope est a te deus/ tecum est, intus est.*[21] In addition to the similar length these two cola exhibit closely related clausulae. One may wonder whether the three preceding clauses (*ut nos ad aurem simulacri/ quasi magis exaudiri possimus/ admittat,*) should not be counted as one; certainly the pauses within it are weak. The result would be an interesting combination of two pairs (6-7 and 11-12) with a longer colon in between. However, the rearrangement (which would make the passage comparable to e.g. 1.54-56 quoted

---

[19] Isocola: 1.21-22; 1.55-56; 26.19-20; 26.70-71; 26.78-79; 26.111-112; 41.11-12; 41.21-22; 41.53-54; 41.56-57; 41.78-79; 41.97-98; 41.116-117; 75.2-3; 75.8-9; 75.20-21; 75.29-30; 75.74-75; 75.129-130; 75.144-145; 75.171-172; 75.182-183; 75.185-186; 80.13-14; 80.16-17; 80.34-35; 80.37-38; 80.66-67; 80.91-92; 80.98-99; 80.101-102; 100.11-12; 100.19-20; 100.22-23; 100.61-62; 100.87-88; 100.107-108; 122.7-8; 122.141-142; 122.159-160; 122.175-176; 122.201-202; 122.209-210.

tricola: 1.25-27; 26.75-77; 41.42-44; 75.14-16; 75.32-34; 75.173-175; 80.103-105; 100.122-124; 100.126-128; 122.56-58; 122.180-182.

tetracola: 1.60-63; 75.13-16(?); 80.51-54(?).

symmetries: *lsl* 1.45-47; 26.38-40; 26.64-66; 75.84-86; 75.147-149; 75.163-165; 80.18-20; 100.38-40; 100.84-86; 122.215-217; *sls* 1.51-53; 75.49-51; 75.64-66; 75.150-152; 80.21-23; 80.78-80; 80.112-114; 100.33-35; 100.90-92.

contrasts: *ls* 75.67-68; 75.91-92; 75.93-94; 75.105-106; 80.55-56; 80.57-58; 100.14-15; 100.41-42; 122.184-185; 122.187-188; *sl* 26.85-86; 75.169-170; 80.3-4; 100.161-162; *slsl* 26.1-4; 26.88-91; 26.104-107; 41.68-71(-73); 41.109-112; 75.58-61; 75.154-157; 100.109-112; *lsls* 26.15-18; 26.21-24; 122.21-24; 122.133-136.

waxing: 41.65-67; 122.83-86; 122.148-150.

decreasing: 41.106-108; 75.4-6; 75.80-82; 122.11-13; 122.42-44.

[20] These fall, all, under the definition of Isocolon as given in *Ad Her.* 4.20.27. It would seem that my rule of thumb of not allowing more than one syllable difference is somewhat stricter than even the Auctor has it. See also above p. 87, n. 11.

[21] We may, of course, prefer *tecum est/intus est,* in which case the combination 11-12 should be listed under those tricola in which the combined lengths of 2 + 3 equals that of 1. Cf. p. 95. However, the similar clausulae of 11 and 12 provide a defence for those who wish to treat 12 as a single colon.

above p. 89) makes very little difference for the main aspect of this group, viz. the emphatic finality created by an isocolon of very short clauses with identical or very similar clausulae.

On several occasions similar pairs constitute short periods. E.g. letter 80.66-67: *si vis scire quam nihil in illa mali sit,/ compara inter se pauperum et divitum vultus.* Another, even better, example is found *ibidem* 70-71: *etiam si qua incidit cura,/ velut nubes levis transit.* Here the two cola exhibit the same clausula as well as similar length. These examples are very different from the ones quoted above, in so far as the entire paragraph is arranged in groups of two, an arrangement that may be thought of as illustrating the subject matter (a comparison of the attitudes of the rich and the poor) and which as a matter of fact is in subtle counterpoint with it. For that reason we should not regard 69-71 as a tricolon. Moreover, of the three pairs of related clausulae only the one mentioned strengthens a pair of cola. The other two overlap pairs (at 67-68 and 73-74). This type of *variatio* which takes into account some three aspects of form is, it would seem, part and parcel of the strength of Seneca's style.

b. Tricola and tetracola.[22]

A good example of a tricolon is found in letter 75.14-15-16: *nec supploderem pedem/ nec manu iactarem/ nec attollerem vocem.*

---

[22] In this chapter tricolon is used for all groups of three cola, tetracolon for groups of four cola. Such groups need not form a complete period or other type of sentence. It is obvious, however, that tricola of special types are being used to create special effects. Amongst these the isocolic tricolon is the most important, i.e. the tricolon in which all cola have the same length, give or take a syllable, and in which the cola are often tied together by other similarities as well. Such a tricolon is quoted by Quintilian 9.3.77: *vicit/pudorem libido,/ timorem audacia,/ rationem amentia.* Wordorder, rhyme of *-orem, -ia* ensure a pause after *vicit.* In the same paragraph Quintilian admits tetracola and even longer groups, though he avoids the terminology, but he makes it very clear that it is not the three members but the additional element that stamps these as Figures. (Cf. 98). One may ask the question whether the mere fact of equal length, given the sharp rhythmic ear of the ancients, would be worthy of sufficient note to single out the group. Not so, it would seem, according to Quintilian, cf. *ibid.* 80, certainly so according to the Auctor ad Her. 4.20.27, cf. his example of isocolon: *In proelio mortem parens oppetebat,/domi filius nuptias conparabat;/haec omina gravis casus administrabant.* In this group the additional elements are very light (hardly homoioteleuton *-bat*, hardly chiasm *mortem parens filius nuptias*; acc. to Prof. Leeman chiasm is not a Figure anyway; no clausula repetition). It would seem then that the twins and the triplets should not be absent from our inventory even if they were not dressed in identical or similar clothes.

Why Thraede (*Grundzüge* pp. 33, 34, 66, 77[105], 85[135], 87, 111, 122, 140, 163[301],

The wordorder of 14 and 16 is the same, 15 acts as an element of *variatio*, as do the differing clausulae. The purpose of the arrangement seems to be directly illustrative of the content—that at least is the suggestion of the next clause : *sed ista oratoribus reliquissem*. One may, of course, react to the irony of the situation, as Norden did when remarking on a very similar tricolon at 75.32-34 (*quod sentimus loquamur,/ quod loquimur sentiamus ;/ concordet sermo cum vita*) "aber wird es uns nicht schwer einem zu glauben, der eben diese *propositi summa* in ein pointiertes σχῆμα kleidet?". I am not sure that this is fair comment (even if it is Seneca's own, 80.88 ff.), any more than it is fair comment to say that the ghost in Hamlet is a flesh and blood actor with a few stage effects, since the important thing is that he is the ghost and gets his message across to the audience. Elsewhere (100.122-128) Seneca uses two such tricola in quoting Lucilius' criticism of Fabianus' style, thereby apparently suggesting how precious is Lucilius' own.[23] On occasion the tricolon is almost hidden in a larger group, e.g. 75.173-175 which forms a subgrouping within seven negative clauses.

Letter 1.60-63 may be regarded as a tetracolon : *tu tamen malo serves tua et/ bono tempore incipies./ Nam ut visum est maioribus nostris,/ "sera parsimonia in fundo est ;"* In the context there can be no doubt that the four cola belong more closely together than the full stop

---

167?) restricts his use of the term tricolon to groups with the relation $1+2=3$ ($3=1+2$ being an "inverted tricolon") is not clear to me, unless it is based on a misinterpretation of Hermogenes *Inv.* 4.3 p. 180.16 ff. Rabe. Hermogenes says no more than that there are certain tricolon periods in which one monocolon apodosis suffices for the double protasis. Length of the cola does not enter the picture. Thraede's type does exist and I add a number of examples, though the group is no more important than that of the isocolic type.

[23] Seneca Pater mentions with disapproval the fashionable use of tricola and tetracola. Cf. *Contr.* 2.4.12 (*tricolum tale, qualia sunt quae basilicam infectant*). The least one can do is make sure that all membra make some sense: cf. 9.2(25).27. *Et illud tetracolon: serviebat forum cubiculo, praetor meretrici, carcer convivio, dies nocti. Novissima pars sine sensu dicta est, ut impleretur numerus; quem enim sensum habet: "Serviebat dies nocti?" Hanc ideo sententiam rettuli, quia et in tricolis et in omnibus huius generis sententiis curamus ut numerus constet, non curamus an sensus. Omnia autem genera corruptarum quoque sententiarum de industria pono, quia facilius, et quid imitandum et quid vitandum sit, docemur exemplo.*

Seneca's judgement seems a little harsh here, since "*serviebat dies nocti*" may well obtain its (metaphorical) sense from the previous membra. E. Norden quotes these passages (*Aen. VI* p. 377) to show that *tricolon* and *tetracolon* in the widest sense of the words were particularly fashionable at the time. It is obvious, however, that Seneca's reference is restricted to such pointed schemata as quoted above (n. 22) from Quintilian.

after *incipies* would tend to indicate. The suspended *et* (cf. above
p. 11, n. 1; p. 86) may be regarded as objectionable, but I feel that it
loads *bono tempore* with additional meaning, here at the end of a
letter that deals with time in the sense of your time, my time; and
this meaning is further strengthened by the use of the proverbial
statement. Note that 62-64 also form a unit within which 62-63 roughly
equal 64 in length. There seems to be no reason why the double
function should not have been intended. Another tetracolon, though
not quite as precise, is to be found at letter 80.51-54 (6-6-5-7). Does
Seneca intend to suggest the small size of the amounts involved by
means of the accumulation of very brief cola?

Among non-isocolic arrangements those tricola in which the third
colon is as long as the first two combined are worthy of mention.[24]
Once again we may allow a reasonable margin in the number of
syllables, in keeping with the auditive principle. One instance has
been mentioned above (1.62ff.). Letter 26.82-84 provides another good
one in so far as the longer clause deals emphatically with both the
statement and the question of the shorter ones. What seems at first
a striking instance occurs at 41.13-15: *Ita dico, Lucili:/ sacer intra
nos spiritus sedet,/ malorum bonorumque nostrorum observator et custos*;
the length of these cola is in step with the increasing emphasis. Yet
the instance is almost too good, for the third colon may also be
combined with the subsequent lines: *hic prout a nobis tractatus est,/
ita nos ipse tractat.* Thus the passage could also have been mentioned
under *symmetries*, below p. 98. There is an unmistakable hint that
the length of the clauses has indeed been put to work to enhance,
underscore and emphasize the content. With this example in mind
we may wonder whether a similar arrangement is tried out in the
first five cola of the letter. If so, it is remarkable that *bonam mentem*
at 41.3 and *observator et custos* at 41.15 occupy parallel places. Indeed,
the first sentence of the letter merits some further analysis. *Facis rem
optimam et/ tibi salutarem,/ si, ut scribis, perseveras ire ad bonam
mentem,/ quam stultum est optare,/ cum possis a te impetrare.* We have
a structure here, that, (apart from *ut scribis*) operates on four gram-
matical levels: 1. *facis-salutarem* (main), 2. *si-mentem* (1st subordination), 3. *quam-optare* (2nd subordination), 4. *cum-inpetrare (3rd subordination).* It is reasonably obvious that the level of subordination

---

[24] Apart from the instances mentioned e.g. 26.29-31; 26.108-110; 75.70-72; 75.118-120.
In inverted order e.g. 100.18-20; 122.229-231.

has little to do with the level of importance and that the more important
pause in the sentence as a whole does not lie at *salutarem* but at *mentem*,
after which a new thought is added. Yet it would seem that the
element of subordination has a stylistic importance of its own, one
that lies in the very contrast with the paratactic structure of the
parallel group of cola at the beginning of the next paragraph.[25] In
inverted order this type of tricolon is found e.g. 1.8-10. The
instance is a very suggestive one in that the first and longest clause
hints at robbery with violence, the second at stealthy theft, and the
third, the shortest, at unnoticed loss. Is the last one the least important,
then? Certainly not. Seneca continues with a short period, resounding
in the contrast : *turpissima tamen est iactura/ quae per neglegentiam.
fit.* The function of the entire arrangement seems to be to express
the countertheme, the reverse of *vindica, serva*, with an appropriate
emphasis. This type of tricolon, whether the long or the short clauses
precede, may either be regarded as a dissembling isocolon, or as a
special case of that common occurrence in Latin Literature, the
Waxing Group. Indeed our seven letters provide several examples
to illustrate the Law of the Waxing Members, which Leumann-
Hofmann-Szantyr state is observable in Seneca (p. 722). It is however
of little more than secondary importance among the many effects
Seneca uses.[26] Moreover, groups of what may be called Waning
Members also occur.[27] I quote 80.3-5 : *Nemo inrumpet/ nemo cogi-
tationem meam impediet,/ quae hac ipsa fiducia procedit audacius.*
The example contains its own element of *variatio*, in so far as the
expected *nemo*+future indicative does not materialize the third time.
Indeed none of the examples quoted in note 26 have additional stylistic

---

[25] It seems, then, that, keeping the definition of period in mind as it will be
given below (p. 100), we must view this sentence as two periods, twice εὐκαταστρόφως,
and yet we feel little inclination to place a period after *bonam mentem* since what
follows is so obviously its qualification. A double periodic structure, therefore, within
one sentence. Cf. 41.58f. for a very similar situation. That a periodic structure may
be part of a larger whole should not be cause for surprise. There seem to be several
examples in these seven letters alone. E.g. 41.16-17 is a period that belongs to a group
stretching from 1-5.

[26] Cf. Leumann-Hofmann-Szantyr, *Lateinische Syntax u. Stylistik* 1965 p. 722ff.
(The term stems from Behaghel IF 25, 1909 p. 110ff.); our sample provides examples
at 1.57-59 (3-6-11); 26.48-50 (but cf. 51); 41.13-15; 41.41-49; 75.23-25/6; 75.52-54;
75.70-72; 75.130-132 (with an obvious lack of rhetorical impact); 100.30-32; 100.51-54;
100.70-72; 122.101-104; 122.105-108; 122.177-179.

[27] 1.8-10 (cf. above for the inclusion of this passage among inverted anisocolic
tricola); 1.35; 26.25-27; 26.41-43; 75.4-6; 75.80-82; 100.48-50; 122.127-130.

traits to as noticeable an extent as the isocolic tricola quoted above. For that reason the only criterion for inclusion has been the number of syllables. This, of course, is not to say that no stylistic figures may be observed in Waxing Groups.

A number of the instances is somewhat formally correct and uninteresting, but there are certain passages in which the increase is strikingly in tune with the thought of the passage. Among these paragraph 4 of letter 41 takes a curious place. We have to do with a period that embraces the entire paragraph, starting with a protasis of three words (6 syllables): *si hominem videris*. Seneca lingers on the qualification of *hominem*, first by means of an isocolic tricolon (above p. 92, n. 19) of 8-9-8 syllables; the tension thus created is subsequently heightened first by a single qualification of twelve, next by a double qualification of seventeen syllables. The apodosis consists of a very effective simple question of eleven syllables. After this, almost unexpectedly, but doubly effective in its excessive length (cf. above p. 89), follows a second apodosis, again in the form of a question— introduced by *non dices*.

Now, when we ask why Seneca uses this somewhat heavy battery of effects, it is not quite enough to suggest that after all the Wise Man is central in the author's thought. It is also necessary to be fully aware of the fact that the paragraph is not isolated, that the conditional form employed here is the third in a series, a series that is carefully interrupted by the Group at 41.37-40, which constitutes an element of *variatio* in the form of the overall argument that stretches over paragraphs 3 and 4. And finally we must realize that the two clinching questions of the final double apodosis are not only in contrast with one another, but are also varying the format of apodosis that had been used twice in the preceding paragraph (the homoiote- leuton *faciet...percutiet* is only one of several characteristics those apodoses have in common). It is clear, then, that Seneca has indeed the Wise Man in the centre of his attention here, but that it is a Wise Man who in the gradual accumulation of his characteristics is fully integrated in this particular letter, which is often quoted for its "*sacer intra nos spiritus sedet*".

Next to the Waxing Members the Waning Members should be mentioned. The instance at 41.96-100 is rather suggestive if cola 97-98 belong together: *Familiam formonsam habet et domum pulchram,/ multum serit, (/) multum fenerat:/ nihil horum in ipso est/ sed circa ipsum*. A relationship between form and content seems to be observable here, but with the other instances this is the case to no greater degree than with the increasing groups.[28]

Finally, above p. 95, two instances were mentioned of anisocolic tricolon and inverted anisocolic tricolon combined. It was suggested that those passages could equally well have been treated in the next section, under *symmetries*. The same is true of a few additional passages that show a combination of increase and decrease, e.g. 1.1-5 and 1.41-44 (decrease + increase). It may be however, that the reverse, to see the symmetries as waxing and waning, or waning and waxing, is felt to be more descriptive of the effect created, since we are dealing with auditive rather than visual rhythms.

c. *Symmetries and contrasts*

Among symmetries the one quoted above (1.45-47, cf. p. 91) is almost immediately followed by another: 1.51-53, *Non possum dicere nihil perdere/ sed quid perdam et quare et quemadmodum dicam;/ causas paupertatis meae reddam.* This group, in its turn, is followed by another group of three cola, this time arranged in a long-short-short sequence (cf. p. 93 for the closing effect of the isocolon). In between the two symmetries, however, there is a further group of three, which, though it does not qualify as an absolute symmetry on technical grounds (the syllable lengths are 7-15-10), is otherwise comparable to the groups it separates. Thus we have a set of three groups which are sufficiently similar to one another to set up a certain cadence that is then broken by the finality of the last group. This, it seems, is all that Seneca can say in his own defence. However, the next paragraph starts with a 3-6-11 sequence in order to raise the almost despairing tone at the end of paragraph 4 and introduces a new contrast. Further symmetries may be found e.g. at 80.112-114 where the simplicity of the proper object *te* is contrasted with the involved hindrances. More obvious is the pictorial effect at 100.90-92 or even the impatience at 75.64-66. Cf. p. 90 above.

For contrasting lengths I discuss only one further example: 1.17-20, *quem mihi dabis/ qui aliquod pretium tempori ponat,/ qui diem aestimet, qui intellegat se cotidie mori.* The lengths are 5-11-5-11. No doubt such an arrangement had an immediately audible rhythmic effect. It is noteworthy, however, that the meaning structure is 1:3 (*quem-*

---

[28] Cf. above p. 96 n. 27.

qui-qui-qui), whereas the clausulae are 1,1,4,4. So one may say that the contrast of clause-lengths is contrapuntal with the meaning structure and that the clausulae play a third melody against the other two, effecting a double counterpoint. This sentence winds up a set of very carefully composed groups whose main function is to emphasize the main notion of this letter : time. See above p. 96, in particular below p. 103 f. for an analysis of those groups.

There has long been a classification of styles according to the prevalence of the types of sentences prevalent in them. Thus Lausberg[29] quotes from Demetrius 12 a style called κατεστραμμένη of which the period is characteristic, and one called διῃρημένη which is described as ἡ εἰς κῶλα λελυμένη, and from 193 a διαλελυμένη λέξις of which Heraclitus' obscure disjointedness is an example. Lausberg respectively connects these with Quintilian's *oratio vincta atque contexta* (9.4.19), Aquila's *oratio perpetua* (18) and *oratio soluta* (*ibidem* ; cf. Quintilian 2.20.7 : *oratio concisa*). Thus he builds up a tripartition (cf. Aquila 18), which, however, is not entirely satisfactory in so far as the distinction between *oratio perpetua* and *oratio soluta* (respectively : zufällig-kunstlose Nebeneinanderstellung, gewollt koordinierende Nebeneinanderstellung) remains somewhat vague. Yet even this rather vague distinction has its importance since the ancient authors were conscious of some relationship between the prevalence of a certain type of sentence and the genre they were writing in.[30] The periodic style has always been closely related with oratory ; Quintilian 9.4.19 connects the *oratio soluta* by way of example with *sermo* (conversational style) and *epistulae*. He continues : "nisi cum aliquid supra naturam suam tractant, ut de philosophia,. de republica, similibus. Quod non eo dico, quia non illud quoque solutum habeat suos quosdam et forsitan difficiliores etiam pedes ; neque enim aut hiare semper vocalibus aut destitui temporibus volunt sermo atque epistula ; sed non fluunt nec cohaerent nec verba verbis trahunt, ut potius laxiora in his vincula quam nulla sint". In Seneca's letters, then, we may look for a fair degree of *oratio vincta atque contexta*. But in order to discuss the details of this style I prefer to replace Lausberg's too vague distinction of sentence types by Primmer's more precise elaboration. Primmer,[31] too, bases his tripartition essentially on the Aristides-

---

[29] Sections 912-947.

[30] Thus Aquila 18 feels that the *oratio perpetua* fits *historia* and *descriptio* in particular.

[31] A. Primmer, *Cicero numerosus*, p. 118 ff., against Norden *Aen. VI* p. 376 ff.

Romanus pattern.[32] In view of the fact that he also provides certain statistics with which our sample may be fruitfully compared, I may be permitted to adopt Primmer's system with a minor modification only[33] in particular since in the present study the sentence typology plays only a minor part. The main characteristics of each type (Periode, Satzgefüge, Gruppe, here rendered period, complex sentence, group) are as follows.

1. Period

The sense is complete only then, when we have come to the end of the last colon. A special characteristic is the καμπή, the aspect contained in the word εὐκαταστρόφως.[34] From the seven letters studied here I may cite the following instances:

41.41-49 : *Si hominem videris/ interritum periculis/ intactum cupiditatibus/ inter adversa felicem/ in mediis tempestatibus placidum/ ex superiore loco homines videntem, ex aequo deos// non subibit te veneratio eius?/ non dices/ "ista res maior est altiorque quam ut credi similis huic in quo est corpusculo possit"?///* The example may seem badly chosen in so far as one may say that the *sensus* could finish after *veneratio eius* ; however, the rising series of qualifications in the protasis would cause such a finish to fall flat on its face. A much simpler example, but one that fulfills all the requirements, is to be found in 41.16-17 : *hic prout a nobis tractatus est,/ ita nos ipse tractat.* If this

---

[32] Aquila Romanus, *De fig. sent. et eloc. liber*, 18 (Rhet. Lat. Min. ed. Halm, Teubner 1863, p. 27). See also Aristides *Techn. Rhet.* 167 (p. 63.5 Schm., 507 Sp.). Cf. Schenkeveld p. 38f. (more lucid than Lausberg 912 ff.).

[33] Primmer adds a distinction *concinnus-inconcinnus* based on the presence or absence of what he calls the *Numerus* element, by which he means "etwa die Gliederung einer Aussage durch parallele Gedankenführung, durch Periodisierung, durch Figuren der Wortstellung wie Anapher und Homoioteleuton. (...) sein wesentliches Merkmal (...): dass durch den Numerus Harmonie und Ordnung hergestellt wird".
Cf. the discussion of concinnity p. 66ff. (and e.g. Cicero, Orator 44.149, Brutus 83.287). It appears, then, that the classification "inconcinnus" essentially means "I do not recognize any particular rhetorical element". I doubt whether such a classification is at all useful. Indeed we do well to remember the wisdom of Mr. Laughton's remark in his review of Fraenkel's *Leseproben* (p. 194): " 'concinnitas' ...was not confined to any one period or to particular authors, or even to consciously literary expression, but was a normal characteristic of educated speech; moreover ... this natural and almost involuntary concinnity extended even to the rhythm-patterns of individual phrases".

[34] Primmer, *op. cit.*, p. 52: "durch diese differentia specifica unterscheidet sich die Periode von anderen Gebilden, die auch von Kola zusammengesetzt sind". The definition is based on Demetrius 10 which contains the notions εὐκαταστρόφως and καμπή, signifying the rounded quality of the period.

example should arouse the aristotelian objection of excessive brevity, it may be useful to quote Cicero (Orator 225): *extrema sequitur comprehensio, sed ex duobus membris, qua non potest esse brevior: "quem quaeso nostrum fefellit ita vos esse facturos?"* An example in which the καμπή is less centrally placed,[35] but which must count as a period for all that, may be found in the same letter, 41.31-36: *Si quis specus/ saxis penitus exesis/ montem suspenderit/ non manu factus/ sed naturalibus causis in tantam laxitatem excavatus// animum tuum quadam religionis suspicione percutiet.///*

2. Complex sentence

The main characteristics are a far less tight meaning structure coupled with syntactical subordination: syntactically dependent clauses add elements of meaning rather than being indispensable for the basic meaning. An example may be found in 1.45-47: *Interrogabis fortasse/ quid ego faciam/ qui tibi ista praecipio//.* The final colon is not indispensable for the meaning, though one must admit that once it has been said it has added a whole dimension. If for that reason the example is thought to be somewhat unfortunate, a better one may perhaps be found in 80.21-27: *cogito mecum/ quam multi corpora exerceant/ ingenia quam pauci/ quantus ad spectaculum non fidele et lusorium fiat concursus/ quanta sit circa artes bonas solitudo/ quam inbecilli animo sint/ quorum lacertos umerosque miramur//* Its noteworthy rhetorical structure (visible in the double anaphora *quam-quam-quantus-quanta-quam,* audible in the length of the clauses that follow each of these—the pause at *animo sint/ quorum* being obviously less marked than the others) includes none of the characteristics of the period as stated above, and though almost the whole set of cola is subordinated to *cogito mecum* not one of the subordinate clauses is really indispensable. Another instance, difficult in its colometry, is furnished by 75.48-51: *Non quaerit aeger medicum eloquentem,/ sed si ita competit, ut idem ille qui sanare potest compte de iis quae facienda sunt disserat,/ boni consulet.* The sentence could have been complete without the entire portion *si-disserat.*

---

[35] Yet it would not do to apply the adjective *inconcinnus,* since a certain balance between the initial description of the cavern (cola $31+32+33 = 18$ syllables) and its natural aspect ($34+35 = 23$ syllables) may well have been felt by an ancient reader/ hearer.

3. Group

Its characteristic is properly indicated by its name : it is a group of syntactically independent clauses, which together form an identifiable totality. The phenomenon was properly observed by Gercke (*Seneca Studien* 1895, p. 155): "Nicht selten gehören... eine ganze Reihe kleiner Sätzchen inhaltlich zusammen und bilden bald grammatisch bald nur logisch eine Periode." *Ep.* 75.31-34 furnishes an instance : *Haec sit propositi nostri summa :| quod sentimus loquamur,| quod loquimur sentiamus ;| concordet sermo cum vita.* Another instance, one in which the *Sätzchen* show a certain complexity within themselves, occurs at 100.21-23 : *Sed ita, ut vis, esse credamus :| mores ille, non verba composuit| et animis scripsit ista, non auribus.* It is perhaps interesting—though premature—to note that Seneca is often at his rhetorical best in these groups.[36]

These types have been marked in the margin of the text with P (period), S (complex sentence) and G (group) or combinations of these symbols for mixed instances. Single cola, not obviously linked with any of the above structures, have been marked Cl. Mr. Primmer has developed his system on the basis of Cicero's speeches and there can be no guarantee that we shall be able to employ it for Seneca without adjustment. Indeed in view of the difference not only of author but of genre, it is not surprising that I found it not always easy to classify the instances. In fact I assign rather larger percentages to mixed categories than Primmer does even in the small specimens from Cicero's second Catilinarian that I have added to the table for the sake of comparison. The latter's distinction *concinnus/inconcinnus* has been omitted. The table shows the results both for the individual letters and in overall percentages. For the sake of comparison I have added a count of Servius Sulpicius Rufus' consolatory letter to Cicero (*Ad fam.* IV 5, written in March 45 B.C.) as well as Fraenkel's first two Leseproben. All of these are based on a counting of the cola. It may be thought that the colon is not a very uniform unit for counting purposes, and that therefore it would be useful to rework the figures based on cola into figures based on a unit such as single words or lines of print. Primmer uses the latter. After reworking the figures of four letters into figures based on lines of print, it appeared that the differences in percentage were negligible. For that reason Primmer's figures were converted into percentages and added to the table without further ado.

---

[36] See below p. 104.

TABLE II

	1	26	41	75	80	100	122	overall %	Ad fam. IV 5	Lesepr. 1+2	Pro Sestio (Primmer)
P	23%	21	27	16	19	13	22.5	ca.20.0%	30	36	(50.2)
S	11	32	9	12	21.5	26	20	ca.18.0%	28	31.5	(30.8)
G	37	33	37	52	34	46.5	31	ca.40.0%	23	13	(16.0)
PG	11	55	16	5	6	9	8	ca. 8.0%	13	12 }	(2)
PS	0	0	0	8	0	3.5	4	ca. 2.0%	0	0 }	
GS	20	5	6	2	13	8	7	ca. 8.0%	2	6	
CL	0	2	2	3	6	3.5	4	ca. 2.0%	2	0	(0.6)

The difference in distribution is hardly startling, is in fact a confirmation of what a simple reading of Cicero's speech and Seneca's letters might lead one to suspect. But if the distribution might, at first sight, seem to support also the criticism of Seneca's style in Caligula's scornful "harena sine calce", in Quintilian's *minutissimae sententiae*, and in a late echo of the latter in John of Salisbury, who refers to the *commaticum genus dicendi*,[37] we must ask whether the distribution reflects the author's style, or rather the genre he was writing in. And, once more as suspected, a rough count yields for a number of letters of Pliny:[38] P 30%, S 22% and G 54%, and for Cicero's letters[39] P 20%, S 26% and G 57%. These counts are rough since they have not been preceded by a close colometric study of the texts involved. For that reason even the mixed categories have been omitted. But even with those restrictions the figures support the point that the distribution of periods, complex sentences and groups is useful as a genre characteristic.[40]

It is necessary to note one feature of the table with some care: even if the natural divergence due to the small amounts of material has been taken into account, it seems curious that letters 75 and 100, the two letters in which Seneca is currently occupied with stylistic matters, should show a rather larger percentage of G and a rather smaller percentage of P elements than even the average of the entire group. To study this phenomenon properly we need comparative

---

[37] Caligula apud Suetonium *Cal.* 53.2; Quintilian *Inst.* 10.1.130, John of Salisbury, *Metalogicon* 1.22; the latter quoted by Norden, *Kunstprosa* p. 307. Cf. Rauschning p. 2 f.

[38] 1.13; 1.15; 2.1; 2.6; 2.11; 2.20.

[39] Numbers 787-792, 794, 795, 798, 799 in Tyrrell and Purser, *Correspondence* vol. VI.

[40] I am fully aware that it is possible to criticize these statistical statements as based on too small a sample of material. I should like to see each of them treated, for that reason, as a useful hypothesis.

statistics for *a.* all letters dealing with stylistic matters and *b.* an equally large group of letters dealing with subjects of a different nature. To prepare such statistics falls outside the scope of the present study: nec pietas moram rugis et instanti senectae adferet...

From the figures above it is obvious that G is characteristic of the letter style, Seneca's as well as Pliny's and Cicero's, though it is equally clear that considerable divergences occur within the genre. Thus, e.g., it is noteworthy that Servius Sulpicius' formal letter of consolation should show a much smaller G and a much larger P count than the Seneca group or the Cicero group.

If we then return to the text of e.g. Letter 1.1, we find that indeed the overriding impression is one of coordination rather than subordination, but also of the rhetorical effect achieved by means of this coordination. There is no mistaking the "rhythmical" quality of the paragraph as a whole with its three groups of repetitions. We note further that the qualification of *tempus* in the second line consists of one of these groups and shows cola of respectively 9,7 and 5 syllables. The second of the groups is a tricolon in which the second and third members roughly equal the first and shows a triple anaphora of *quaedam* which in turn qualifies *tempora*. The final group, tied together by a triple *agentibus*, equally has time for its subject, in the very sense in which *tempus* of line 2 is to be interpreted: *vita*.

It is obvious that the group-material has been carefully arranged so as to underscore the basic notion of the paragraph and its proper interpretation. There is little doubt in our minds that time-life is the basic concept of the paragraph. It still is, for much the same reason, at the start of the next paragraph.

If the group is characteristic of the letter style, that must not be taken to mean that the periods and complex sentences are structurally and stylistically unimportant. It is best, perhaps, to demonstrate the importance by means of another analysis: 80.10. This paragraph shows a very careful arrangement. The first colon (106, *Cl.* indicating that it has no hypotactic or paratactic connection with the previous or succeeding cola) is balanced by the central colon of the paragraph, the question *Quid de aliis loquor* (111), which by means of that position achieves a pungency of its own. It, too, is marked as *Cl.* Both of these cola are followed by a period in four cola. These periods are of a type that may be called "broken" in that the apodosis consists of a paratactic construction of which the members are really needed to supplement one another. To that extent, we have here a stylistic *repetitio*, whose rhythmic effect is essentially strengthened by the length of the clauses involved. Seneca, however, applies two elements of *variatio*. The first is the different inner arrangements of the two conditional periods. Period one consists of a protasis in two cola and an apodosis of as many, period two has a protasis of one colon and an apodosis of three cola. The other element of variation lies in the management of the clausulae. We have three pairs, the first ties cola 106-107 (after all *illum* refers back to *regem*) the third ties cola 111-112: once again the question with the protasis of the conditional. Whether cola 110 and 114 may be tied together by their similar clausulae is a matter to be considered later on.[41]

---

[41] See p. 128.

CLAUSULAE, STATISTICS AND USAGE

Among the various systems in use to denote the rhythms with which Latin authors of the Golden and Silver Ages were wont to close their phrases, I have chosen what seems to me the most neutral one with respect to the question whether or not these rhythms consist of (verse)feet applied to prose.[1] I do not intend to discuss this question, since it would inevitably lead to speculation concerning the nature of rhythm and metre—speculation which I am not at all convinced would be helpful in the present enquiry. Nor do I wish to spend a great deal of time on the question at which point in the phrase the clausula started, since in the nature of things we are more interested in its closing effect. It can hardly be necessary for the hearer of a prose passage or phrase to know where exactly the closing effect has started, provided it has had its effect. And if, then, there are instances in which rhythms frequently employed in closing a phrase start in the middle of a word, I would submit that a closing rhythm not cut off, but flowing from the phrase in a natural manner, shows greater art than cases (some of them stock phrases like *esse videatur*) in which a syntactical break announces the approaching end. Quintilian's treatment certainly points in that direction.[2]

The notation used is essentially the traditional one developed by Zielinski, Hagendahl, Primmer[3]:

1   denotes $\_ \cup \_ \_ \, \infty$
2   denotes $\_ \cup \_ \_ \cup \, \infty$

---

[1] I get the impression that e.g. Quintilian is entirely indifferent to the names he gives certain sequences of longs and shorts. Thus he allows for *Brute, dubitavi* both "prior paean + spond." and "dactyl + bacchius".

[2] Quintilian starts his treatment of the clausula as such with the notation that long syllables produce a firm ending, though short syllables are also employed in producing endings. He acknowledges the theory of the final *anceps* but leaves us in no doubt that to his own ears long or short makes a difference, (9.4.93-94). Having discussed the question he continues: "*Retrorsum autem neque plus tribus ... repetendi sunt*". Obviously he starts from the end, and first counts the final groups. Nowhere does he evince any of the anxiety concerning the beginning of the clausula that characterizes several modern discussions. It seems to me that the problem has been stated in the wrong way. The audience will know when the closing rhythm has done its work without having been made aware of it at the start. Indeed one might say that not those who start clausulae in the middle of a word, but those who feel that they cannot but start at the beginning of a word are wielding the instrument with which whole cloth is cut.

[3] *Cicero Numerosus* p. 153 ff.

3   denotes (...) $\_\cup\_\sim$

4   denotes $\_\cup\_\cup\sim$

Each of these has derived forms which are marked by the following symbols :

1^1, 2^1 etc. denotes resolution of the first long : $\cup\cup$.

1^2, 2^2 etc. denotes resolution of the second long syllable. Similarly 1^3 etc.

Double figures are used to indicate lengthening of the first short; 1^{tr} etc. marks doubling of the first short. Combinations of these symbols may occur. The Greek characters following the symbol indicate wordendings within the clausula. In the case of type 3 wordendings start being counted from three syllables before the clausula proper.[4]

I have felt it would be useful to adhere to this elaborated (and somewhat elaborate) system of notation, even though I shall not make use of all its facets in the present study. I have however taken the liberty to omit the system whereby Primmer notes elisions, but I have added an s wherever synaloephe smoothed out all word endings within a clausula, since it seems that in such a case we approach rather closely the difference between *criminis causa* and *archipiratae* or *balneatori* (Quint. 9.4.98).

Synaloephe has been accepted as the rule within the cola, as it is the rule within contemporary verse. It is to be noted that it occurs rather more frequently than in Seneca's own tragedy. Our sample of ca. 1000 cola shows 546 instances, whereas the Hercules Furens has 377 instances in 1344 lines. This fits the general impression that the closer we are to everyday language the more frequently synaloephe occurs.[5] A considerable number of scholars[6] claim that synaloephe

---

[4] However, I felt that to enter the questions concerning the shape or shapes of clausula 3 when those three syllables are taken into account would lead me too far from the aim of the present study.

[5] The most intensive study of synaloephe is the one by J. Soubiran, *l'Elision dans la poésie latine*. Thèse, Paris 1966, who modestly proposes the following paragraph for textbooks of Latin Metre: "Quand une voyelle finale (ou une syllabe en -m) rencontrait en poésie une initiale vocalique, la finale était comptée pour zéro dans la mesure du vers (élision), mais elle continuait d'être entendue: les deux voyelles en contact étaient prononcées d'une seule émission de voix (synalèphe). Trois exceptions: les enclitiques, dont l'élision était totale; le monosyllabe *est* qui, précédé de finale élidable, se réduisait le plus souvent à *st*; un monosyllabe élidable suivi de voyelle brève, rencontre qui, parfois, aboutissait à une syllabe longue (phénomène improprement nommé "hiatus prosodique")". Cf. Drexler's review in *Gnomon* 1967, p. 145ff. Concerning the frequency of synaloephe see Crusius p. 15, and, in greater detail, Soubiran p. 148 who demonstrates statistically that where Vergil avoids, or at least reduces, the number of instances, Cicero is indifferent to the phenomenon.

may cause a shift of accent : the hypothesis is to save the coincidence of ictus and accent e.g. in Terence *And.* 1 ..*ánimum ad scríbendum áppulit.* E. Fraenkel (*Lesepr.* 195f.) when opposing Zielinski's law of the shifted accent (formulated in order to accommodate the type *complúres vénerant in* ‿‿‿‿‿‿) makes an exception ("selbstverständlich") for the recession caused by synaloephe. Two years before Fraenkel's *Leseproben* appeared, however, Soubiran had directed a spirited attack against the whole idea (o.c. p. 457-480) arguing that it rests on the postulate it is designed to prove and that the applicability-at-will is an absurdity. In the case of our prose sample an attempt has been made to assign the clausulae keeping in mind the rule that the main word accent should not occur *in thesi*. This has been possible in all but a very few cases :

41.84 *non sine timore aspici* 44

The symbol 44 hints at *tímore*. If Soubiran (and his predecessors) are right the symbol should be 22^1 which does not elsewhere occur in our sample. See also p. 27 n. 1

80.102 *lenocinio abscondunt* 1^{tr}

The symbol 1^{tr} presumes *lenócinio*. *Lenocínio-* results in 33^1 also unparalleled in our sample, unless we assume synizesis. See also p. 51 n. 1

100.34 *iudicium abstulit* 4^{tr}

4^{tr} assumes *iúdiciábstulit*. *Iudícium-* is hard to catch under the net of the system chosen; if we insist, *qui iudicium_abstulit* may be given the symbol 22^2 αβ, equally unparalleled in our sample; synizesis would simplify to simple 4.

122. 21 *in eádem_urbe_antípodes* 11^3

This instance causes little trouble: *in eadem úrbe antipodes* produces 33^2, only slightly less common than 11^3. In the other cases we have to decide whether a unique clausula is sufficient reason to assume a somewhat drastic departure from the usual pronunciation. The present sample is, of course, too small to base such a decision on. Upon examination, however, it appears that the examples K. Müller gives (*o.c.* p. 769) are not all of them compelling : Curtius 9.5.11 (*múcrone hausit*) may well be read as $11β$ *subiecto mucróne hausit.* 6.5.4 *Aléxandro*

---

[6] Soubiran p. 457 gives a brief history of the question. Drexler, *Einf.* p. 17 n. 17 is not convinced and points out that "das Beispiel animadvertere ... die Antwort auf die umstrittene Frage der Akzentverscheibung bei Synaloephe (gibt): sie musste notwendig eintreten". I do not understand the word *notwendig* in view of e.g. K. Müller (*o.c.* p. 769: Bei Synaloephe *kann* der Akzent vorrücken).

essent and 9.2.34 *imperátorem essent* are more difficult, but in our Seneca sample we find 26.60 *de me iudicaturus sum* in which the enclitic presumably adds an accent to *-us*, but surely it leaves at least a secondary one on *tu-*; cf. 75.37 *videbimus qualis sit*. See also p. 110 on the question of a possible cretic+molossus. For Curtius 6.4.8 *prope óccisum ab eo*; 4.13.10 *cómpertum habeo*; 10.5.35 *in potéstate habuit*, add Seneca *De ira* 3.22.14 *si in castris meis Silenum habeo* (Zander indeed accentuates *Si*), a counterindication may be found in *De ira* 3.43.5 *ínterim dùm tráhimus*. See also Fraenkel, *Leseproben* 119 on *praecepta velis*.

The question of prosodic hiatus is a hard one. On the whole I am inclined to side with those scholars who feel that with monosyllabics of the type sī, sē etc. preceding a short vowel something in the nature of a halfway synaloephe takes place. The resulting time is more like two *morae* than one. Accordingly I have marked ‿‿ , but in the clausulae I count as long. The same applies to the monosyllabics in -m, though there presumably some nasal effect remained in the pronunciation. Examples occur at 1.18 ; 1.29 ; 26.11 ; 26.30 ; 26.77 ; 26.98 ; 41.41 ; 41.69 ; 41.71 ; 41.73 ; 41.108 ; 75.49 ; 75.50 (doubtful) ; 75.65 ; 75.85 ; 75.89 ; 75.149 ; 80.56 ; 80.60 ; 80.111 ; 100.69 ; 122.97 ; 122.228.

I have not accepted hiatus where similar monosyllabics precede a long [7], though such hiatus often occurs e.g. in Plautus. 26.98 presents a curious problem : quī ait or quī ait? In view of the few certain cases of ait, the first possibility seems preferable. (See also Appendix on 80.89).

Table 1 gives the statistics for the individual letters in numbers of actual occurrences, which seemed to me of primary importance in view of the possibility of basic differences between letters. Obviously the table would have been much more useful could it have contained evidence from whole groups of letters from different parts of the corpus. Since, however, the present study represents but a πάρεργον, I was unwilling to spend the time needed for preparing full statistics— a task which in any case had better be performed with the help of a computer.

On the whole, the table will provide no difficulties, if one is willing

---

[7] It is not entirely clear to me why K. Müller (*o.c.* p. 769) accepts hiatus at Curtius 9.3.9. nostra vis iam in fine est (1 αβγδ) where synaloephe —‿— ——— (tr 33 βγδ) gives an acceptable clausula as well. Cf. Soubiran p. 432 f. It is a pity that the latter did not provide us with samples of his prose scansion.

to admit that all closing rhythms, even if employed only once, are clausulae. Some, of course, are a great deal more frequent than others, but it is rather unwise to pretend that the others are not there. The following comparative list of notations may be found convenient.

	Fraenkel, *Leseproben* p. 15f.	Müller	Table III
I	Cretic + −⌣	A1-A13	1
	each of the longs may be resolved		1¹,1²,1³
	cretic replaced by choriamb		1ᵗʳ
II	dicretic −∪−−∪⌣	B1-B10	2
	first and second long may be resolved		2¹,2²
	first cretic may be replaced by choriamb or molossus		2ᵗʳ
			22
III	ditrochee −∪−⌣	C1-C4	3
	both longs may be resolved		3¹,3²
IV	double spondee −−−⌣	D1-D4	33 or h (see below p. 113) also "cretic+molossus"
	third long resolved		33²
V	So-called hypodochmius −∪−∪⌣	E1-E3	4
	(resolutions)		4¹ etc.
VI	Edite regibus −∪∪−∪⌣	E4	4ᵗʳ
VII	Dochmius ∪−−∪⌣	F1	p

The table also contains a count of all those small elements that somehow refused to submit to the system; a list follows immediately after. It will eventually prove interesting to compare their frequency here with the frequencies in other letters and in Seneca's further writings. However, their numbers are too small in the present sample to show any trends to speak of. Even now, however, Fraenkel's discussion (*Leseproben* pp. 17-18) is entirely relevant. See also below p. 112f. It may cause some surprise that I have added cretic+molossus in this place: I felt comparison of the frequencies of this rhythm, too, might be interesting; and even with our small numbers the impression created is −∪−/−−− rather than −∪/−−−−

TABLE III

	1	1^{tr}	1^1	1^2	1^3	1^{1+2}	1^{1+3}	1^{tr+3}	11	11^1	11^2	11^3	11^{2+3}	subtotals
Letter 1	15	1	1		4			1	6		1			29
Letter 26	19	2	3	3	8	1			5		2			43
Letter 41	23		8		9	1			4	1				46
Letter 75	31	4	3	3	8	1	1	1	6					58
Letter 80	30	2	3		9				3		1			48
Letter 100	43		2	3	8		1		3		4			64
Letter 122	42	1	9	4	12	1	2	2	16	1	4	1		95
	203	10	29	13	58	4	4	4	43	2	12	1		383

	2	2^{tr}	2^1	2^2	2^3				22					subtotals
Letter 1	8		2	2					4					16
Letter 26	14	1							8					23
Letter 41	14	1							4					19
Letter 75	22				1				5					28
Letter 80	14			1	1				2					18
Letter 100	16	1	2						7					26
Letter 122	16	1	1						11					29
	104	4	5	3	2				41					159

	3	3^{tr}	3^1	3^2	3^3	3^{1+2}		3^{tr+2}	33		33^2			subtotals
Letter 1	3				1				4		1			9
Letter 26	10	1	1	3					1		1			17
Letter 41	10	1	1	4					5					21
Letter 75	30	6	1	5					10		3			55
Letter 80	14	1		2	1				5					23
Letter 100	22	4	1	2					2					31
Letter 122	26	10	2	4	1			1	8		1			53
	115	23	6	20	3			1	35		6			209

	4	4^{tr}	4^1	4^2		4^{1+2}		4^{tr+1}	44	44^1				subtotals
Letter 1	3	2	2											7
Letter 26	6	2	1					1	6	1				17
Letter 41	4		3			1			6	1				15
Letter 75	17	1	1	1					7					27
Letter 80	3	4							2					9
Letter 100	8	3	4	1					5					21
Letter 122	11	3	1						15					30
	52	15	12	2		1		1	41	2				126

transport subtotal = 877

transport subtotal 877

	a	b	c	d	e	f	g	h	i	j	k	l	m	n	o	p	q	r	s	t	u	v	cr+m	verse	
Letter 1	1							1		1	1														44
Letter 26	1	2		1	5	1	1	2	2	3	1	1		1	2	1	1						4		29
Letter 41	1				2			3	1	1			3			1						1	2	1	16
Letter 75	1			3	1	1		2		1		1	2	1	1	2							6		22
Letter 80	1		1	1		1	1									3							5	4	18
Letter 100	2	2	1		1			2		1	2	1		1		1		1	1		1		4		22
Letter 122	1	1	1	1	2	1	2	6		1			1			1				1			4	9	32
	8	5	3	6	11	4	4	16	3	7	4	3	6	3	3	9	1	1	1	1	1	1	25	14	140

1017

Several of the main clausula rhythms may also serve as the rhythm of a closed colon or comma. Thus we find

$-\cup--\sim$ 1.6 ; 1.17 ; 1.39 ; 1.56 ; 41.34 ; 75.12 ; 75.106 ; 80.21 ; 80.109 ; 100.20 ; 100.53 ; 100.128 ; 100.146 ; 122.50 ; 122.57 ; 122.58 ; 122.118 ; 122.212 (= 18 ×)

$-\cup--\cup\sim$ 1.38 ; 1.58 ; 41.23 ; 41.79 ; 75.73 ; 75.78 ; 75.92 ; 100.107 ; 122.176 ; (= 9 ×)

$-\cup-\sim$ 41.101 ; 75.42 ; 75.79 (= 3 ×)

$-\cup-\cup\sim$ 1.19 (= 1 ×)

In several derived forms they occur at 1.46 ; 26.36 ; 26.52 ; 26.56 ; 26.65 ; 26.106 ; 26.111 ; 41.12 ; 41.28 ; 41.87 ; 75.10 ; 75.83 ; 75.172 ; 100.33 ; 100.61 ; 100.90 ; 100.92. This list does not include groups that may be analysed as 33, since they are listed as dispondee.

In several cases we find these with an additional syllable at the beginning, which may possibly be termed anacrusis:[8] e.g. 26.13 ; 26.94 ; 41.2 ; 41.11 ; 75.6 ; 75.94 ; 75.96 ; 75.113 ; 75.124 ; 75.138 ; 75.164 ; 75.179 ; 80.13 ; 80.51 ; 100.19 ; 100.44 ; 100.59 ; 100.147 ; 122.24 ; 122.27 ; 122.65 ; 122.74 ; 122.176.

The frequency with which clausula and colon coincide need not surprise in view of the relative frequency of short clauses. Cf. the statistic, above p. 87f.

There are, however, also a fairly large number of short cola whose rhythms do not coincide with the rhythms of well known clausulae.

---

[8] The term is used here much in the sense in which Drexler uses "Auftakt" (e.g. Einf. p. 159, 180). I should like to confine the term, though, to those situations in which a clausula rhythm coincides with a colon bar one extra syllable at the beginning. See J.B. Hall (Gnomon 41, 1969 p. 471) for a criticism of Drexler's use of the term "Auftakt". Fraenkel uses the word in a different sense, cf. Noch einm. K.u.S. p. 67; Leseproben p. 181.

They are listed here with the symbols that mark them in the presentation
of the text :

a ∪−   100.121 and 7 × *vale* (8 ×)
b −∪̣   26.34 ; 26.98 ; 100.93 ; 100.97 ; 122.111 (5 ×)
c ∪∪∾   80.12 ; 100.135 ; 122.200 (3 ×)
d −∪−   26.39 ; 75.39 ; 80.86 ; 75.154 ; 75.156 ; 80.86 (5 ×)
e −−∾   26.27 ; 26.43 ; 26.47 ; 26.85 ; 26.109 ; 41.10 ; 41.48 ; 75.38 ;
            100.115 ; 122.159 ; 122.160 (11 ×) Cf. Fraenkel 29,41,70f.,93
f ∪−∾   1.57 ; 26.83 ; 75.70 ; 122.113 Cf. Fraenkel 59 (4 ×)
g ∪∪∪∾   (26.77[9]) ; 100.125 ; 122.130 ; 122.208 (4 ×) Cf. Fraenkel 148
h −−−∾   26.104 ; 26.114 ; 41.65 ; 41.100 ; 41.104 ; 75.77 ; 75.181 ;
            80.3 ; 100.42 ; 100.45 ; 122.76 ; 122.77 ; 122.115 ; 122.152 ;
            122.188 ; 122.196 (16 ×)

            The dispondee of course allows the symbol 33, but in view
            of its relative frequency as a closed colon it seemed a
            useful practice to give it its own symbol, all the more since
            another group of dispondees may have to be analysed
            altogether differently, cf. above p. 110 on the cretic+
            molossus. For the dispondee see also Fraenkel type IV).

i ∪−∪∾   26.37 ; 26.75 ; 100.51 (3 ×) Cf. Fraenkel p. 191
j ∪−−∾   26.24 ; 26.48 ; 26.119 ; 41.109 ; 75.56 ; 100.62 ; 122.216
            Cf. Fraenkel 142f., 144,162 (7 ×)
k −∪∪∾   26.3 ; 80.40 ; 100.24 ; 100.103 (4 ×) Cf. Fraenkel 38,47f.
l ∪∪−∾   1.40 ; 26.69 ; 41.52 (3 ×) Cf. Fraenkel 99f.,149,155
m −−∪∾   1.10 ; 41.97 ; 75.127 ; 80.47 ; 100.15 ; 122.136 (6 ×) Cf.
            Fraenkel 18, 30f., 58, 91ff., 190
n −−∪∪∾   26.22 ; 100.35 ; 122.92 (3 ×) Cf. Fraenkel 30 n. 9, 137 n. 5
o ∪−∪∪∾   26.124 ; 26.127 ; 75.110 (3 ×) Cf. Fraenkel 143 n. 2
p ∪−−∪∾   26.31 ; 41.1 ; 41.25 ; 41.95 ; 75.51 ; 75.166 ; 80.14 ; 80.58 ;
            80.91 (9 ×) Fraenkel VII and p. 43 (Cic. Or. 218)
q ∪∪∪∪∾   26.82 (1 ×) Cf. Fraenkel 45f.
r ∪∪−∪∾   75.142 (1 ×) Cf. Fraenkel 190f., 192
s ∪∪−−∾   100.127 (1 ×) Cf. Fraenkel 38f., 58
t ∪∪∪−∾   122.203 (1 ×) Not in Fraenkel's index
u ∪∪−∪∪∾   75.109 (1 ×) Cf. Fraenkel 104 n. 2 and 184
v ∪∪∪∪−∾   100.70 (1 ×) Cf. Fraenkel 137, 152

Table IV deals with the frequency of the various rhythms at pauses of
various levels of strength. The table rests on a rather subjective element

---

[9] Prosodic hiatus gives ∪∪∪∪∾. See above p. 109.

of interpretation : what is a strong, and what is a weak pause? More difficult even, which are the gradations between those two? Once again the question is somewhat less difficult in practice than it appears in theory. The strongest pauses are given with the ends of periods, complex sentences and groups. Individual clauses provide a certain amount of hesitation, and so do, within subordinate structures, the adjectival clauses in particular.

Perhaps the most curious aspect of this table is the almost even distribution of the various types over the various levels of strength. It is true that I have not included the further distinction of word endings in the table, and it may be that that would make a difference. On the whole I am inclined to think that that would only be the the case if the material were increased to about ten times the present size. It would not surprize me, however, if after a careful elaboration of such increased material the present even distribution would prove to hold for Seneca's style in general, though most probably with some variations to be explained by differences of chronology and genre.

But if little use can be made of this table for the present enquiry, matters are different in the case of the fifth table.

TABLE IV

This table does not include *vale* and lines of verse, and other special items.

Levels %

	1	1^{tr}	1^1	1^2	1^3	1^{1+2}	1^{1+3}	1^{tr+3}	11	11^1	11^3	11^{2+3}	11^2
1	5.6	0.4	0.7	0.2	1.3				0.3	1	0.4		
2	3.1		0.6		0.8		0.1	0.1	0.3		0.1		
3	4.6	0.4	0.5		1.1		0.2		0.8		0.2		
4	3.0		0.3	0.1	1.0	0.3	0.2	0.1	0.9		0.2	0.1	
5	3.5	0.3	0.6		1.4				1.6		0.4		0.1

	2	2^{tr}	2^1	2^2	22
1	2.6	0.1	0.3		1.1
2	1.5				0.9
3	2.1		0.1	0.1	0.7
4	2.3	0.1	0.1		0.6
5	2.1	0.1	0.1	0.2	0.8

	3	3^{tr}	3^1	3^2	3^{1+2}	3^{tr+2}	33	33^2
1	1.9	0.3		0.3			0.4	
2	2.1	0.2					0.4	0.1
3	2.7	0.6		0.6	0.1	0.1	0.7	0.2
4	2.2	0.7	0.4	0.3			1.0	
5	2.9	0.4	0.2	0.5	0.1		1.0	0.4

Levels %

	4	4^{tr}	4^1	4^2	4^{1+2}	4^{tr+1}	44	44^1	44^2
1	0.9	0.2	0.3				0.8		
2	0.4	0.2	0.1		0.1		0.2		
3	0.1	0.5	0.3	0.2			0.8		
4	1.1	0.3	0.2	0.1			1.0		0.1
5	1.6	0.4	0.2			0.1	1.3	1.0	

cr + m (instances)

1	3
2	2
3	3
4	12
5	4

types

	a	b	c	d	e	f	g	h	i	j	k	l	m	n	o	p	q	r	s	t	u	v
1				1	2			3		1			1		1	4						
2		1		2	1	1	1	1	1	1			2	1								
3		2	1	1	3	3		4					2	2	1	1					1	1
4	1			1	2		1	5	1	3	1	1	1		1			1		1	1	
5	3			2	2		2	5	1	1	3		1	2	1	3						

A fifth table deals with the clausulae that are used in cola containing an immediate reference to the main theme of the letter in which they occur. It is obvious that the basis of this statistic is even more subjective than that of any of the others. In every case there was an interpretation to be made, and in many cases the decision was not easy. For that reason the table presents two sets of figures. The first figure of each pair represents a reasonably conservative count—if in doubt do not—, the second a more generous count—if in doubt do include. For reasons of economy all derived forms of each of the four main types have been lumped together under the asterisked figure.

TABLE V

Clausula :	1	1*	2	2*	3	3*	4	4*	other
Letter 1	10/12	4/5	2/4	4/5	3/2	0/0	1/2	0/3	1/1
Letter 26	8/12	2/2	4/4	3/3	2/2	1/1	1/1	0/0	1/3
Letter 41	17/21	9/9	5/8	3/3	6/7	3/6	3/3	7/7	4/6

Clausula:	1	1*	2	2*	3	3*	4	4*	other
Letter 75	25/28	15/21	6/8	1/3	4/7	4/3	1/2	2/3	1/4
Letter 80	24/28	9/10	6/9	0/2	3/5	1/0	0/1	2/4	1/1
Letter 100	21/29	7/10	3/6	5/7	8/11	0/0	1/2	1/2	4/9
Letter 122	23/29	8/14	2/3	1/3	7/9	2/4	2/5	3/4	0/5
Total	128/159	56/71	28/43	17/27	33/43	11/14	9/16	15/23	12/29
Percent	41.5/37.5	18.1/16.7	9/10	5.5/6.3	10.7/10	3.5/3.3	3/3.7	4.8/5.4	3.8/6.8

One of the most striking sets of figures in this table is that of clausula one in its basic form. Even in the conservative count it appears that a good deal more than half of the actual number of instances has a close connection with the main theme of the letter, but more strikingly, the relative frequency is for both the more conservative and the more generous counts considerably more than the frequency one might expect if the subject matter were of no importance for the clausula. For in that case we would have the same relative frequency for the clausulae expressing the main thought as for the letters in general, i.e. 20%. Instead, we find 41.5% (128 instances) in the more conservative, 37.5 (159 instances) in the less conservative column. The discrepancy needs an explanation.

If we wish to explain this phenomenon, we must try to imagine the mentality of an author who works with clausulae, indeed with prose-rhythm, not so much because he made the decision to do so at a specific moment, starting from point zero, but partly because he consciously wishes to do so, partly because it happens to be part and parcel of the usual writing techniques of his age. In such a situation, I believe, it would be wrong to accept mere automatism on the part of the author, but on the other hand the clausula would not in each case be the result of ponderous decision after lengthy reflection either. And it might well be that in the case of the main subject of his piece of prose he would be just a little more careful, a little more reflective, in composing his cola. Imagining—and I am fully conscious of offering but speculation—such a situation, I find it possible to understand that Seneca precisely here uses the clausula of his preference relatively more often than elsewhere.[10]

---

[10] Cicero, *Brutus* 33, uses the telling words "dedita opera", doubtless referring to the training needed to reach proper results; in the next paragraph he deplores both a *defici* and a *laborare* in this respect. The latter is also rejected *de oratore* 3.193: *...nec nos id, quod faciemus, opera dedita facere videamur*. See also *Orator* 170; 193. Cf. Dion. Halic. *Comp.* 134: ἔχει δέ τινα χάριν ἐν τοῖς τοιούτοις καὶ τὸ οὕτω

It is rather more difficult to see what conclusions can be drawn from the observed facts. May we say, for instance, that the clausula obtains, by its very distribution, a referential value? In other words, may we turn matters around and state that, if Seneca prefers to use a certain clausula for his main thought, the sensitive listener is meant to treat each instance of the clausula as a roadsign flashing the warning "here is a link with my central message"?

Secondly, if one of the four main types of the clausulae has a direct link with an element of content, may such links be observed for the other clausulae as well? Are they, for instance, used in phrases related to one another by (however subordinate a) topic? The next section will attempt to deal with these questions.

b. Usage

In order to investigate the questions raised above, I shall start by cautiously assuming a distinction between the various types of form 1. Those forms will be treated as related to one another, rather than as identical.

Above, p. 89, I referred to the obvious fact that time is the central notion in letter 1. Forthwith a question must be raised: 1.18 *tempori ponat* (1αδ) is typologically the equivalent of 1.6 *collige et serva*, Is this accidental, or is the equivalence related to the fact that much the same notion is presented once more? In other words, is it possible that Seneca uses the clausula with referential force? The present letter is of course too short to allow us to decide the question. The instances quoted are the only ones where this precise clausula occurs. It is true that a closely related clausula occurs in 1.2: *te tibi et tempus* (1βδ) which may well—if I am allowed to look ahead to my next chapter for a moment—be balanced by 1.53 *causas paupertatis meae reddam*, which shows the same clausula exactly, and which in the scheme of the letter as a whole is another item in a series of contrasts between Lucilius and Seneca himself. Colon 1.3 *auferebatur* (1α) also has its clear reference to *tempus*. On the other hand 1.4 *subripiebatur* (1ᵗʳα) which has an equally clear relationship with *tempus* is not nearly as closely related a clausula, and 1.5 *excidebat* (3γδ) is not related at all. Related clausulae occur once again in

συγκείμενον ὥστε μὴ συγκεῖσθαι δοκεῖν. The *dissimulatio artis* is here (as in Cicero), the main thought. Cf. e.g. Karin Pohl, *Die Lehre von den drei Wortfügungsarten, Unters. z. Dion. v. Halic. De comp. verb.* Diss. Tübingen 1968, pp. 54,76.

1.30 *vita transcurrit* (1αγ), 1.33 *natura non misit* (1γδ), 1.42 *tempus accepit* (1αγ), 1.43 *cum interim hoc unum est* (1αδ), 1.50 *constat impensae* (1αγ), 1.56 *nemo succurrit* (1αγ). And is it too fanciful to suggest in passing that *vita transcurrit* and *nemo succurrit* have been placed in their respective positions with a clear reference to each other? Finally then also the proverbial expression 1.63 *sera parsimonia in fundo est* (1δ). All of these might with a great—and possibly excessive—deal of goodwill be regarded as related in sense. Colon 1.52 *quemadmodum dicam* (1δ) at first seems a clear counterinstance, until one realizes that what Seneca loses is time. There is a counterinstance in 1.17 *quem mihi dabis* (1αβδ) which shows at least that not all related clausulae must, of necessity, have an immediate connection with *tempus*. But the relationship between clausula and main theme is remarkably close if we define the clausula morphologically rather than typologically. Indeed that is what both Cicero and Quintilian usually do.

However, it may well be that letter 1 is so brief, so compact and single-minded a letter that the tendency described gives us an entirely twisted picture of this aspect of Seneca's technique.

In letter 26 we start with colon 2 *in conspectu esse me senectutis* (1αβ) and we are struck by the fact that the next time 1αβ appears the subject-matter is once again *senectus*: 17 *mihi facit controversiam de senectute*. However, no further instances of this clausula—defined typologically—occur, and *senectus* occurs 26.4, 26.8, *senuerunt* 26.14 in cola closed with entirely different sequences.

But it is noteworthy that in this letter Seneca starts with *senectus* only to reject the notion for another one : 3-4 *iam vereor ne senectutem post me reliquerim* and he winds up with a formula that is much closer to the core of the letter, 10 *..extrema tangentis* (1γ).[11] The only other instance of 1γ occurs at 26.45 *e vita repentinus excessus*.[12]

---

[11] It looks as if Seneca emphasizes and announces the change of subject by means of the change of clausula.

[12] Colon 44 reads *non quia aliquid mali ictus* in ω; Beltrami added <est> at the end of the colon, producing 4βε, but certain recentiores had *non quia aliquid mali est ictus*: 1βδ. Naturally the latter reading would fit in well with the duties suggested for clausula 1 in this letter, but it is much more likely, as Reynolds suggests, that ω is right. Préchac borrows *non quia aliquid mali sit ictus* from a correction in P. That reading would add an item to our list of cretic+molossus. See p. 110.

There are however numerous instances of other forms of clausula 1. Thus we note 1αε at 26.57 *morti crediturus sum*; 1s at 26.68, *mors de te pronuntiatura est*. Add 1α at 26.49 (*experimentum*); 1δ at 26.33 (*incommodum summum est*); 1β at 26.87 *itaque tu illam omni loco expecta*. All of these are expressions of or closely related to the core thought of the letter. But there are also a number of instances where that link is less clear or even obviously absent. 26.20 *bono suo utatur* (1β) reveals its relationship after some reflection. The *animus* is subject and part and parcel of its proper *bonum* is to be free from the body (above 26.15 *non multum sibi esse cum corpore*) and one might add the exclamation in the coda, 26.115 *quid ad illum carcer et custodia et claustra?* (1δ). Is all this not a little too far removed? Or should we say on the contrary that Seneca hints at this link by means of his use of the clausulae? 26.28 shows, in Kronenberg's conjecture, 1αγδ; the uncertain state of the text may serve as a good excuse for not immediately counting the colon as a heavy counterindication. No such excuse exists for 26.71 *sapientium verba collecta* (1αγ) and 26.74 (*oratio*)...*timidissimis audax* (1δ). However, in the case of 26.90-91 Seneca is playing a little game (see below p. 140) and it seems possible to suggest that one element of the game is a play on the word *viaticum* which in Plaut. *Poen.* 71 (*ipse abit ad Acheruntem sine viatico*) and Apuleius *Met.* 6.18 (142,9 Helm *set moriens pauper viaticum debet quaerere*) refers to the price to be paid for the final crossing. These coins have to be amassed and they consist of ..a *verbum sapientis selectum*.

The connection between the various phrases with clausula 1—with extreme goodwill one might also add 26.100—is very tenuous: a gossamer spun rather than a chain forged. A contemplation of the other clausulae may well blow it away. The various forms of 4 will not cause the wind : they might even, whether together with or apart from the counter theme suggested above p. 118 n. 11, show their own connection. However, 26.50 *et ille laturus sententiam de omnibus annis meis dies venerit* (2βδ), a heavy colon qua length and content, one that expresses an element of the core thought, shows that clausula 1 does not occupy a position of monopoly, and this impression is strengthened by 26.58 *componor ad illum diem* (2ᵖβγε) ff.

In letter 41 the situation is also somewhat less obvious than it is in letter 1. To be sure we find, here too, a rather interesting frequency of clausulae of form 1 in close connection with the main notion of the letter, but there is as interesting a frequency, it seems, of counterinstances. There can be little objection to the thesis that the *vis divina* of 41.50 in its connection with the *vir bonus* (and the *mens bona* of 41.3) constitutes the basic notion of this letter. In 41.44 he is *inter adversa felicem* (1γ), hardly startling until we find that 41.50 *divina descendit*, 54 *optamusque ridentem*, 57 *unde descendit*, 59 *unde mittuntur*, and 62 *divina nossemus* all show exactly the same clausula. It is hard to believe that this can be accidental. Indeed this one paragraph shows two more clausulae that are closely related : 56 *numinis stare* (1αδ) and 58 *contingunt quidem terram* (1δ). The latter clausula had also appeared in 49 *corpusculo possit*, which in context appears to be another reference to the basic notion.

On the other hand 1γ does not show up anywhere else as a clausula in this letter, except in 71 *aliena laudare*. At first sight this colon must count as a severe counter indication against the theory, for *aliena* are the very opposite of that *vis divina* that is a *bona mens*. But that, surely, is the very point that Seneca makes in his sentence "Quid enim est stultius quam in homine aliena laudare?"—only, he makes the point in negative form, and it may well be that it is for that very reason he needs a clausula here that has achieved the referential force 1γ did in § 5. The same reasoning may apply to the next clausula : 73 *protinus possunt* (1δ). Of course, by this time these clausulae have been used for "*aliena*" as well, and so no longer surprise in the example 74 *non faciunt meliorem equum aurei freni* (1δ) or even in 77 *cogitur fatigatus* (1β). Colon 96 *et domum pulchram* (1αβδ) belongs in this group as well. We subsequently note that 3 *ire ad bonam mentem* (1βδ) shows a related clausula, as do 14 *sacer intra nos spiritus sedet* (1αδ), 15 *observator et custos* (1γδ). But we are a little more hesitant in paragraph 3. The examples are 24 *solitam altitudinem egressis* (1s), 27 *proceritas silvae et* (1δ) both of which are perfectly unimportant clausulae (if clausulae they are at all) and we may reason that they find their justification in the phrase 30 *fidem tibi numinis faciet*. Whether Seneca would have felt that the latter clausula (1^3αδ) is closely related to the various types of form 1, I am not, at this juncture, prepared to say, but it is something worth investigating on a much larger sample of material than I am here dealing with. The two other examples of related clausulae in this paragraph are more easily comparable to the core notion of the letter ; they are 34 *non manu factus* (1αβδ) and 39 *calentium fontes* (1δ), both of which illustrate the notion of *numen* even more obviously than the examples above.

It appears then, that if we are prepared to admit opposites or negatives, something of a case can be made in this letter for linking these clausulae. But once again we need to enter the caution that not all cola which express a thought related to the central notion of the letter also exhibit the clausula, witness e.g. 41.19, or the series 41.41-49.

In the case of letter 75 I believe the search for a meaningful coherence of clausulae of identical type must be abandoned, but a meaningful coherence of clausulae of the same morphology seems to be found, here too. The letter exhibits a long series of cola of form 1 in its various types, all of them dealing with or mentioning *adfectus* or *morbus animi*. There is, however, a shorter series, equally of form 1, that is occupied with the rhetorical simplicity Seneca claims for his letters. Furthermore there are a few such cola that refer to Seneca's preference for the philosophical rather than the rhetorical ideal, and finally there are those that combine these themes. It may be useful to examine these series a little more closely.

The letter starts with the rhetorical simplicity and we find clausula 1α in cola 5/6 *si una desideremus / aut ambularemus*, a subordinate position (for table IV I marked both as level 4). The three instances in the next paragraph are weightier: 12 *quam loqui mallem* (1αβδ), 16 *nec attollerem vocem* (1δ), 17 *sed ista oratoribus reliquissem* (1β). At this point it seems the list is abandoned with the subject.[13] But it returns with great emphasis in paragraph 4, when the ideal is stated in 35/6 *Ille promissum suum implevit* (1β) / *qui et cum videas illum et cum audias idem est* (1αδ), *videas* referring to the *vita*, *audias* to the *sermo* of colon 34.

In the meantime, however, clausula 1 has been employed once more: 26 *satis apparet adfectus* (1γ) and this colon foreshadows the discussion of *adfectus* and *morbus animi* from paragraph 9 onwards. Clausula 1 appears in 82 *tamen etiam quod prope est extra est* (1αβδ)—the absence of *adfectus* is the very definition of this high degree of proficiency. From colon 100 onwards (*et adhuc in lubrico stare* 1αδ) the list speaks for itself—102, 104 (with a pointer to sapientia), 106 (possibly to be read with, certainly a natural outflow of the previous colon), 112, 123, 129 (with a pointer to the ideal), 138, 146, 157, 159 and, once more in connection with an expression of the ideal, 183 *tranquillitas*

---

[13] I suspect that Seneca almost playfully refers back to this list in 96 *de quo locutus sum* (1αβε); cf. 2 *loquitur*, 3 *loqui*, 4 *sermo*, 12 *loqui*, 21 *dicerem*.

animi et expulsis erroribus absoluta libertas (1γ). Three times, then, the
list combines the *adfectus* or *morbus* with its absence. Such a combination had appeared earlier : in colon 40 Seneca had said *non
delectent verba nostra sed prosint* (1αγδ), a philosophical in comparison
with a rhetorical ideal, a comparison that returns in 56/57 *quid
oblectas/ aliud agitur, urendus, secandus, abstinendus sum* (1αε) and
62/63 *circa verba occupatus es?/ iamdudum gaude si sufficis rebus* (1αδ).
Sufficere rebus is defined in 89 *iam ibi sunt unde non est retro lapsus*
(1αβδ), a colon I believe must be read in close connection with 82 :
these people are at the top, but not quite. But this is the ideal which
in the other list was combined-in-contrast with the presence of *adfectus/
morbus animi.* Here we may fit in colon 150 as well : *magna felicitate
naturae* (1γ), and 169 *at quam grande praemium expectat* (1α). Cola 182
and 183 (see above) and in particular 187 *in se ipsum habere maximam
potestatem* (1β) finally combine the two series.

It would seem, then, that in letter 75 various themes are linked
in a series of cola with clausula 1. That the impression we get of the
use of this clausula in this letter differs from the other letters we
have seen so far, fits in very well with the fact that its structure
differs also in other respects, as we shall see in chapter 5.

Matters appear to be different again in letter 80. We may state
that *quidquid facere te potest bonum tecum est* (paragraph 3) is to
be regarded as the central theme of the letter ; see the discussion
below p. 153. The statement has clausula 1βδ. The precise clausula
occurs on several occasions ; I list them here noting with an asterisk
those which in my opinion fit the mold suggested by the central theme.

    32 madens diem ducat[14]
    45 quid autem melius potes velle*
    56 qui te in illa putas natum (sc. libertate)*
    63 libera te primum metu mortis*
    71 velut nubes levis transit (sc. cura)*
    97 solvi iubes stratum*

From this list I obtain the suggestion that *..bonum tecum est* is very
closely connected with the idea of naked, unveiled, unhidden. And
indeed 42 *tibi continget virtus sine apparatu, sine inpensa* which occurs
just before the statement of the central theme, shows a closely related
clausula (1β). It may also be claimed, then, that other related clausulae
were chosen to underscore closely related notions. For instance :

---

[14] Is there a suggestion here of naked being? (cf. *48 condicionis extremae*).

44 *quid tibi opus est ut sis bonus? velle* (1αβδ). The colon immediately precedes *quid autem melius potes velle*, which was quoted above, and it seems obvious that related clausulae were chosen in this particular case in order to enhance the impact of *velle*, the very nakedness of which is subsequently illustrated by two more related clausulae, 48 *condicionis extremae* (1γ) and 49 *in his sordibus nata* (1αδ).

It is equally interesting to note that *libera te primum metu mortis* (also quoted above) is immediately followed by 64 *illa nobis iugum imponit* (1β). And does 71 *nubes levis transit* referring to the *pauper* suggest that 67 *divitum vultus* (1αδ) is more heavily clouded? Certainly : 68 *saepius pauper et fidelius ridet* (1δ); thus the thought that Seneca uses this clausula with its typological variations for the purpose of emphasizing basic connections and relationships becomes rather more marked.

There are however, here too, some counter indications. One clear case is 93 *omnibus dicas* (1αδ), but the phrase that precedes, winding up the mime section of the letter, 92 *in centunculo dormit* (1δ) has an unveiling, denuding function that is very similar to the function of *velle* earlier on. It may be significant that the mime section also starts with three clausulae : 78 *exemplo mihi utendum est* (1β); 80 *partes quas male agamus adsignat* (1γ) and 81 *in scaena latus incedit* (1αγ). Colon 94 *lectica suspendit* (1γ) might also be regarded as a counter indication, but I should prefer to regard the *lectica* as serving a function similar to that of *stratum* or *fasciam* (resp. 97 and 109), both of them occurring in clausulae of type 1.

Finally we are hardly surprised when we find that 105 *tibi corpus ostendi* (1αγ) and 108 *scire qualis sit* (1αγε) show related clausulae as well.

There are three clausulae of type one left : 27 *umerosque miramur* (1γ) which may be a counter indication unless someone wishes to argue that the nakedness of those athletic muscles is underlined by the clausula, or, better, that the *umeri* serve as a veil for the *animus* ; 17 *sine interpellatore secretum* (1γ) and 7 *non adlevabitur velum* (1δ). I suspect very strongly that the last-mentioned phrase is given this particular clausula in order to announce, or at least underscore the veil, the covering, the theme of hiding that seems to pervade the letter as a whole, and that colon 17 fits in the same corner.

In letter 100 we are dealing once more with the relationship between style and conduct, and even a first reading of the large number of cola showing clausula 1, shows that both style and conduct are amply represented among them. Indeed in the cautious count of table V I have counted about half of the cola with clausula 1 as related to the main theme of the letter. If we start, for once, at the beginning of the letter and, without paying attention to the types, list the clausulae of form 1, we note two examples in the announcement of the subject-matter : colon 3 *legisse te cupidissime scribis* (1δ), in which the word *cupidissime* warns us that we may have to do with a case of emotional involvement in the judgment, a judgment which turns out to be unfavourable : colon 6 *compositionem eius accusas* (1γ). The next two clauses repeat and rephrase the judgment, respectively using 1γδ and 1αγδ. Subsequently this judgment is qualified : 10 *est decor proprius orationis leniter lapsae* (1αδ). Already the function of the clausula seems to gel in its application to style judgement ; it is not necessary to quote all the instances in full ; the list : 18, 19, 20, even the concessive 21, refer to Lucilius' judgment, and so does (after a slight hesitation on our part) 36. But then suddenly 39 and 40 effect a transition from the style to the man : *ubi tandem erit fortis et constans* (1αγδ) definitely refers to a moral judgment, whereas *ubi periculum sui faciet qui timet verbis* (1αβδ) links the moral judgment to the stylistic one. Cola 50 and 52, 53, 54 (the latter three a tricolon with rhythmic rhyme in which the final member is equivalent in length to the first two combined) belong to the list on style, but 59-60 seem at first to belong in a different atmosphere, until the truth dawns : the judgment is being expressed by a metaphor.[15]

The list continues without difficulties in 63, 64, 65, 72, 74. At 82 *sed placida et ad animi tenorem quietum compositumque formata* (1γ) we note that we are both at the central point, numerically speaking, and at the core thought of the letter (see p. 157 below). The next colon repeats and confirms (1γδ). Also 85 (Lucilius' wishes in the matter of style) belongs in the list. Colon 99 *in re tanta eminere est post duos esse* also presents a style judgment, but one expressed in a somewhat unusual wordorder in which the subject and predicate are inverted in order to achieve both emphasis on "post duos esse", and on "eminere" as well as the desired clausula (1αβδ).[16] Next we encounter 112 ; 116-117 (the tetracolon is not entirely expressed in the same rhythm, and we remember Cicero's warning against a too

---

[15] Those who prefer to read 61/62 as one colon must add it to the metaphor. Whether Seneca felt that ◡___ (j) was related to _◡___, I do not know.

[16] J. Marouzeau, *L'ordre des mots dans la phrase latine, II. Le verbe*, Paris, Les Belles Lettres 1938, p. 9 ff. ; L.-H.-Sz. p. 402.

persistent repetition, *Orator* 213), the tricolon 122-124 ends with 1δ, the next tricolon with 1α. Colon 129 sums up these stylistic desires and 130 adds the ideal as represented by Fabianus. When after a concession (134) we next come across form 1, it is to express first one combination of literary judgment with statement of ideal (141 : *ut liqueat tibi illum sensisse quae scripsit*), then another: 146-147; and even in the last paragraph where much of the subject-matter is of a slightly different nature (Seneca explains that he is working by memory and speaks of Fabianus' didactic qualities) two cola appear with stylistic judgments : 154 and 161, both still in the chosen form.

Letter 122 has as its central subject the perversity of those who turn day into night and night into day. It is reasonably easy to list, as was done in the case of letter 100, those cola which both show a clausula of form 1 and a connection with that subject. We pass by cola 1 and 4 for a moment and pause at 9 "*et adhoc multis hoc antelucanum est* (1α). If we may read 25 and 27 together, they certainly belong in the list, as does 33. In the case of 36 we hesitate a little, but on the whole I think it must be included on the grounds of its close connection-in-contrast with 35. The next colon with clausula 1 is 47, a well known crux ; nevertheless it seems that whatever the right reading the perversity of nightlife is being illustrated. There are no difficulties concerning 49, 50, whereas 57-58 in which the heavily emphasized *ille* (sc. *animus*) is dark, obscured to the extent of being envious of the blind, express the perversion in full force. Colon 65, *gaudere perversis*, creates no problems. The subsequent cola, of which 66 and 68 also have clausula 1 and in which *gaudere perversis* is situated in the moral scheme of things, fit in very well. We are then presented with a number of examples : 71 *qui vinum recipiunt inanibus venis*, cf. 79 ; the perverse judgment that only rustics drink after the meal 82 *et verae voluptatis ignari*. Next 88 *qui commutant cum feminis vestem* cf. 93 ; 103, 104 treed roofs and now 109 the general perversion : *cum instituerunt omnia contra naturae consuetudinem velle*. The examples that follow are 118 the perverted dinner time, cf. 121, 126 (*qui ad faces et cereos vivunt*). However, cola 133 and 142, both having a clausula of form one, do not contain immediately recognizable perversions unless the pun of 142 may count as such: the slight joke at 151 might point in that direction, and the pointer just might be strengthened by the clausula. And if we may argue from context, 153 "*incipit Buta dormire*" may equally count as a perversion, cf. 161. I am more doubtful about 163, though a case could well be made

for the perversion in the use of *egerunt* here, in particular in view
of the previous colon. Colon 167 indeed allows itself to be fitted
into a list of perversions, but we have more difficulty with 174 *quod
excitet famam*. I think, however, that the context shows quite clearly
that the urge to cause a stir by excentricity is indeed felt to be perverse.
Three more cola (197-199) illustrate another instance of the perverse
use of time and colon 228 finally sums up all this in *qui ut ita
dicam retro vivunt* (1βδ) which stands in sharp contrast to 230 (*via*)
quam natura praescripsit. We remember that it was indeed something
natural that was stated, some decent activity that was suggested at
the start of this letter in cola 1 and 4 : *detrimentum iam dies sensit* :
it is autumn and the best you can do is to get up early : *liberale..
spatium... si quis cum ipso, ut ita dicam, die surgat* (1βδ).

Though it is possible to do in the case of this letter what was
done in that of the others, it is quite clear that we need to formulate
the main objection : it may be true that clausula 1 occurs both
absolutely and relatively with greater frequency than the others, it may
be true that all (or almost all) instances of that clausula can be
linked together, but in all cases there are also other clausulae that
are used for that chain of meaning.

The objection loses some of its force if reasons can be suggested
for the use of such alternative clausulae, but the strongest support
for the theory that we have to do with a specific technique purposely
applied by the author must come from a negative consideration, i.e.
one's inability to suggest a similarly coherent use of the other clausulae,
other than in small bits and pieces. And such support is not really very
strong.

The usage of clausula 4 in letter 1 may give us a good example.
At the end of the first paragraph we find the sequence *male agentibus—nihil agentibus—aliud agentibus*. Seneca hardly stated these in
this manner because he could not have done otherwise (c.q. because
he could not have fitted a sequence involving clausula 1 in the
passage), but rather because he has a subordinate theme here that
is important to him (and that occurs elsewhere with some frequency).
It is quite true, of course, that that theme is connected with the
main theme of the letter, but does Seneca not indicate here, not
only by the rhyming repetition, but also by the sequence $4^{tr}β$-$4β$-$4β$
that, related though these clauses are, they are different?

Letter 1 shows too few clausulae of type 4 to enable us to draw
any conclusions concerning the question whether they, too, are meant

to connect a thematically related group of phrases. The possibility is not excluded : 19 *qui diem aestimet* (4β), 20 *intellegat se cotidie mori* (4δ) shows an interesting repetition as well, and one may claim that the fact that its content is contrasted with the repetition of 1 argues a link ; 31 *omnia, Lucili, aliena sunt* (4^{tr}ε) can easily be related to the *male—nihil—aliud* sequence of 14-16. I must repeat however that the number of instances involved is far too small to draw any conclusions.

As was indicated above (p. 118 n. 11) letter 26, too, seems to use in its first paragraph an interchange of clausula 1 and others to indicate and emphasize change of definition. If we check whether clausula 44 which occurs three times in this first paragraph is assigned special duties in this respect, it appears that it is used for unconnected themes: 1 *modo dicebam tibi* (44αδ), 6 *certe huic corpori* (44αγ), 9 *non fractae nomen est* (44αγε), 56 *quid profecerim* (44αβ), 80 *haec mecum loquor* (44αβδ) 93 *unde sumpturus sim mutuum* (44βγ). Even if two pairs suggest themselves (1+80, 6+9), cola 56 and 93 show that these must be accidental. It is more likely therefore that the clausula is used for local variation.

If we list the instances of clausula 4 in the same way, we obtain much the same lack of result. Derived forms are added in brackets.

4 *ne senectutem post me reliquerim* (4αβ)

(12 *non sentio in animo aetatis iniuriam* (4^{tr}γ))

(44 see above p. 118 n. 12)

51 *ita me observo et adloquor* (4γ)

63 *quidquid contra fortunam iactavi verborum contumacium* (4)

(65 *dubia semper est* (4^{1}αγε))

(96 *et de domo fiet numeratio* (4^{tr}β))

102 *supervacuum forsitan putas* (4αδ)

113 *supra omnem potentiam est* (4β)

(121 *ita minuendus est* (4^{1+tr}αβε))

No link suggests itself, though for a moment we try to pair off 4+12 with (above) 6+9 and 51 with (above) 80. Such vague suggestions are shown to be accidental when not supported by the other instances.

On the other hand letter 26 shows one or two interesting sequences of clausula 1[3] : 64, 66, 70 seem to be connected in content, and so are 111, 112, 116. This type of employment may well have been conscious. But letter 100, cola 136/139 uses the same clausula to express opposite observations. Do we dare, then, affirm anything about 148/9, 162?

Similarly I find that I am unable to suggest any connecting link for clausula 2. This is not to say that there are no interesting observations to be made about its use. I list a few instances :

1.24 ff. There may be an intended connection between : *quidquid aetatis retro est mors tenet* (2βδε), *sic fiet ut ex crastino pendeas* (2αδ) and *si hodierno manum inieceris* (2β). The last two form a contrast within one sentence, and their connection is obvious, but together they may be seen as contrasting with the first phrase.

26.13 + 15 : verbal anaphora causes rhythmic anaphora and precludes conclusions as to intention.

26.38 ff. : the smooth path down to death may be illustrated by clausula 2 (see cola 40 and 46 ; if we were to read 39 immediately with 38, the impression would be strengthened—but I feel the pause is rather too strong). I am hesitant to suggest that colon 50 stilll belongs in this series.

41.75 ff. provide a good example of the type of instance that creates difficulties : *aliter leo aurata iuba mittitur* (2βδ), a few lines further on *integri spiritus* (2βδ) and *speciosus ex horrido* (2γδ). One can plead contrast or one can argue similarity, but one must not use both arguments at once. Cf. 112 ff. where something very similar happens : *secundum naturam suam vivere* (2δ), *communis insania* (2γ), *in vitia alter alterum trudimus* (2αδ).

75.80 ff. *sapientiam nondum habent* (2δ), *inexperta fiducia est* (2γ), *scire se nesciunt* (2αγδ) may show a common clausula because they state the merely negative side of the *primus proficiens*.

Paragraph 15 in the same letter shows an interesting list of clausulae as well as colometrically interesting items. One might—but no more than half seriously—suggest that 151 *intentione studii* (2ε) has an element of self-congratulation, explained by 152 *secundus occupatur gradus* (2ε)—Seneca's own level of achievement?—but in need of being tempered in words *and* rhythm by 153 *sed ne hic quidem contemnendus est color tertius* (2δ)—Lucilius' level?— ; if one may read all this into these cola, the end of the paragraph has a rather obvious reminder in the clausula of 161 *si inter pessimos non sumus* (2αδε).

80.57 *ad arcam tuam respicis* (2βδ), 60 *nec qui emerunt habent* (2αβε), 62 *istud bonum a te petas* (2βδε) seem to show a progression that could possibly have been intended. If so, 87 *et quinque denarios* (2αγ) just might refer back to this progression. 80.110 and 114, however, are too isolated to count as a convincing instance of connection illustrated or even underscored by clausula. Cf. p. 105 above.

Letter 122 is perhaps the most promising of the group if we wish to investigate whether clausula 3 is used with special connotations. I list as I have done with clausula 1 :

23 *nec orientem umquam solem viderunt* (3γε)
24 *nec occidentem* (3αδε)
29 *in quam se vivi condiderunt* (3αβε)
30 *tam infausti ominis quam nocturnae aves sunt* (3βγθ)
41 *et aliquid ex illa in diem transferatur* (3βδ)
42 *aves quae in conviviis comparantur* (3δ)
44 *in obscuro continentur* (3δ)
52 *languidi et evanidi albent* (3βγζ)
53 *et in vivis caro morticina est* (3βδ)
61 *aversandi diem et totam vitam in noctem transferendi* (3βδ)

Possibly 55 may be compared. The list suddenly fails until 99 *et locorum apta mutatione* (3γ), 107 *et delicate natare ipsi sibi non videntur* (3βδε) which do not regard the dark at all—darkness simply not being discussed here. Nor are the last two instances of the clausula connected with one another as are 114 and 116 (*nunc exerceamur* 3βγ // *nunc prandeamus* 3γδ). Cf. 123, 124. Indeed, though there are many examples still of clausula 3, it is no longer possible to suggest a common rationale. This means that in paragraphs 3 and 4 we have to do with a slightly extended example of local connections.

I do not intend to produce an exhaustive list of such examples. Indeed the grey area of instances that might or might not be so interpreted is of necessity rather large. I merely add a small selection of further instances of clausula 3.

1.5. *aut excidebat* (3γδ) and 12 *iactura quae per neglegentiam fit* (3βη). But if there is intent here, we are hard put to explain 10 *quaedam effluunt* (m) which is one of those awkward clauses that do not seem to fit a known clausula. (See above p. 112f.).

75.1. *mitti quereris* (3^2γ) and 2 *accurate loquitur* (33^2ε) provide a striking letter opening.

75.71 *nulli gradus sunt* (3γεη) and 79 *dividuntur* (3δ) may establish an intended relationship.

75.118 shows with *nimis inminere leviter petendis* (3βε), 119 *vel ex toto non petendis* (3αβδε) one of the author's many rhyming repetitions ; there is another one in this very paragraph : 115 *tamquam valde expetenda sint* (4ε), 116 *quae leviter expetenda sunt* (4αε). Together they make more of a case for the principle of *variatio* than for the referential value of the subordinate clausulae.

80.11 *non ergo sequor priores* (3αγε) and 13 *non servio illis* (3γδ) show an interesting similarity, which just possibly might have a somewhat naughty connection with *ad sphaeromachian avocavit* (3δ) earlier in the paragraph : in both cases Seneca asserts his independence, but the implied comparison of the *molesti* with the *priores* may be too much to expect even of this master of subtle hints.

80.66 *nihil in illa mali sit* (3βγεη) and 69 *nulla sollicitudo in alto est* (3αζ) may in their similarity have set up a sufficiently strong expectation for 76 *cor ipsum exedentes* (3βγ) to jar in contrast.

80.106 *capitis decorum* (3βε) ; 107 *illum aestimare* (3αβγ) and *domum, dignitatem* (3βδ) have enough in common to be somewhat striking. It is awkward that what they have in common seems to fit beautifully into the mold of clausula 1 for this letter, with the result that we need to strain the function *variatio* somewhat strongly.
Cf. below p. 152f.

100.86-88 : although we have a rhythmic anaphora, only 87 and 88 are clearly related in sense.

If we check the results of this discussion against the questions asked above (p. 117), it is clear that they cannot all be answered in the affirmative. Notably any suggested functions of clausulae of types 2, 3 and 4 in connection with content disappear upon closer inspection, except perhaps the function *variatio* (at best a vague entity).

Nor can it be proven that the observed links between cola ending in cretic + trochee show an intended referential value for that clausula with respect to content. For such referential value we would expect either all cola with clausula 1 to have a link with the core thought or core sequence, or all cola with such a link to have clausula 1. In fact, though the percentages in both cases are high, neither of these obtains. For the explanation of those high percentages, then, we have to fall back on some such description of the author's practice as was imagined on p. 116. We have to do not so much with roadsigns carefully put in in order to help the reader, as with an element of compositional technique that gives away some of the author's thought processes. The link of clausula 1 with content, I maintain, is there ; but the link originates at a rather lower level of consciousness than would be required for intended references.

If referential intention has to be rejected with respect to Seneca's use of clausulae matters are different with his arrangement of subject-matter, as we shall see in the next chapter.

ARRANGEMENT

Almost a century and a half ago Ludolph Dissen caused a great deal of sometimes heated discussion by his Pindar edition (1830) and the principles of interpretation discussed in the introduction.[1] If in those discussions it was the position of the myths in Pindar's poetry that was the more important, we are interested in the structural patterns he described as περιπλοκή (aba and derivatives) and ἐμπλοκή (abab or abacbc etc.). In so far as I know he was the first to use this notation for sequences of motifs.[2] Next Rudolf Westphal described the thematic correspondence in Catullus 68[b] in terms of the Nomos of Terpander/Pollux.[3] Westphal taught that the "Terpandrische Compositionsnorm" occurs frequently in Pindar and the choral odes of Aeschylus, that it continued into and beyond the Alexandrian period but was used for the last time by Catullus. The central portion of a Terpandrian nomos is called *omphalos* and, though the Westphalian theory was dropped very soon, this element of his terminology stuck in the scholarly discussions, partly through the agency of Ellis' edition of the Catullan corpus.[4] Westphal, however, also used the expression *mesodische Responsion der Theile*[5] (p. 75) and the term *mesodic* equally continued in use. In addition a great number of other terms has been invented by a prolific scholarly imagination as similar compositional

---

[1] *Pindari carmina quae supersunt cum deperditorum fragmentis selectis ex recensione Boeckhii commentario perpetuo illustravit Ludolphus Dissenius, professor Gottingensis.* Sect. I, Gothae et Erfordiae, MDCCCXXX pp. LXVI-LXXXVIII. In the second edition of this work, edited by Schneidewin in 1843, the relevant section occurs pp. XLV-LXII. Schneidewin added a brief note with bibliographical details concerning the reception of the work. See e.g. G. Hermann, Opuscula VII 1839 p. 111. It is fascinating to note that five years later Dissen discovers similar structures in Tibullus: *Albii Tibulli Carmina ex rec. C. Lachmanni passim mutata explicuit Ludolphus Dissen, Pars Prior,* Gott. MDCCCXXXV e.g. pp. CIV ff.
[2] It had been used before to denote strophic correspondences.
[3] R. Westphal, *Catulls Gedichte in ihrem geschichtlichen Zusammenhange,* Breslau (Leuckart) 1867 pp. 73-92. For Terpander see now also E. Turolla, *Struttura simmetrica nella redazione rapsodica dei poemi omerici; I. L'Iliade; II. L'Odissea* GIF XVI 1963 243-261 and 314-325.
[4] R. Ellis, *Catulli Veronensis liber. Iterum recognovit...,* Oxon. Clar. MDCCCLXXVIII p. 255ff., in particular p. 272ff. with the discussion of Westphal's theories.
[5] The term mesodic was picked up by F. Skutsch, RhM 47 (1892), 138-151 = *Kleine Schriften* p. 46ff. The word probably derives from Hephaistion *Poem.* 4 μεσῳδικὰ δέ, ἐν οἷς περιέχει μὲν τὰ ὅμοια, μέσον δὲ τὸ ἀνόμοιον τέτακται. Hephaistion is speaking in a context of metrical analysis.

sequences began to be discovered, not only in the authors and periods mentioned by Westphal but far more widely.[6] One of those terms is ring composition. This is a rather unfortunate term in so far as it does not distinguish between compositions that show several concentric rings and those that show only one inset and one frame. The question arises forthwith whether the phenomena *Rahmenerzählung* and *Zwiebelschalenkomposition* are related, and if so, to what degree. On the whole I incline to the view that the difference is one of degree rather than kind, but that different genres often seem to show different compositional techniques which in essence are no

---

[6] I have not yet compiled a satisfactory bibliography. I simply list some ancient authors in which scholars have detected related phenomena and add a reference or two fully realizing that neither list nor references come anywhere near being full. Aeschylus, E. B. Holtsmark, *Ringcomposition and the Persae of Aeschylus*, SO 1970 p. 5.23, Catullus, D. Thomson, CJ 57 (1961/2) p. 50. H. Bardon, *Propositions sur Catulle*, Bruxelles, Coll. Latomus 118, p. 37 ff. See however J. Jachmann in *Gnomon* I, 1925, p. 212; J.P. Elder, HSPh 60 (1951) p. 103, Herodotus, H.R. Immerwahr, *Form and thought in Herodotus*, Philol. monogr. publ. by the APA, 23, 1966 p. 54 and *passim*, a bibliographical note on p. 54, n. 28. Ingrid Beck, *Die Ringkomposition bei Herodot und ihre Bedeutung für die Beweistechnik*, Spudasmata 25 Hildesheim 1971, Homer, W.A.A. van Otterlo (cf. Bibliography p. 175 below), Cedric H. Whitman, *Homer and the heroic tradition*, Cambridge, Mass. 1958, p. 249 ff. Horace, G. Blangez, *La composition mésodique et l'ode d'Horace*, REL 42, 1964, p. 262-272, M. Owen Lee, *Horace Odes 1.4, A sonic circle*, CQ 1965 p. 268 ff. Lucretius, P.H. Schrijvers, *Lucrèce*, Amsterdam 1970, p. 148 ff. Ovid, Brooks Otis, *Ovid as an epic Poet*, Cambridge UP, 1966, p. 83 ff., K. Gieseking, *Die Rahmenerzählung in Ovids Metamorphosen*, Diss. Tübingen 1964, see in particular his definition, p. 10 f. H.O. Kröner, *Aufbau und Ziel der Elegie Ovids Trist. I 2*, Emerita 38, 1970, pp. 163-197. Pindar, David C. Young, *Three Odes of Pindar*, Mnemosyne, Suppl. IX, p. 111; p. 121 ff. (with bibliographical note). See also L. Illig, *Zur Form der pindarischen Erzählung*, Berlin 1932 p. 62. Propertius, Th.A. Suits TAPA 96 (1965) p. 427-437; TAPA 100 (1969), pp. 475-486. On the question of numerical responsion cf. J.P. Boucher, *Études sur Properce, Problèmes d'inspiration et d'art*, Paris 1965, p. 366 ff. (a survey of symmetries in note 1, p. 367, older work, p. 368, n. 1), Seneca, cf. Karlhans Abel, *Bauformen in Senecas Dial.*, p. 68, 75, 83, 143 (ring composition). Sophocles, A. Lesky *Die tragische Dichtung*, 1972³, p. 195 (Antig. 11-17), Theocritus, C. Cessi, *La tecnica dell' 'incorniciamento' e delle 'metà' e l'arte di Teocrito*, Atti del Reale Ist. Veneto di Sc. Lettere ed Arte 83.2 (1923/4), 797-812; 84,2 (1924/5), 95-119, U. Ott, *Die kunst des Gegensatzes in Theokrits Hirtengedichten*, Spudasmata 22, 1969, p. 38, 44, 204 see also F.O. Copley in TAPA 71 (1940), 56. Tibullus, R. Hanslik in Forsch. z. römischen Lit., Festschr. Büchner, Wiesbaden 1970, p. 138-145 (see however C. Campbell, Yale Class. Studies 23, 1973, p. 148, n. 7 and 155, n. 12). H. Merklin in Festschr. Büchner, p. 301-314 (Tib. 2.5), Vergil, G.E. Duckworth, *Structural patterns and proportions in Vergil's Aeneid*, Ann Arbor 1962, p. 21 ff., K.H. Pridik, *Vergils Georgica, Strukturanalytische Interpretationen*, Diss. Tübingen, 1971. In general see also F. Cupaiolo, *Tra poesia e poetica, Collana di Studi Latini XV* Napoli 1966, p. 98 ff. and note 94. For the history of ring composition proper also B.A. v. Groningen, *La composition*, p. 51 ff.

more than adapted compositional techniques.[7] Indeed it seems to me that the subject needs an overall treatment showing in how far genre affects the choice of elements (motifs, stories, topoi) arranged in single, double or multiple (concentric) "rings". That the word "rings" involves a metaphor is so obvious that it is often forgotten. A study as intended would have to deal also with the perception of the compositional form, the more so since it has been said that structures as detected by Whitman in Homer could not have been appreciated by an ancient audience, in particular the audience for which the epics were originally intended.[8] Only in this way the precise value of the metaphor and its appropriateness to the phenomenon can be estimated. This, of course, holds true for the other metaphors in use. I have found—and I am sure that my list is far from complete—: ἀναβολή (Illig), Chinese Ball (Ellis), Chinese Box (Wheeler), Circular composition (Cupaiolo, Immerwahr), Einschachtelung (Riese, Kroll), embrassé (Bardon), framework pattern (Otis), incorniciamento (Cessi), mesodisch (Westphal, Skutsch), metà (Cessi), omphalos composition (Westphal, Ellis, Abel), pediment composition (Myres), Rahmenerzählung (general), recessed panel pattern (Duckworth), ring composition (v. Otterlo), Schleifengang (Fraenkel), Zwiebelschalenkomposition (Kröner).[9] In most cases the name in brackets represents not the only but one of several users of the term involved. It is sufficiently clear from the mere choice of terms that both the phenomena described by them and the points of view of the describers differed in various respects.[10]

---

[7] In this respect I have changed my mind since my paper in Lampas 7,1, March 1974, p. 11. Immerwahr insists on a difference in kind between ring composition and circular composition.

[8] See my Lampas paper quoted above, note 4.

[9] It may be interesting to compare to the Zwiebelschalenkomposition a phenomenon in the visual arts recently described by Gilbert-Charles Picard, Mélanges de l'École Française de Rome, Antiquité, 85, 1973, p. 162-195. M. Picard speaks of *composition héraldique* which he defines as follows: «une composition comprise dans un seul plan dans laquelle des êtres, humains, animaux ou mythiques, ou des objets en nombre pair, strictement identiques deux à deux, se répondent symétriquement de part et d'autre d'un axe qui est généralement matérialisé soit par un personnage en position frontale, soit par un objet plus haut que large (arbre, pilier etc.) soit encore par un objet arrondi (bouclier, masque) qui est souvent soutenu par les deux personnages ou êtres les plus proches de lui". The author notes that this type occurs regularly in Italian compositions of the first cent. B.C. (p. 170).

[10] The entire question may be placed in the more general context of symmetry in ancient literature. See e.g. the bibliographical note in E.R. Schwinge, *Die Verwendung der Stychomythie in den Dramen des Euripides*, Heidelberg, Winter, 1968, p. 13, n. 6.

In this context the *technopaegnia* of Greek bucolic poetry may be of particular

When in the subsequent pages similar compositional sequences are noted in some of our Seneca letters, these are based not on verbal correspondences so much (though on occasion these, too, occur) as on notions, ideas, motifs. This is to be expected in letters dealing with moral subjects. Furthermore it is obvious that strict numerical correspondences are equally out of the question, though Seneca repeatedly marks the middle of his letter (below p. 136 f.). The correspondences within a letter are not in all cases continued into subordinate detail as they are in letter 1.

Finally, it is important to note that this particular compositional approach is no more used in all cases than it is in e.g. Pindar or Horace : the interpreter cannot assume a rigid scheme ; once the scheme has been found, however, he may use it to support points of detailed interpretation.

It will be noted that the subsequent analyses show somewhat divergent approaches : this is due to a desire to allow the letters themselves to dictate the approach rather than attempting to impose a ready-made scheme upon them.

a. Letter 1

Ita fac, mi Lucili : vindica te tibi ... Several aspects of the first phrase are obvious. Seneca replies, or pretends to reply, to a communication from Lucilius. The nature of this communication does not become clear until after the middle of par. 2 *scribis* : Lucilius has written a letter.[11] Seneca, then, whether in reality or pretence,[12] picks his theme from his correspondent. This theme is stated twice : *vindica te tibi* and (par. 2) *omnes horas conplectere.*[13] The two are closely related. The expression *vindica te tibi*—possibly because it was felt to be a little startling and perhaps even obscure, in any case in need of

---

interest, see G. Wojaczek, *Daphnis, Untersuchungen zur griechischen Bukolik*, Beitr. z. Kl. Phil. 34, Meisenheim am Glan 1969 (p. 67 ff. for Simias' wing, egg, axe etc.); an appendix contains these forms visualised in written forms for which modern parallels may be found in Paul van Ostaijen, Dylan Thomas and many others.

[11] The technique is somewhat different from e.g. *epp.* 2, 3, 7 (*quaeris*, cf. *De prov.* 1.1.), 8, 9 etc. where Lucilius' letter or communication is mentioned forthwith. Implied replies are to be found e.g. in *epp.* 4, 5, 10 etc.

[12] Cf. Maurach *passim* and Karlhans Abel's review in Gymnasium 1972, 83-86. The latter believes Seneca's correspondence with Lucilius was a historical rather than a fictitious one.

[13] Maurach, *Der Bau von Senecas Epistulae Morales*, Heidelberg 1970, p. 25 ff., misses this point with the result that he mistakes the emphasis of the letter as a whole.

explanation [14]—is clarified forthwith by the further injunction *tempus...* *collige et serva*. The phrase is joined to the preceding one by an explicative *et*.

Indeed the advice "*tempus...collige et serva*" is the content of *vindica te tibi*. The *vindicatio sui* consists in a preservation of time, which, it is suggested at the beginning of par. 3, is the only thing that is really ours. For that reason the legal "claim yourself for yourself" is the first connotation of *vindicare* rather than an aspect of liberation.[15] *Ep*. 82.5, which has been quoted[16] as a parallel in order to support the notion of liberation, does not provide the support claimed: the burden of its imagery makes Noblot's translation "se défend" perfectly acceptable. The latter notion, however, does not fit our passage either, since we are not dealing with an onslaught of the enemy. The relevant type of onslaught—if any—is suggested by the three words *auferebatur, subripiebatur, excidebat*. Seneca himself dismisses the first two in the sentence "*turpissima tamen est iactura quae per neglegentiam fit*" thereby introducing his more special theme. That should not close our eyes, however, to the fact that *auferri* and *subripi* are strengthened in the next lines by *eripiuntur* and *subducuntur*, words that respectively suggest more or less violent robbery and stealthy theft.[17]

In such a context *vindica te tibi* can hardly be thought to mean "free yourself".[18] Rather it denotes the sort of things that we read in *Ad Pol*. 15.5: *exercitum... corpus Drusi sibi vindicantem*, or *ibidem* 8.2: *tunc te illae (sc. litterae) antistitem et cultorem suum vindicent*, and in particular *De otio* 5.7: *etiam si illud (sc. tempus totum) sibi vindicat*.[19] This "legal" interpretation of *vindicare* is strengthened by the fact that almost the entire letter is written in the vocabulary of property.[20] The expression *si hodierno manum*

---

[14] Imputing intentions or motives to an author is, of course, highly dangerous. The fact that a clarification follows does not prove that the author has been thinking (merely) in terms of clarification. He may have wished to introduce a new element by means of his "clarification".

[15] Gummere translates: "set yourself free", so does Pohlenz, *Die Stoa* p. 318: "Mache dich für dichselber frei", Noblot on the other hand "revendique tes droits sur toi-même".

[16] Maurach, *l.c.* p. 26.

[17] Cf. the distinction in the XII tables (8,12-17) between *furtum manifestum* and *furtum non manifestum*, Zulueta, *The Inst. of Gaius*, Part II, p. 199.

[18] Cf. n. 15.

[19] Cf. Noblot, note 2.

[20] I hesitate to use the word "imagery". Apart from the items mentioned above,

inieceris (col. 29) for instance has certainly retained its heavily legal connotations.[21] The picture is that of the creditor claiming what is his own.

These initial notes enable us to study the arrangement of the letter as a whole. It is remarkable, then, that this letter starts and finishes with words that denote saving, preserving and managing,[22] whereas the item that is to be saved, preserved, is placed in the very centre (17th line in 32 of the OCT and 32nd colon in the text printed above : *tempus tantum nostrum est*). But *servare* is not the only notion that serves as a frame. If *vindica te tibi* in the sense suggested is said to Lucilius, a good case can be made for interpreting the proverbial[23] "*sera parsimonia in fundo est*" as referring to Seneca himself. He has already admitted that he is still losing time (par. 4 : *non possum dicere nihil perdere*) but he advances a number of reasons (or excuses?) that may be adduced to absolve him from blame : 1. he can account for the losses (*causas paupertatis meae reddam*), 2. the losses are not his fault, 3. since what little is left is enough, the appellation poverty does not apply and, finally 4. (applicable to his old age, not Lucilius' younger years) it is too late to do anything about it in any case. Number two is particularly interesting, since it contains the words *non suo vitio* which, as it were as an aside *sotto voce* and hidden in a clause of unusual length,[24] pick up the

---

the list is as follows: *pretium* (18), *aestimet* (19), *tenet* (24), *conplectere* (27: here one might actually think of the manner in which a child claims and protects a piece of property. See also OLD *sub voce* 3), *manum ieneceris* (29) see above, *nostrum* (32), *possessionem* (33), *inpetravere* (39), *debere* (41), *accepit* (42), *reddere* (44), *ratio mihi constat impensae* (50), *perdere* (51).

[21] It is, of course, not easy to decide whether Seneca has in mind the old *manus iniectio* as a *legis actio* (cf. Zulueta, part II, p. 231, 242 ff. and his distinction of various kinds of *manus iniectio*) or some weakened expression of common parlance that ultimately derives from that source. I base my preference for the strictly legal connotation on a. the general impression that Seneca is highly conscious of the basic connotations of the words he uses and b. on the accumulation of legal terms in this letter (e.g. *mittere in possessionem*, *expellere*). This interpretation is also supported by such expressions as *ep.* 20.1 *fias tuus*, *ep.* 62.1 *meus sum*.

[22] Noblot's translation of *serves* : recueille ce capital et menage-le, catches the precise connotations much better than Gummere's rather weak "keep".

[23] Cf. A. Otto, *Sprichwörter der Römer* p. 149 s.v. *fundus* 2., Nachträge p. 166. Seneca may refer to Hesiod *Erga* 368 f. :

ἀρχομένου δὲ πίθου καὶ λήγοντος κορέσασθαι,

μεσσόθι φείδεσθαι : δειλὴ δ' ἐν πυθμένι φειδώ.

Sinclair ad loc. quotes our Seneca passage and "It is too late to spare / When the bottom is bare". Hesiod's lines are discussed by Plutarch, *Quaest. Conviv.* 7.3.701 d f. and Macrobius *Saturn.* 7,12,13.

[24] Cf. table I, p. 87 f., and the discussion on p. 89.

notions that had been announced in *auferebatur/subripiebatur* and were repeated a line or so later only to be brusquely dismissed in favour of the theme of *neglegentia*. *Neglegentia* is *turpissima*, whereas on the other hand Seneca's own situation is one that everybody regards as forgivable (*omnes ignoscunt*). Seneca's own situation, however, is also described in the near-oxymoron "luxuriosum sed diligentem" with its solution *ratio mihi impensae constat*. But this description is the answer given to the interjected question of Lucilius, which itself balances Seneca's own rhetorical question at the beginning of par. 2 with its implied negative answer. Thus we are beginning to see that the entire letter is arranged in the fashion of a chinese box or as an intricate instance of circular composition. The pattern is one of concepts rather than verbal correspondences. In the following schematic presentation the few verbal frames are italicized. Those concepts that are balanced by their opposites have been marked with an asterisk. (See the diagram on p. 138)

To summarize, then, we saw in ch. III that the clauses were arranged in various formats, not haphazardly, but with a strong indication that those formats were used to advantage. Thus *ep.* 1 par. 1 was shown above (p. 104) to underscore and clarify its central notion by its very arrangement. We may add here that e.g. the periodic statement "turpissima tamen est iactura, quae per neglegentiam fit" gains additional force by its very periodicity. Where we noted the length of 1.33 (above p. 89) and suggested two reasons, it is now also clear that this clause together with the preceding *tempus tantum nostrum est* (which it qualifies) is the very core of the letter. The core, then, is marked not only by the clauselength, but by the place (clause 33 in 65) as well as the clausula, since it was suggested above in chapter IV that the clausulae of this type seemed to receive preferential treatment whenever Seneca approached the core thought. Thus we may claim that for letter 1 at least the structure in all its dimensions (even though not all have been studied here) is wholly functional, that it serves the content in so far as it organizes, emphasizes, balances, but, what is more, also provides footholds for basic interpretation of content.

b. Letter 26

At the very first reading it is clear that letter 26 finds its centre in the passage Seneca addresses to himself (cola 52-79), that these paragraphs

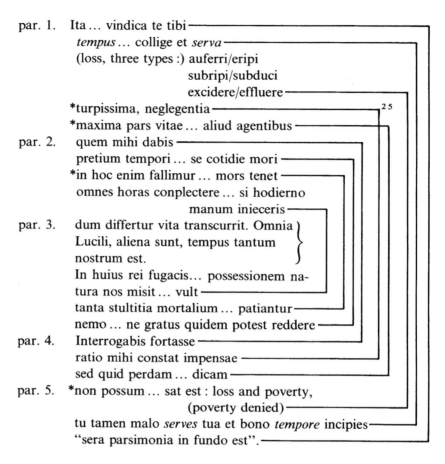

par. 1.   Ita … vindica te tibi
          tempus … collige et serva
          (loss, three types :) auferri/eripi
                      subripi/subduci
                      excidere/effluere
          *turpissima, neglegentia   25
          *maxima pars vitae … aliud agentibus
par. 2.   quem mihi dabis
          pretium tempori … se cotidie mori
          *in hoc enim fallimur … mors tenet
          omnes horas conplectere … si hodierno
                      manum inieceris
par. 3.   dum differtur vita transcurrit. Omnia
          Lucili, aliena sunt, tempus tantum
          nostrum est.
          In huius rei fugacis… possessionem na-
          tura nos misit … vult
          tanta stultitia mortalium … patiantur
          nemo … ne gratus quidem potest reddere
par. 4.   Interrogabis fortasse
          ratio mihi constat impensae
          sed quid perdam … dicam
par. 5.   *non possum … sat est : loss and poverty,
                      (poverty denied)
          tu tamen malo *serves* tua et bono *tempore* incipies
          "sera parsimonia in fundo est".

are introduced by some remarks belonging in the topos *de senectute* and that the addition has been chosen carefully in connection with the subject matter of the letter as a whole. When we start determining the latter it soon appears that "death" as a single unified notion will not do as an indication of the central subject. The large central section leaves no doubt that it is rather the day of our death as the moment of truth vis à vis the life we have lived that Seneca spotlights in this letter. Nor is the encore singleminded : it shows at least two different elements, the element of preparation, *askesis*, and the element of death as liberation—a liberation that one may have to provide for oneself.

---

[25] The inversion of corresponding items of detail hardly invalidates the scheme as a whole.

The first of these two elements does not occur for the first time in the letter: in cola 21 ff. the *animus* had ordered a *cogitatio*. It is interesting to see how this *cogitatio* is sketched in a carefully built group of dependent questions rounded off by a rhetorical one:

> Ire in cogitationem iubet
>> et dispicere
>> *qui*d ex hac tran*qui*llitate ac modestia morum sapientiae
>>>> debeam
>> *qui*d aetati
> et diligenter excutere
>> *qu*ae *non possim* facere
>> *qu*ae *nolim*
>>> proinde habiturus at*que* si *nolim*
>>> *qui*d*qui*d *non posse me gaudeo.*
> *Qu*ae enim *qu*erela est
> *qu*od incommodum
>> si *qui*d*qui*d *d*ebebat *d*esinere *d*efecit?

Apart from alliteration, assonance, anaphora and parallelism we notice the chiastic grouping of *non possim, nolim, nolim* and *non posse me gaudeo* (I take these words together as the expression of a reasonably unified notion). The chiasm contains an element of variation that is functional in so far as the last member reaches a high point which in turn is rounded off in the contrasting rhetorical question.[26] The rhetorical question in its turn provides in *incommodum* the link with the subsequent objection. We experience the objection as weak and whining. The gradually diminishing strength is employed as (the usual) reason for thinking old age an *incommodum*. But this reason is promptly used (in a slightly modified wording) to reject the objection.

An identical sequence is found in paragraphs 8-9 (cola 99-107): exhortation to reflect, followed by an objection whose foundation is immediately changed into the basis for rejecting the objection. These cola, then, may be said to show an obvious correspondence with cola 21 ff. (paragraphs 3-4). The elaborated *meditatio mortis* of paragraphs 4-5 (cola 52-79) is enclosed by a very simple frame (51 : *ita*

---

[26] In a small way we have an example here of what Brooks Otis calls the law of symmetrical progression: "though the episodes after each central panel correspond to those before it, they also reveal a significant change which almost insensibly prepares the reader for the next major section". (*Ovid as an Epic Poet*, p. 86).

me observo et adloquor and 80/81: *Haec mecum loquor/ sed tecum quoque me locutum puta*). The passage itself has two sections that may be formally distinguished in that the first person is used in the first, the imperative and second person in the second section. They contrast the reality of the act with the make believe of the word. The first section employs a rather forceful metaphor: first *pignora animi.. multis.. involuta lenociniis*, then the picture shifts from the brothel to the cathedra: *remotis strophis ac fucis*; it is all about *me*. These images give the reality of contemporary culture (neatly sketched in par. 6) an unmistakable colouring. The word *remotis* is picked up in *remove* (with anaphora!). To be removed is first of all the involvement in what other people think (cf. colon 55 *lenociniis*), next the involvement in *studia tota vita tractata* (cf. 59 *strophis ac fucis*); it is all about *te*. Those *studia* are then further qualified as various forms of literary-rhetorical activity that have noting to do with a real *agere*; that which it is all about is *quid egeris*.

Subsequently we notice that also part of the light play element in the introduction of Epicurus' exhortation has a corresponding section. There are three motifs in this playful passage: a. the *viaticum* motif which the letter has in common with e.g. letter 12.10 (*peculium*) but which is here given a double bottom (cf. above p. 119), b. the *mutuum* motif, that which is borrowed with its contrast, c. "soon from my own stores". In cola 21 ff., too, Seneca contrasts wisdom obtained from outside and wisdom gained from inside.[27] Thus we may state that paragraphs 3 and 8, 4 and 9 correspond, or, better, that the progression 3-4 corresponds with the progression 8-9. The exhortation itself corresponds with the exhortation of the *animus* in 3 but has exchanged places with the correspondent of the *mutuum* motif. When Seneca finally elaborates Epicurus' advice (cola 108-128) this closing portion of the letter too aims at *agere*, at one's readiness for the final act. Seneca indicates very succinctly what it is that keeps us from this final act: *amor vitae*. We must not be overcome by this lust for life: *ut non est abiciendus, ita minuendus est ut* etc. Is there any danger that the author is overcome by this *amor vitae*? Hardly. At the start of the letter he speaks of his own age as *lassa aetas*,

---

[27] One may add that "*proinde habiturus atque si* etc. also contains a playful element but it is to be remembered that it is Kronenberg's emendation of a much discussed *crux*. Reynolds' apparatus does not show how much the place has been doctored, cf. Hense and Beltrami[2]. Among the various proposals Kronenberg's is doubtless the most economical.

and this expression being insufficient it is emended to *fracta aetas*.

At this point the impression imposes itself that this *fracta aetas* which is, in so many words, linked with the state of the body, is given its intentional counterpart at the end of the letter in *amor vitae*, in which expression *vita* also refers to the life of the body. And whereas at the end of the letter the contrasting notion is freedom, at the beginning the contrasting notion is *animus*—and the latter turns up in the middle section in the expression *verum robur animi* (colon 73). Moreover, it is now clear, if it was not from the immediate context, that the *bonum suum* of the *animus* in colon 20 is very closely related to *libertas* in the final paragraph. Thus the main correspondences in this letter may be organised in the following diagram :

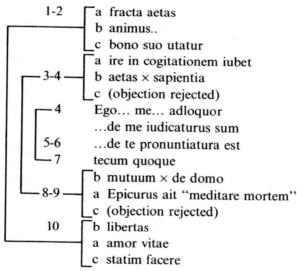

```
1-2        a  fracta aetas
           b  animus..
           c  bono suo utatur
           a  ire in cogitationem iubet
 3-4       b  aetas × sapientia
           c  (objection rejected)
 4         Ego... me... adloquor
           ...de me iudicaturus sum
 5-6       ...de te pronuntiatura est
 7         tecum quoque
           b  mutuum × de domo
 8-9       a  Epicurus ait "meditare mortem"
           c  (objection rejected)
 10        b  libertas
           a  amor vitae
           c  statim facere
```

However, there is a tension in the letter that is not fully represented in the diagram, viz. the tension between body and soul, between the tired, broken body and the mind whose activity is the purer as the body can be less active (cf. paragr. 2 *gaudet, exultat, bono suo utatur*, 3 *iubet..gaudeo*, 4 *ego..me observo et adloquor*—to ask who exactly is speaking to whom, what exactly is the relationship between *ego* and *me* would be rather unfair on Seneca in so far as such a question takes its cue from Descartes or Sartre : it ought to be sufficiently clear that the *vox rationis* addresses the man.) In paragr. 5 the author drops the bodily element as such and replaces it by mental activities of a non-essential type, *fallacia pignora animi*, just saying as against really experiencing, the undependable opinions of others, rhetorical *studia*. All of these are to be contrasted with a *verum robur animi*. At the end of this rising line we encounter the fittingly impressive isocolon :

> *accipio condicionem*
> *non reformido iudicium.*

Thus far the part of the letter in which Seneca is busy with himself. Follows a break that does not seem to fit the diagram at all (paragr. 7)[28] but which has a double function. It transfers the attention from the first person to the second, from the I to the you, and as a result the element death, originally introduced in connection with the autobiographical *fracta aetas*, is severed from it in order that a purely general *meditatio mortis* may follow in the last paragraph.

Thus we have three meditations, or rather a *cogitatio*, an *allocutio* and a *meditatio* in this letter. They represent the *agere* of the mind, an activity which, as said above, results in that readiness to *statim facere* which was placed so obviously at the end to form a balance against *lassa/fracta aetas* of paragraph 1.

c. Letter 41

In this letter we need not wait very long before being presented with the principal subject. Seneca half-quotes Lucilius in the very first period : *perseveras ire ad bonam mentem*. The *bona mens* will play a central role. The words *perseveras ire ad* are commented upon in the sentence (6) *non sunt ad caelum elevandae manus e.q.s.*, but the comment seems somewhat out of place since, in so far as *we* are concerned, there is no suggestion that Lucilius' road is the one of stupid, though pious, prayer—prayer that is wrongly addressed at that (4: *quam stultum est e.q.s.*). But Seneca acts as if it is and he has a solid structural reason for so doing. For the suggestion eases the transition to *prope est a te deus e.q.s.* (11f.) and at the same time emphasizes that most central of doctrines in Senecan Stoicism viz. the notion that the *bona mens* is the kin (as well as the equal) of the divine mind. But at this point in the letter the emphasis is merely preliminary.

This is not the place to discuss the full import of the first sentence

---

[28] Here, too, there may be a reference to a previous letter (24.20. G. Maurach, *Der Bau*, p. 103, shows that the entire letter is closely linked with letter 24).

of paragr. 2 (13ff.) and its connection with the notion of *conscientia*,[29] but let us note that it effectively links the *bona mens* of paragr. 1 with the *bonus vir* of cola 18ff. Seneca subsequently feels that it is incumbent upon him to give some proof of his main assertion that a divine spirit resides in the good man, and so he provides us in the next paragraph (cola 23-40) with three areas of nature, each of which arouses a religious emotion in people: the forest with a *lucus* (23-30), a remarkable cave-formation in the mountains (31-36) and, third, the waters of riverheads, hot springs and (even) certain stagnant pools (37-40). The religious emotions aroused are heaped up here (*fidem numinis... religionis suspicione... veneramur... aras habet... coluntur... sacravit*) so as to make it impossible to treat the questions of paragr. 4 as other than rhetorical.[30] But these rhetorical questions deal with the core subject of the letter: the *bonus vir* in his relationship with God.

The first sentence of paragr. 5 spells out that relationship and it contains the central message of the letter. Though we are not dealing here with the content of the statement so much as with its form, it must be noted that the wording suggests a rather transcendental, even neo-platonic, world-view. We should ask, then, whether the rhetoric of the passage as a whole has occasioned this impression—in other words, whether the images have run away with Seneca—or whether Seneca has a design. It would seem that the latter is the case (as might be expected).[31] In paragr. 1 Seneca had said *non sunt ad caelum elevandae* manus (6). Now, in contrast, we find an immediate line of communication between heaven and the *vir bonus*. The tension created by this apparent contradiction must, and of course will, be solved in the remainder of the letter. But before it is indeed solved, a second element of tension is introduced by the sun-simile which takes up the remainder of paragr. 5 (cola 58-67). The wide divergence between the wise man's heavenly origin and earthly presence is akin to and strengthens the earlier element of tension. The opening sentence of paragr. 6 works like an implosion: *Quis est ergo hic animus? qui nullo bono nisi suo nitet* (68-69). Both tensions, but especially

---

[29] Cf. G. Molenaar in Mnemosyne IV, 22 (1969), pp. 170-180 and my reaction in Mnemosyne IV 23 (1970) p. 190. An exhaustive treatment is still lacking.

[30] Cf. W. Trillitzsch, *Senecas Beweisführung*, Berlin 1962, p. 84. The author mistakes the passage by asserting that the Vergil quotation of paragr. 2 is part of the proof. On the contrary, it is part of the thesis and indeed its second statement. Paragraphs 3 and 4 furnish the proof.

[31] Compare the tenor of my paper in Theta-Pi 2 (1973), pp. 40-59.

the first, have found their resolution. The good is not to be sought outside (*non sunt ad caelum elevandae manus*) and the sun-simile appears to have been what it was, a simile. The basic element that remains is the element *suum*. In its turn this element suggests its opposite : *alienum*. The contrast between the two is illustrated with three examples from the realm of nature in paragraphs 6 and 7 : the horse with the golden rein, the lions—one tame with gilded mane, one with his mane all tangled but full of spirit—, the vines—one loaded with grape clusters, the other a golden fake—. The fertility of the natural vine provides an easy transition to human virtue, which can only be defined in terms of the *proprium hominis*, in other words : *animus et ratio in animo perfecta* (105).

It is clear that once again we are dealing with a circular composition, one which may be visualized in the following diagram.

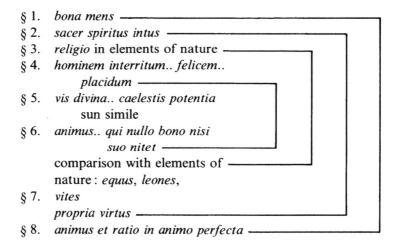

§ 1. *bona mens*
§ 2. *sacer spiritus intus*
§ 3. *religio* in elements of nature
§ 4. *hominem interritum.. felicem..*
          placidum
§ 5. *vis divina.. caelestis potentia*
          sun simile
§ 6. *animus.. qui nullo bono nisi*
              suo nitet
       comparison with elements of
       nature : *equus, leones,*
§ 7. *vites*
       propria virtus
§ 8. *animus et ratio in animo perfecta*

In this letter paragr. 5 is the truly central statement both from a spatial point of view (cola 50-67 in 118) and with respect to content. This, however, is also the paragraph that contains the greatest concentration of clausulae of type 1 (7 in 16) in the letter as a whole. Their function has been discussed above p. 119f. And if we are disappointed that this core paragraph does not seem to contain a hint that clauselength, too, marks the core thought as it did in letter 1, we should not lose sight of the fact that essentially paragr. 5 qualifies the rhetorical questions of the end of paragr. 4. The second of these consists of one of the longest cola in our sample of seven letters and deals with the very core notion : the wise man as an object of religious awe. But we also found that Seneca, in this letter perhaps even more obviously than elsewhere, works with lengths of cola in relation to one another, and, above p. 95, it was pointed out that the notions *bona mens* and *observator-custos* (which together constitute the core thought) were marked by their parallel positions in sets of waxing and waning members.

We may, then, claim for letter 41 as well that the structural and stylistic elements are functioning so as to enhance, balance and interpret the basic message.

d. Letter 75

Albertini has qualified the unity of letter 75 as *précaire*.[32] On the contrary the letter is carefully tied together. First Seneca insists in par. 1 that his epistolary style is meant to be just like the conversational style he would use if they were together. One is forcibly reminded of Demetrius *On style* 227: σχεδὸν γὰρ εἰκόνα ἕκαστος τῆς ἑαυτοῦ ψυχῆς γράφει τὴν ἐπιστολήν.[33]

This theme is elaborated in the next few paragraphs (colon 34: *concordet sermo cum vita*), but this elaboration is preliminary. It ends (paragr. 7, colon 69) with *non est beatus qui scit illa, sed <qui> facit*, the demand for coincidence of knowledge and action. The harshness of the transition at paragr. 8 to the discussion of the three classes of *proficientes* does not indicate bad composition on Seneca's part but onesided reading on the part of his critics. Paragraphs 1-7 deal with epistolary and literary style, but not exclusively. They deal as much with the appropriate use a philosopher, and a fortiori a *beatus*, makes of style, and this philosopher-beatus is central throughout this part of the letter but most explicitly so in paragraphs 4 and 7 (second half).

If then this first major part of the letter deals with the unity, indivisibility of a wise man's life and language, then the last thought of the letter as a whole, *inaestimabile bonum est suum fieri*, is closely related with the matter of the beginning. Not to see them as related is tantamount to imagining that for Seneca a man's style did not

---

[32] E. Albertini, *La Composition*, p. 144. Cf. also Maurach, *Der Bau*, p. 158. The latter speaks of a "seltsam schroffem Übergang" between paragraphs 7 and 8.
[33] Cancik, *Unters.*, p. 60, calls it *Selbstzeugnis*.

say much about the man's moral situation.[34] What is more, the
terminology of the last paragraph is, it appears, chosen very carefully
to convey a hint of an under-surface reference to style, since each
of the words *faex, sublime, excelsum, tranquillitas, error, libertas* has
its (in some cases common) rhetorical application,[35] as do *turpia*
and *nimia* (colon 186).

But the letter consists of more than a beginning and an end.
The entire section of paragraphs 8-14 consists of a discussion of the
three classes of *proficientes*, in a decreasing order of perfection.
The decreasing order is repeated in paragr. 15. It is interesting to
see that each of the three classes is defined in terms of incomplete
selfpossession (par. 9 has *scire se nesciunt* with a reference to letter 71.4 ;
par. 13 mentions *non.. securitatis suae certa possessio* ; par. 14 spells
it out in contrasts by way of examples).

Structurally the excursus of paragraphs 10, 11, 12 is most troublesome.
That it is indeed meant as an excursus is, in my opinion, shown
sufficiently by the fact that the content of the beginning of par. 10
is repeated at the end of 12 (cola 95-99 × 129-130). If we regard the

---

[34] Cf. e.g. 114.1 *talis hominibus fuit oratio qualis vita.* Parallels in A.D. Leeman,
Orationis Ratio, vol. II, p. 475, n. 81.

[35] FAEX: Seneca does not use the word often (e.g. *ep.* 58.33-34; 108.26; *De ben.*
7.9.1; *Ad Marc.* 23.1, and then usually with the connotation of Epictetus' πηλός
(*Diatr.* 1.1.11 etc.). However, Seneca may well remember Cic. *Brutus* 244 *tu quidem
de faece hauris* an accusation in which *faex* refers to bad orators. SUBLIME in literary
context needs little more than a reference to Horace's *quodsi me lyricis vatibus inseres,/
sublimi feriam sidera vertice.* Add for good measure Quint. 8.3.18; 8.3.74; 11.1.3 etc.
Curiously enough the word is absent from Cicero's rhetorical works and from the
Ad Herennium if Abbott-Oldfather-Canter are to be trusted. EXCELSUM: cf. in first
instance ThLL *sub voce* B II A 1 b "quasi technice in rhet..." where Cic. *opt. gen.* 12
quicquam excelsum magnificumque is quoted. Cf. Tac. *Dial.* 37, Plin. *Ep.* 1.20.19.
TRANQUILLITAS: cf. Cic. *Or.* 52.176 *est enim* (Isocrates) *ut in transferendis faciendisque
verbis tranquillior, sic in ipsis numeris sedatior.* ERROR: as a technical rhetorical term
it is used in Cic. *de orat.* 3.205 *erroris inductio.* Cf. ThLL *sub voce* col. 817.2. In a more
general sense, but an equally rhetorical context: Cic. *De orat.* 2.83. And once again
we may compare Horace: A.P. 307/8 *...quid alat formetque poetam,/ quid deceat, quid
non, quo virtus, quo ferat error.* LIBERTAS: cf. *Brutus* 47.173 *summa libertas in oratione.*
This instance may possibly be used as a parallel in the sense intended, as may *ibidem*
77.267, but neither instance is as satisfactory as Quint. 10.1.28: *meminerimus tamen non
per omnia poetas esse oratori sequendos nec libertate verborum nec licentia figurarum.*
TURPIA: Cic. *De inv.* 1.49.92 neatly defines the sense we are seeking: *turpe est quod
aut eo loco in quo dicitur, aut eo homine qui dicit, aut eo tempore quo dicitur, aut iis
qui audiunt, aut ea re qua de agitur, indignum... videtur.* Cf. *Brutus* 8,34. And let us
not forget Seneca's own criticism of Maecenas' style in *ep.* 114.5. NIMIA: cf.
Quintilian 12.10.80: *sic erunt magna, non nimia; sublimia, non abrupta* e.q.s.; also the
adjectival use in Cic. *Part. or.* 81.

three paragraphs as a clarification of par. 9, however, their function seems to be similar to that of paragraphs 5-7 which, with the *exemplum* of the medical man, serve that very purpose of clarifying as well as strengthening that which preceded. And it may well be that we are justified in regarding the function of the final paragraphs as comparable, too, though the word application, rather than clarification seems to be the more apt.

Thus far, then, the structure of the letter appears to be as follows:

1-4   statement (style)
5-7   clarification
8   statement (three classes of proficientes)
9   statement (first class)
10-12 clarification
13   statement (second class)
14   statement (third class)
15-18 application.

Apart from this scheme there is also a swing-of-the-pendulum structure throughout the letter which tends to strengthen the balanced effect of the letter as a whole. In the first few paragraphs Seneca contrasts the notions of careful and less careful styles with the demand *concordet sermo cum vita* as its final balance (par. 4). In the clarifying section (par. 5-7) the initial contrast is the one of *delectare-prodesse* which is skilfully and gradually shifted to the one of *scire-facere* at the end of par. 7. In the meantime the good man, who had been introduced as early as par. 4 has, by the time we have reached the final contrast of par. 7, been defined as the one who is *beatus* because he encompasses both poles of the contrast. The question that follows in par. 8 is not unnatural. The wise man has been introduced and the unnamed interpellator asks whether there are identifiable steps on the road towards wisdom. The answer is both positive and orthodox. As might be expected Seneca subsequently discusses the three classes of *proficientes* by contrasting what each of them has in common with and in how far each falls short of the ideal. The first class is discussed in par. 9 and we find that Seneca twice contrasts a couple of positive statements with a couple of negative ones until the final contrast before the clarification of par. 10-12. That section is as clearly designated an interruption of the thread of the letter by the interruption of the pendulum effect prevalent

Par.

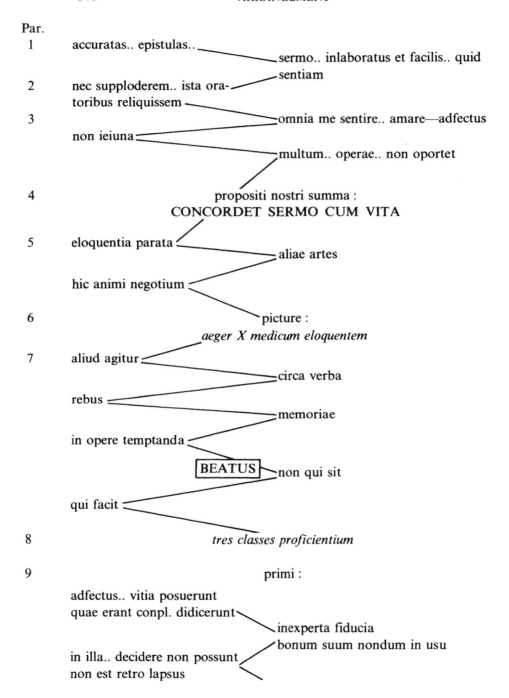

1   accuratas.. epistulas..

sermo.. inlaboratus et facilis.. quid sentiam

2   nec supploderem.. ista ora-toribus reliquissem

3   omnia me sentire.. amare—adfectus

non ieiuna

multum.. operae.. non oportet

4   propositi nostri summa :
CONCORDET SERMO CUM VITA

5   eloquentia parata

aliae artes

hic animi negotium

6   picture :
aeger X medicum eloquentem

7   aliud agitur

circa verba

rebus

memoriae

in opere temptanda

BEATUS non qui sit

qui facit

8   *tres classes proficientium*

9   primi :

adfectus.. vitia posuerunt
quae erant conpl. didicerunt

inexperta fiducia
bonum suum nondum in usu

in illa.. decidere non possunt
non est retro lapsus

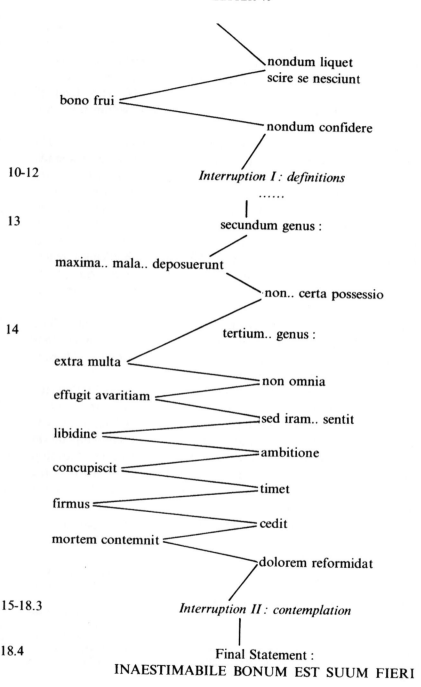

nondum liquet
scire se nesciunt

bono frui

nondum confidere

10-12   *Interruption I : definitions*

......

13   secundum genus :

maxima.. mala.. deposuerunt

non.. certa possessio

14   tertium.. genus :

extra multa

non omnia

effugit avaritiam

sed iram.. sentit

libidine

ambitione

concupiscit

timet

firmus

cedit

mortem contemnit

dolorem reformidat

15-18.3   *Interruption II : contemplation*

18.4   Final Statement :
        INAESTIMABILE BONUM EST SUUM FIERI

in the remainder, as by the element of ring composition mentioned above. Within that frame there is some order in the arrangement of the two motifs (*morbus* and *affectus*) in an ababaabaab sequence.[36] The pendulum effect is resumed in par. 13 with a single stroke and continued in a greatly accelerated manner in par. 14. The effect of speed is reached by the accumulation of six contrasts within five lines of OCT print.

One of the more striking aspects of the final passage (par. 15-18) is that, broadly speaking, each of sections 15, 16 and 17 corresponds with each of 10, 11 and 12. In par. 15 we may regard *mala/nefas/nequitia* as the corresponding terms for *morbus* of par. 10, whereas proficiency (2nd and 3rd class) has an obvious connection with *affectus* in the earlier paragraph. Similarly there is a correspondence between 16 and 11 not only in the words *vitia* and *mala tenacissima* with *morbus* but also in the more formal aspect of the paragraph (Seneca reacts as the typical teacher: "optaverim etc." vis à vis "nunc quoque te admonebo"). Finally, section 12 speaks of the *affectus* in theory and par. 17 gives a list of them.

Furthermore the two passages are framed in similar frames. The frame of 10-12 was mentioned above, the frame of 15-18 consists of the two conditionals *bene.... numerum* and *expectant.... libertas*, similar as they are in both form and content.

Finally the two passages have a comparable function in that the first invites us to stop for a moment and concentrate our attention on the question of the relationship between *morbi* and *affectus*. The second passage makes the invitation to stop and contemplate in explicit form. In the case of the first passage, however, the stop precedes the downward move of paragraphs 13 and 14, whereas the other contemplative passage precedes and indeed introduces the distinct upswing of the final passage.

The diagram on pp. 148f. may help illustrate the arrangement.

---

[36] So clearly have paragraphs 10-12 been marked off that one well may wonder about the presence of the section in this letter. In both paragraphs 9 and 13 Seneca speaks of proficientes who *affectus (de)posuerunt*, whereas in the paragraphs under discussion they have not yet escaped the *affectus* and are indeed still feeling them. A case might be made for the notion that Seneca wrote these paragraphs as a later addition, but perhaps it is better to think of them as a kind of footnote to the question of the *proficientes*. If that is the correct approach the apparent structure mentioned above has some significance. If it is indeed a later addition that structure would appear to have been accidental.

It has been suggested above (p. 94) that Norden's judgement, repeated by Thraede,[37] may not be fair comment, that what Seneca indeed seeks in this letter is to define a middle between extremes of *ornatio* and *abiectio*,[38] between a credibility gap caused by overstatement in a rhetorical sense of the word, and understatement. To base a moral judgement on the use of rhetorical techniques implies that we would know at a given moment in Roman Literary History what is and what is not overdone. I am convinced that Leeman in his *Orationis Ratio* presents a saner view.[39] If that view is correct, then, Seneca is stating that he follows the demands of his school. This in turn makes the unity of the letter more visible than it, apparently, was, not only in so far as Seneca's rhetorical practice is thereby linked to his philosophical activity in general, but also in so far as this link can be demonstrated in this very letter. Several passages have been quoted that suggest the very link between form and immediate content that we are looking for. It has also been shown that the arrangement of the letter as a whole has been handled with a care similar to the care spent on the other letters in our sample. However, to a larger degree than in letter 80 (and a fortiori those that show concentric rings) it is hard to find a single and simply identifiable point of focus. And so we had to admit that clausula 1, though linked to a group of related notions, was less safely so anchored than in the other letters. Yet there was a suggestion (above p. 121 f.) that it was connected with *affectus* and the state of the *proficiens*. In that light it is interesting to note that cola 93 f., the arithmetical center of this letter at the end of par. 9, deals with that very notion. The point, however, is neither reinforced by the clausula, nor by clauselength, and so the occurrence may be simply accidental.[40]

e. Letter 80

In his first paragraph Seneca announces several themes that will be seen to be of some importance in the remainder of this short letter.

---

[37] Thraede p. 72: "Die Unwahrhaftigkeit der Aüsserung, ihr 'rhetorischer' Zuschnitt, liegt auf der Hand, wenn man auf die Stilisierung gerade auch dieses Textes achtet". Such a judgment is only possible in an age that mistrusts rhetoric profoundly.

[38] For the rhetorical value of these terms see e.g. Cic. *De orat.* 3.26.104.

[39] Our passage is discussed on p. 270 and an overall assessment of Seneca's practice occurs on p. 277.

[40] I have one reservation: the colon occurs just before the first interruption, and its placement at the break may be just the reinforcement needed.

In the word *vaco*[41] we find Seneca released from the straightjacket of his usual situation, and he says with some emphasis that this is due not to himself, but to the outward and faintly childish circumstance that everyone has gone off to a ball game.[42]

The game is at first referred to as a *spectaculum* and the people who have gone to watch are described as *molesti*. The next section is introduced with a chuckle and the joke is on Seneca himself. It contains the important words *me non excutit mihi*[43] which determine the place of Seneca as the spectator in the midst of much stage imagery. Seneca then starts speaking of the *spectaculum* (*non fidele et lusorium*) which is compared with the *bonae artes*. The third paragraph gives an elaboration of this theme taking the form of a comparison of body and soul, more precisely the body's ability to be educated to withstand the blows of an adversary and the *animus'* ability to take the blows of fortune. The body needs much in the way of external material, the *animus* needs nothing,[44] except (par. 4) *velle eripere te servituti*. The qualification added after the word "servituti" is to be noted: *quae omnes premit*. The comparison between slavery in this sense and conventional slavery results in a comparison of real *libertas* and conventional *libertas* (par. 5). The former consists in freedom from the fear of death and poverty. The fear of death is left without elaboration except the words "illa nobis iugum imponit",[45] but the *metus paupertatis* produces a comparison of the *vultus* of the poor and the rich, the real laughter of the former and the play-acting of the latter. This brings Seneca back (*saepius!*) to the example of the stage and the *humanae vitae mimus*.[46] The actor on the stage is but a slave in real life, and that comparison between semblance and reality is continued in par. 8. Semblance is represented by setting and dress: *contemnes illos si despoliaveris*. Paragraph 9 shifts the ground to the

---

[41] Cf. *Ep.* 62.1; 106,1.

[42] Gummere translates "boxing-match", Noblot "championnat officiel de ballon". The parallel at Statius' *Silvae* 4 *praef. in fine*: "*sed et sphaeromachias spectamus et palaris lusio admittit*", though quoted since Lipsius, is not very helpful, in particular since its text is not very certain (*pilaris... admittitur* in the recentiores).

[43] The same picture is involved here as in *ep.* 1.1 *vindica te tibi*.

[44] *Virtus sine apparatu, sine inpensa*; there is an obvious connection with both the *apparatus* of the stage and the *inpensa* of the athlete.

[45] Albertini's summary, therefore, overemphasizes this element. Trillitzsch, *Beweisführung*, p. 70, too, mistakes the emphasis ('erstes Erfordernis'). Better Maurach, *Der Bau*, p. 173: the absence of elaboration of the point shows that Seneca planned the letter together with the group *epp. 63-80*.

[46] Cf. my paper *Drama in Seneca's Stoicism*, TAPA 97, 1966, pp. 246 f.

market place and the common practice of sellers to dress up their wares (horse, slaves) to hide defects. One wishes to see *ipsum corpus*. The final section gives a particular example of some Scythian or Sarmatian king with his turban, and ends with the application to Lucilius, who is to divest himself of all outward things : *intus te ipse considera*.

Seneca finishes the letter with a somewhat harsh judgement concerning Lucilius : *nunc qualis sis aliis credis*, which may be paraphrased as follows : "as it is you trust others and accept their judgement concerning your qualities".

The fact, that this judgement is not particularly original (cf. Horace *Ep.* 1.16.19 *vereor ne cui de te plus quam tibi credas*, quoted by Noblot) does not engage us at the present time. We must ask, however, whether this judgement can tell us anything about the organization of this letter.

The question is to be answered in the affirmative. Once again it would seem that the end of the letter harks back to the beginning, but this time in the very contrast between the situations of the two men. Indeed contrast is the operative principle of organization within the letter as a whole, with the result that the pattern is not as simple nor as obvious as were the patterns of letters 1, 26 and 41, though it is not quite as involved as that of letter 75.

As on several other occasions[47] Seneca starts with a kind of medallion describing his own situation. The description is increasingly internalized up to the words *non servio* which denote an internal freedom that is very closely related to the very core concepts of the letter. But the internal freedom has only been mentioned in contradistinction to the external freedom expressed in the words *mihi vaco*. As soon as Seneca has mentioned internal freedom, he revises, recants the external freedom, reasserts the internal freedom and starts a zig-zag comparison of corporal and mental exercise, which ends (par. 3 cola 39 ff.) with the slight but sudden change of direction in *Illis... tibi*. The latter contrast serves to introduce the core thought of the letter : *quidquid facere te potest bonum tecum est*. Follows another zig-zag comparison of internal and external *servitus* and *libertas*. That comparison contains an obvious reference to the core thought (*tibi des oportet istud bonum*). The comparison ends with the introduction

---

[47] Cf. *Epp.* 12 (a somewhat extended instance), 26 (referring back to 12), 53, 54, 55, 56, 57, 65, 84, 86, 104, 123.

Par.

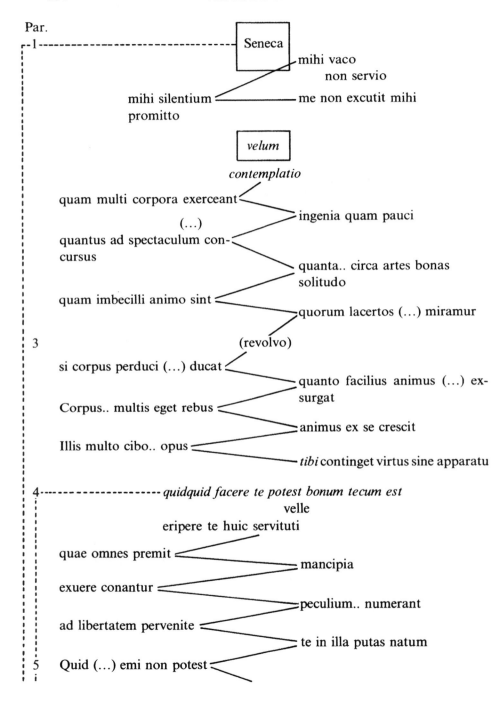

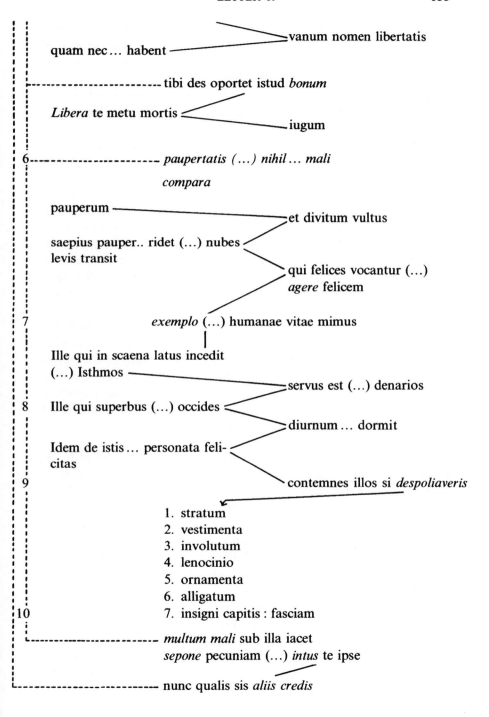

quam nec... habent ————————————————vanum nomen libertatis

------------------------ tibi des oportet istud *bonum*

Libera te metu mortis ⟨

————iugum

6-------------------- *paupertatis (...) nihil ... mali*

compara

pauperum ————————————————————et divitum vultus

saepius pauper.. ridet (...) nubes
levis transit

qui felices vocantur (...)
agere felicem

7   *exemplo* (...) humanae vitae mimus

Ille qui in scaena latus incedit
(...) Isthmos ————————————————
                                        servus est (...) denarios

8   Ille qui superbus (...) occides ⟨

diurnum ... dormit

Idem de istis... personata feli-
citas

9   contemnes illos si *despoliaveris*

        1. stratum
        2. vestimenta
        3. involutum
        4. lenocinio
        5. ornamenta
        6. alligatum
10   7. insigni capitis : fasciam

----------------- *multum mali* sub illa iacet
        sepone pecuniam (...) *intus* te ipse

----------------- nunc qualis sis *aliis credis*

of the notion *paupertas*. The qualification *nihil mali* joins *paupertas*
in a negative link with the core thought. A brief comparison of
pauperes and *divites*, the latter play-acting their happiness, may be
regarded as the first swing of a third zig-zag that moves between
the actor on stage and his slave's reality. The zig-zag ends in denuding
the *delicati* (can there be anything more Senecan?) of their false beauty.
A series of similar *falsa* ends with the *fascia* of an Oriental prince.
It is at this point that we realize with something of a shock that the
velum of par. 1 must have a connection with these *fascia*, and that
Seneca is saying that he is *tutus* because in more ways than one the
velum is not lifted. Surely Seneca is capable of that much irony?
Certainly the clausula underpins this interpretation. See above p. 123.
Multum mali... latet under the fascia. *Multum mali* gives an obvious
link with *nihil mali* above, and, through it, with the core thought,
thus serving to tie up the final injunction, *intus te ipse considera*,
with the backbone of the letter. At the same time the last few lines
refer to the opening frame of the letter, not only abstractly in the
contrast referred to above, but concretely in so far as *pecuniam*,
domum, *dignitatem* are precisely the sort of thing that Seneca's
molesti would be concerned about on his behalf. *Intus te ipse considera*
is the very activity in which Seneca intends to engage when he announces
"mihi vaco". The latter words in themselves announce the freedom
of *non servio* (par. 1, colon 13) which here at the end finds a contrast
in Lucilius' dependence on others : *nunc qualis sis aliis credis.* (115)
The schematic sketch on pp. 154 f. may be useful.

It is useless to pretend that the core statement of letter 80 is to be
found in its arithmetical center, for we have decided that *quidquid
facere te potest bonum tecum est* is the central thought, and it is
clause 43 in 116. But if we look at the arithmetical center, anyway,
we find that the passage within which it is imbedded deals with
the distinction between true and false *libertas*. And indeed that is
what Seneca seems to be doing in this letter : he combines the notions
of *bonum* and *libertas* with the inner self as illustrated by the naked
slave, whereas the opposites, *malum* and *servitus* are sketched by the
very things that tend to hide them : dress and acting.
Once again the clausulae are helpful in the interpretation (above
p. 122 f.). Clauselength, on the other hand, does not seem to have
been employed here with much more than local importance. As the
text is printed above, the first clause is the longest, but under the

text an alternative suggestion is made. Therefore no claims can or ought to be made on this score.

In this, rather complex, letter then, we must still admit that all structural elements mentioned have their function in presenting and clarifying the thought (cf. e.g. the use of periodic structures in the final paragraph, above p.104), but in the nature of things they do not converge upon one single point to the same extent that they did in letters 1 and 41.

f. Letter 100

In letter 100 we have to do with a neatly structured composition. The main subject is the style of Seneca's old teacher Papirius Fabianus. At the beginning of the letter Seneca reacts rather strongly against Lucilius' negative judgment (cola 5ff.). It is not until the end of the letter that we are presented with his own final and much more positive judgment and its presentation is rather subtly moderate. I am convinced that the two contrasting judgments, the first based mainly on form, the second mostly on content, have been placed intentionally at the beginning and the end of the letter: they form an antithesis that embraces many contrasts. (A vs A'). The first of these is again the one of form against content (cola 22ff.: *mores ille, non verba composuit/ et animis scripsit ista, non auribus*). At the other end of the letter there is a corresponding antithesis in cola 145ff.: *ad profectum omnia tendunt, ad bonam mentem: non quaeritur plausus*. Those final words contain a reference to the *recitatio*, or perhaps to the situation vividly painted in letter 108 in which many people come to listen to philosophers by way of a good pastime (*deversorium otii*) sometimes even equipped with notebooks in order to take down striking phrases (*ep.* 108,6). (B vs B'). Subsequently we find in cola 24ff. a contrast between overall impression and careful analysis. This contrast returns in reverse order in cola 132ff. (C vs C'), but the statement that the *oratio sollicita* (= the over-anxious, overly trimmed style) does not befit the philosopher, for the time being remains without an immediately recognizable corresponding element at the other end of the letter (D). The judgment concerning Fabianus' style with the rather nice comparison (cola 41-62) is essentially repeated in cola 106-115 (E vs E'). In both cases the judgment is once again expressed in antitheses. Cola 70ff. deal with the style of others (Pollio is contrasted with Cicero), cola 89ff. do so once again, but this time in order to place the authors mentioned with the addition of Livy (both a historian and a philosopher) above Fabianus. (F vs F'). The latter is the subject matter of the intervening paragraph. (G). This central paragraph consists of the contrasting judgments of Lucilius and Seneca briefly expressed. When Seneca winds up his judgment with the sentence "his *oratio* does not possess but will lend dignity",[48] the very structure of the letter shows that we need to take both the beginning and the end of the letter into account in the interpretation. In the first half of the statement *dignitas* has the rhetorical meaning of Ad Her. IV 18 (*Dignitas est quae reddit ornatam orationem varietate distinguens*), in the second half *dignitas* is obviously linked with the *honestum* just mentioned. That we have to do with an obvious attempt to replace a judgment based on style by one based on content must be clear from colon 5 *oblitus de philosopho agi*. But surely also cola 156 ff. need to be referred to in the interpretation: neither *attollere* nor the *imitatio* on the part of the *adulescens* as mentioned there may be taken in strictly rhetorical, I believe not even in largely rhetorical sense.

One passage remains to act as the correspondent of *oratio sollicita* (D), the quote from Lucilius in cola 116 ff. In my opinion this passage is very precisely characterised by the words *oratio sollicita* and may be taken as an example of it.[49] Within 30 words we find one tetracolon and two tricola in which there are some metrical correspondences in addition.

It may be useful to look briefly at the content of the passage :

"You are missing (you say)
a rugged statement against vice
a courageous one against danger
a proud one against fortune
a scornful one against ambition.
I want luxury to be rebuked
   lust to be exposed
   violence to be broken.

---

[48] The phrase has created difficulties: mss. *debet*, Lips. *dabit*; the editors are right in following Lipsius.

[49] I have considered the possibility that Seneca is playing with a caricature of his own style, but it seems unlikely that he possessed the sense of humour for it. In any case we have to do with a quotation, or at least with a passage that is presented as a quotation of his (younger) disciple; and did not Quintilian (*Inst.* 10.1.125 f.) say that those younger disciples were inclined to imitate the faults in particular?

Let there be something of the orator's sharpness
                    tragedy's grandeur
                    comedy's subtlety.

At first sight these expressions might seem directed against the content
of Fabianus' work as well, but the last sentence in particular banishes
that interpretation from our minds; here the terminology is entirely
rhetorical. In this connection the sentence Seneca Pater writes about
Fabianus (*Contr.* 2.2.) is significant: "*cum veros compressisset adfectus
et iram doloremque procul expulisset, parum bene imitari poterat quae
effugerat.*" Seneca Pater characterises Fabianus' delivery, but the
judgment runs precisely parallel to Lucilius' judgment concerning
the style of Fabianus' written work.

Once we have ordered the letter in a concentric scheme in this
manner, one passage remains that has not been mentioned: viz. the
introduction of par. 7 (the different styles of Cicero and Pollio).
In it Seneca points out that judgments of style differ but he does not
enter into the question why this should be so. To some extent the
thought is left unfinished in the present letter, and it would seem
that there is good cause to treat the passage as a kind of reference
to the extensive treatment of the question in *ep.* 114. Similar
references occur elsewhere.[50]

A mere arrangement of the material in concentric fashion is not
all, however. Seneca appears to add a certain element of progression,
an element of tension. Where in A Lucilius' judgment is presented
and provisionally dealt with, we get in A' a very important addition
in the pedagogical element (*adhortatio efficacissima*) whereby the
purely stylistic judgment is shown to be shortsighted—on the other
hand that shortsightedness had been briefly announced in colon 5
oblitus de philosopho agi.

The correspondence between B and B' also goes beyond the primary
thought noted above. A secondary thought follows: in B this secondary
thought is that one was kept spellbound by the *summa* of Fabianus'
speech, in B' Seneca makes clear that he, too, no longer remembers
all the details, but that the *color* remained with him *summatim.*
Perversely the secondary thoughts have been interchanged: the rhetorical aspect is mentioned in B', the philosophical aspect in B.
On second thoughts, is the arrangement perverse? Is not this rather

---

[50] See below on letter 122.167 *gravis malae conscientiae lux est* (p. 165f.).

a good illustration of the tenor of the letter? "This is how it has to be, the main content stays with you, and in second place perhaps also something of the rhetorical hue."

In C' also *illum sensisse quod scripsit* represents an extra element over against C. Not, it is true, entirely new, but briefly announced in E *sensus honestos* (48). D' does not only present an example of *oratio sollicita*. At the end of the passage Seneca shows what he has up his sleeve in the pointed contrast between that which Lucilius wants (a *pusilla res : verba*) and that which Fabianus devotes himself to, the *magnitudo rerum*. Here *eloquentia* is given its proper place : it is no more than a kind of *umbra* of the truly important things. In F' Livy is the addition if we compare with F, where Cicero and Pollio only appeared. But there is another addition, one that might be even more important. In the cases of both Cicero and Livy philosophical works are mentioned. Asinius, however, is only briefly alluded to. There is a good reason, since in the case of Asinius we do not know of any philosophical works.[51] The addition of the genre fits in very well in the series of corrective elements that appear in the second half of the letter when compared with the first half.

g. Letter 122

Just as Seneca in letter 51 deals with the combination of *luxuria* and *locus*, thus letter 122, towards the end that is of the corpus as we possess it now, treats a combination of *tempus* (in the sense of *diei dispositio*) with luxury. Both subjects had been touched upon throughout the collection of letters, sometimes at length and in detail, sometimes in general and by the way. Letters 1, 49 and 101 e.g. deal with time, whereas 86, 90, 95, 114 and many others broach the topos luxury in extensive passages. It is useful to keep the possibility in mind that a letter's position in the corpus has an effect on its inner structure. Thus 122.3 (cola 28f.) *Et hi mortem timent in quam se vivi condiderunt* does not find its entire explanation within the letter. The element *mors*, if need be, may be explained by referring to the series *iusta sibi faciunt* (35), *mortuis* (36), *caro morticina* (53) and the *defuncti* of colon 123, but the element *timent* remains isolated until we remember 121.19 *nullum animal ad vitam prodit sine metu mortis*, a statement that is closely interwoven within the structure of that letter. Letter 121 may be regarded as a complementary pendant

---

[51] Cf. M. Schanz, *Gesch. d. Röm. Lit.*, II 1, p. 572, Anm. 4.

of 122. Where 122 deals with perversions, 121 deals with natural functions and tendencies.[52] Letter 123 may be meant as another complementary pendant : 122 exhibits *vitia* that are the result of an urge to seem different, 123 on the other hand spends some thought on the phenomenon of fashion.[53]

This indication of the surroundings, too brief as it is, must suffice since we are here dealing with the inner structure of the letter. The central subject is obvious, it is the perversity of those who change day into night, night into day. The letter is subdivided as follows. The topical material is exhibited in the first four paragraphs. Seneca starts by distinguishing between the correct and the incorrect use of daylight. Drinking bouts are hinted at (*hesterna graves crapula*, colon 12). A Vergil quotation linked with one from Cato serves to elevate the exchange of day for night to the status of utter perversity ; the dinner at night is compared with a death rite. An active life during daylight is contrasted by means of a comparison with birds fattened in a cage with on the one hand the bodies, on the other the souls of these nightbirds. In general it might be said that a number of satellites group themselves around the basic notions of good and evil. They are active-passive, day-night, light-dark, life-death, singleness-diversity. These notions then start to function as references to the basic notions. This, however, is looking ahead a little.

The main structure of the letter is determined by the position of two individual examples, the one of Acilius Buta and the other of Sextus Papinius. These are separated by the more theoretical paragraph 14 and are flanked on both sides by a diversity of perversities. In paragraphs 6-9 Seneca speaks of drunkenness on an empty stomach, prostitution of boys (and, worse, people who for the sake of prostitution attempt to remain boys), abuse of season (roses in winter), of place (trees on the roof, warm baths in the sea), and of time (*lucet: somni tempus est* cola 111-112). On the other side these vices are summarized in the general statement that they are *varia*, that diversity is indeed the essential mark of perversity. The next paragraph gives once again the cause of the special aberration Seneca is dealing with in the present letter (*huius morbi*). That had also been

---

[52] Cf. H. Cancik, *Untersuchungen*, p. 5.

[53] R. Hirzel, *Der Dialog*, 1895, reprint Hildesheim 1963, p. 26, regarded the letters as a "planmässiges Ganzes" and G. Maurach has tried to elaborate the thesis for letters 1-80 in *Der Bau von Senecas Epistulae Morales*, Heidelberg, Winter, 1970. See also my review in Mnemosyne 4,27 (1974), p. 321-323.

the start of the elaboration in paragr. 5 where the question was asked
why people should wish to exchange day for night. A coda, speci-
fically addressed to Lucilius, ends the letter. The subdivision, then,
may be visualised as follows :

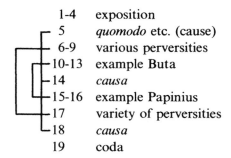

	1-4	exposition
	5	*quomodo* etc. (cause)
	6-9	various perversities
	10-13	example Buta
	14	*causa*
	15-16	example Papinius
	17	variety of perversities
	18	*causa*
	19	coda

Next it is useful to follow various motifs within the letter. It goes
without saying that day/night and light/dark play the largest parts
and are almost continually present except in paragraphs 6-8.[54] It is,
therefore, interesting to see how Seneca directly at the start of the
letter prepares a bit of tension between pretext and actual content.
The proper interpretation of *detrimentum iam dies sensit* appears from
the subsequent sentence. But if some other sentence had followed,
the phrase could have been used in the sense of "the day has become
less important", something which we notice only when we arrive at
the end of the paragraph. In the meantime the reader has been advised
to await the day even before it starts, in other words to lead a very
active life. Seneca does not point out that strictly speaking this is
no more "naturam sequi" than is dining at night. By thus going
beyond the line of the strictly logical the author draws the attention
to the central pair of opposites in the realm of morality : active frugality
versus passive luxury. The fact that the active life is a great deal
less tiring than the exceedingly complicated nightlife is the sort of
subtle paradox that Seneca savours elsewhere[55] but which he restricts
here to an illustration in the example of Papinius. There is a further
reference to the theme *actus* at the end of paragraph 3 and the
expression used (37 *nullus agenti dies longus est*) is sufficiently pregnant

---

[54] The relative frequency is significant: words for day and light occur 24 times,
night and dark 30 times, as against words for life 5 times (but manner of life 16 times),
death 5 times, activity 5 times, passivity as such once.

[55] *Ep.* 55.1 *A gestatione cum maxime venio, non minus fatigatus quam si tantum
ambulassem quantum sedi* etc.

to remind us of letter 1 in which wrong activity was associated with loss of time.[56] But even here the theme does not run out. Instead it is replaced by its opposite, inertia. This counter theme had been first expressed in colon 7 in the words *semisomnus iacet* and was picked up again in paragraph 3 in Cato's antipodes. It culminates in those poor birds who (43f.) *ut inmotae facile pinguescant, in obscuro continentur*. At this point of the letter we need to emphasize the element *inmotae* since this is the aspect of the image that functions as the opposite of *actus* (together with *iners sagina*). Presently certain further aspects will be shown to have their own importance.

By this time the contrast active vs. passive has helped fix an associative link between night and luxury of which latter notion the remainder of the letter will highlight not so much the aspect passive/motionless but rather the aspect different-from-others. The Vergil quotation functions as the announcement (further emphasized by the explicative Cato quote) that here we have to do with the central theme of the letter. Every detail of composition has its function and we notice that the thematically important Cato quotation (cola 23-24) has been expressed in a carefully built phrase in which the light-element (*solem*) is enclosed within the frame *umquam-viderunt* which in its turn is framed by the dual unity *nec orientem ... nec occidentem*. The reference to ep. 121.18 in cola 28-29 shows a similar order though it is less obvious : *et hi* (a) *mortem* (b) *timent* (c) *in quam* (b) *se vivi* (a) *condiderunt*?

It is at the very least noteworthy that both here and in letter 121.18-19 the notion "fear of death" is immediately followed by a discussion of birds that possess a certain clairvoyance. Here the night birds of ill omen serving as a comparison for the people who live at night, there geese and chickens whose instinct, inborn not acquired, enables them to distinguish between friend and enemy. The perverse quality of the birds in our letter is further elaborated in paragraph 4. There we are once again presented with a comparison, this time one with

---

[56] The treatment of *agere* and cognates and of the notion 'action' in Seneca needs a monograph. A few places are mentioned in an earlier paper '*Drama in Seneca's Stoicism*' TAPA 97, 1966, p. 242ff. See also Maurach, p. 47 and 118; furthermore I. Hadot, *Seneca und die griechisch-römische Tradition der Seelenleitung*, Berlin, de Gruyter, 1969, p. 138f. It is a pity that "action" is among the missing items in A.L. Motto, *Seneca Sourcebook : Guide to the Thought of Lucius Annaeus Seneca*, Amsterdam, Hakkert, 1970. Part of the material is to be found in A. Pittet, *Vocabulaire Philosophique de Sénèque*, Paris, Les Belles Lettres, 1937, *sub vocibus actio, activus, actuosus, actus, agilis*; the verb *agere* is lacking.

fattened birds, whose *pigrum corpus* builds the transition to the bad body condition of those dedicated to nightlife.[57] Once more a bird appears in our letter, the *tristis hirundo* who in the Montanus quotation announces the day that will be slept through by Buta (paragraph 12) whereby, as we have learnt in paragr. 10, an *ingens patrimonium* is lost.

It appears next that fear of death plays a small part after all, as material for comparison. A careful reading of ep. 123 shows that there death plays an important part in connection with that ordinary kind of luxury that may be characterised by "eat, drink and be merry, for tomorrow we die" (cf. 123,10f.).[58] In our letter however the unnatural is partly represented by the fact that its special type of *luxuria* is on the contrary rather like death. This is underlined once more in paragraph 10.[59]

In the midst of all this secondary matter it appears that that perversion is the really central subject; it starts with *turpis qui alto sole semisomnus iacet* (colon 7), it then grows by way of the phrase *sunt qui officia lucis noctisque perverterint* (10, more loaded already) and the antipodes, introduced at first in a neutral sense in the Vergil quotation, into the *in eadem urbe antipodes* (colon 21). These are increasingly closely linked with *luxuria* in the manner sketched above. It goes without saying that this luxurious perversity has a contrasting *conditio recta*. Twice the introduction gives expression to the *conditio recta*, first lightly and apparently restricted to the man who gets up normally and on time: *officiosior meliorque si quis illum exspectat*

---

[57] Reynolds writes † *superba umbra* †. Indeed, however attractive Prof. Wagenvoort's interpretation may be (*'t trots gevederte*: the proud plumage), there is in our letter insufficient reason to take *umbra* in the sense of feathers or plumage, unlike Statius, *Silvae* III 4, 29-30. If <*sub*> *superba umbra* is in fact the right reading, we should in connection with the notion of confinement in the dark rather be inclined to interpret "in the tyrannical, cruel dark" (for *superbus*=cruel cf. Vergil *Aen.* VIII 118).

[58] Indeed Seneca writes "*fluunt dies et irreparabilis vita decurrit*". For the Vergil echo see H. Wirth, *De Vergili apud Senecam Philosophum usu*. Diss. Freiburg/Br. 1900, p. 52, who compares *Georg.* III, 284 and *Aen.* X, 467. See also Giancaro Mazzoli, *Seneca e la poesia*, Milano (Ceschina) 1970.

[59] Just for a moment we remember *ep.* 12.3 in which, equally in the context of a proper division of the day, Pacuvius' behaviour is narrated: "*cum vino et illis funebribus epulis sibi parentaverat, sic in cubiculum ferebatur a cena ut inter plausus exoletorum hoc ad symphoniam caneretur*: βεβίωται, βεβίωται. *Nullo non se die extulit*". It is true that this behaviour is represented as caused by *mala conscientia*, but the *luxuria* is obvious. There is also *De tr. an.* 2,15 where it is suggested that some people commit suicide from pure boredom. If we take the word *novissime* in colon 110 seriously, death is indeed close by.

et lucem primam excipit (cola 5-6), then much more heavily and provided with an expletive :[60] *at mehercules nullus agenti dies longus est. Extendamus vitam: huius et officium et argumentum actus est. Circumscribatur nox et aliquid ex illa in diem transferatur.* We learn in paragraph 19 that those who heed this advice are the followers of nature. Their opposites are the *contra illam nitentes* (colon 234) who at the end of the letter are compared with people rowing upstream (*contra aquam remigantes*). This last expression has been chosen, I think, to form a balancing contrast with the subordinate clause (equally used as a comparison) *si quis cum ipso, ut ita dicam, die surgat* at the beginning of the letter (colon 4). This adds the final frame to the diagram given above.

The three paragraphs that deal with the causes of the perversity in question contain two central thoughts. Paragraph 5 indicates that all *vitia* are against nature, that "unnatural" is the very mark of *vitium*. The notion "against custom" is related to the notion "against nature", custom appears as a kind of extension of the natural. It occurs in paragraph 14 (*nihil iuvat solitum*). A second notion, *fama*,[61] is added here: the urge to be noted is the second one these perverted people succumb to. Both thoughts return in paragraph 18.

Paragraph 14, however, shows a third statement, one which we have not been prepared for and hence seems somewhat abrupt: *gravis malae conscientiae lux est.* Seneca does not return to this sentiment in the remainder of the letter either. Nor can the thought immediately following be regarded as an explanation of the previous phrase since the *luxuriosus* who despises all things he need not pay for can hardly be regarded as automatically identifiable with a man bothered by a *mala conscientia.* It seems, then, that we have two thoughts here of which the first is entirely unconnected with the material of the remainder of the letter. The last time *conscientia* had occurred in the

---

[60] Seneca often uses *mehercules*, and, to my knowledge, always with care. On several occasions it underlines the last of a series of examples (e.g. *Helv.* 12,6), or a conclusion after a series (e.g. *Marc.* 23,3), or it supports an unexpected point (e.g. *De v.b.* 13,2). See also *prov.* 3,2; *clem.* 1,5,1; 1,9,10; 2,6,4; *De v.b.* 15,6; *brev. vit.* 5,3; 6,4; 16,3. A more complete list is found in Neue-Wagener II[3], p. 992.

[61] This thought is connected with the dictum in letter 123,8 *sunt quidam qui vitia gestant* but at the same time it contains a reference to 123,6 *gloria vanum et volubile quiddam est auraque mobilius.* In this connection it is to be noted that Seneca elaborates a distinction between *fama, claritas* and *gloria* (*ep.* 102,17) in which *gloria* rests on the judgment of the many, *claritas* on the judgment of the good, whereas *fama* has the neutral sense of "reputation". In our passage *fama* has a bad connotation which is made explicit in paragr. 18 in the word *infamia.*

letters was in ep. 105,8[62] *tutum aliqua res in mala conscientia praestat*[63] and it is clear that one of the things that may give people with a bad conscience a sense of security is the very dark alluded to in our passage. But at the same time I have the impression that Seneca refers to letter 121 as well, for that letter deals with οἰκείωσις. In 121,21 we read *simul enim conciliatur saluti suae quidque et iuvatura petit, laesura formidat.* This attitude of being intent on one's own well-being, this ability to distinguish between the useful and the harmful is precisely what is lacking in the perverse nightbird. Does Seneca make a play on a double meaning of *mala conscientia*, bad conscience and wrong kind of self awareness?[64] If that is the case it is easier to understand how this at first sight incidental remark could be placed at a central spot of the letter.

The two examples of this specific perversity, Acilius Buta and Sextus Papinius, are not entirely equivalent from a formal point of view. In the case of Buta there is a strong admixture of extravagance; moreover Buta eventually wakes up. With Sextus Papinius the description is limited to the nightlife aspect and every element seems to have been chosen in such a manner that a fixed daily occurrence is transformed into a fixed nightly one. Moreover the first example is described from some distance, as one of the *faits divers* of Roman Society, whereas the second is presented from a much closer point of view, from the inside as it were. Variety, then, is not lacking, here no more than in the diversity of perversities which in paragraphs 6-9 is represented by a number of cases, in par. 17 by the plain statement that a great number of possibilities exist. We may suppose, then, that Seneca's art with respect to letter composition consists for a large part in carefully weighing and balancing *varietas* against just enough similarity to allow the structure to be recognizable.[65]

---

[62] Apart from the less important occurrence in *ep.* 117,1.

[63] Cf. *De moribus* 65: *mala conscientia saepe tuta est, secura numquam.* If this is watered down Seneca, it occurs in an even further banalised form in Otloh's *Libellus proverbiorum* (ed. Korfmacher, p. 46): *mala conscientia numquam quiescit secura.*

[64] Seneca plays with two meanings of *conscientia* also in *de tr. an.* 7.3. Cf. G. Molenaar, Mnemosyne 4,22 (1969), p. 173.

[65] Cf. Brooks Otis, *Ovid as an Epic poet*, Cambridge 1966, p. 86: "An original motif, *ab*, never corresponds to an identical *ab* later on, but instead corresponds to a congruous or similar, but different *ab* (or an *a'b'*)". The remark occurs in a quick survey of the structure of the Metamorphoses.

SOME PROBLEMS OF SCANSION

Scansion is not in all cases easy or without controversy. Some of the problems encountered in preparing the preceding pages merit a brief discussion.

I. L. Nougaret (Analyse verbale comparée p. 20)[1] announces that he scans -ĕrunt in the 3rd pl. pf. act. (his book deals with the metrical units of *De signis*). In view of the fact that there are 13 cases in which our Seneca sample shows such a form *in clausula*, it may be interesting to draw up a comparative table of those clausulae scanned with -ērunt and the same scanned with -ĕrunt.[2]

1. 26.14 ministeria senuerunt	1^{1+2}	—◡◡◡ ◡◡◡∾	4^{1+2} (?)
2. 75.81 in vicinia eius constiterunt	3	——— ◡◡∾	11^3
3. 75.84 ac vitia posuerunt	1^{1+2}	—◡◡◡ ◡◡◡∾	4^{1+2} (?)
4. 75.85 complectenda dediderunt	1^2	——— ◡◡◡◡∾	3^{tr+2}
5. 75.111 haec animum implicuerunt	3^{tr}	—◡◡—◡◡◡∾	3^2
6. 75.112 esse coeperunt	1	—◡—◡∾	4
7. 80.52 comparaverunt	1	—◡—◡∾	4
8. 80.60 qui emerunt habent	22	◡◡ ◡—◡∾	4
9. 80.61 nec qui vendiderunt	3	———◡◡∾	$11^3(33^2?)$
10. 122.23 solem viderunt	33	———◡∾	44
11. 122.29 se vivi condiderunt	3	———◡◡∾	11^3
12. 122.49 se tenebris dicaverunt	1	◡◡—◡—◡∾	4
13. 122.163 eodem tempore egerunt	1	—◡—◡∾	4

---

[1] Cf. A. Ernout, *Morphologie historique du latin*, Paris³ 1953, p. 215 f.; also L.R. Palmer, *The Latin Language* 1954, p. 275. R.G. Kent, *Forms of Latin*, 1946, p. 125, has a slightly different acount of the phenomenon.

[2] The wordending symbols have been left out since they do not enter the picture here.

Numbers 1 and 3 show a rare clausula which with -ĕrunt would become even rarer (the one parallel for 4^{1+2} is 41.103 which is accentuated differently: $- \cup \cup \cup \quad \cup \cup \cup \wedge$. The clausula 11^3 (nr. 2) has many parallels, but 3 has many more; for that reason I feel -ĕrunt would change nrs. 2,9,11 for the worse, but at the same time I would not count these as arguing strongly against the proposition. The same applies to nrs. 6, 7, 12, 13. Three cases show a clausula of roughly equal frequency in both columns: 5,8.10. But in the case of nr. 4 there is a definite deterioration of clausula if we read -ĕrunt (12 parallels against one: 122,141).

Thirteen items constitute a very small sample indeed and it appears inconclusive as to the scansion to be chosen. It may be useful, therefore, to compare a further set of instances. I choose, to begin with, the ones Nougaret has scanned with -ĕrunt from *De signis*.

1. 2.3 Messanam accesserunt	11	$- - - - \cup \wedge$	44	
2. 4.7 in bello fuerunt	sp 3	$- - - - \cup \wedge$	3^2	
3. 5.9 tam amentem putaverunt	1	$- - \cup - \cup \wedge$	4	
4. 8.18 ornamenti causa fuerunt	m3	$- - - \cup \cup \wedge$	3^2	
5. 10.22 irati fuerunt	sp 3	$- - - \cup \cup \wedge$	3^2	
6. *ibidem*: prandium saepe fecerunt	1	$- \cup - - \cup - \cup \wedge$	4	
7. 10.23 liberi fuerunt	tr3	$- \cup - \cup \cup \wedge$	1^3	
8. 14.32 qui me ubi viderunt	? tr 33	$- \cup \cup - \cup \wedge$	2	?
9. 16.35 ut exposita fuerunt	$?^3$	$- \cup \cup \cup \cup \wedge$?	3^{1+2}	
10. 20.42 intellexerunt isti	33	$- \cup - - \wedge$	1	
11. 20.44 atque imperio fuerunt	d3	$- \cup \cup - \cup \cup \wedge$	1^{tr+3}	

Once again the results are hardly conclusive. Comparison with Primmer's elaborate table shows that in 6 of the 11 cases the -ĕrunt scansion produces the better clausula, i.e. nrs. 2, 3, 4, 5, 6, 11; in two cases the worse: 1,10; once the two clausulae are equally avoided (7).

---

[3] It is by no means certain that we have to do with a clausula in this case.

Items 8 and 9 involve uncertainties of a different type. More examples are clearly needed. I take them from the first two Catilinarians in order to have once again the benefit of Primmer's table for the purpose of comparison.

Cat. I

1.1	ora voltusque moverunt.	1	—∪——∪—∪∾	4
3.7	causa profugerunt	1	——∪—∪∾	4
4.8	tecum una fuerunt	m3	———∪∪∾	m3²
7.16	ad caedem constituti fuerunt	cr 3	—∪——∪∪∾	33²
	nudam atque inanem reliquerunt	1	∪——∪—∪∾	4
7.18	ferenda non fuerunt	tr 3	—∪—∪∪∾	1³
11.28	a republica defecerunt	cr 33	——∪———∪∾	44
	civium iura tenuerunt	1²	—∪——∪∪∪∪∾	cr 3^{tr+2}
12.31	mollibus sententiis aluerunt	tr3^{tr}	—∪———∪—∪∪∪∾	tr3²
	non credendo conroboraverunt	1	————∪—∪∾	4

Cat. II

3.5	exercitum maluerunt;	cr3	——∪——∪∪∾	33²
5.10	patrimonia sua profuderunt	tri33	∪∪∪∪∪—∪∾	2¹
	suas obligaverunt	1	∪——∪—∪∾	4
6.12	inanem reliquerunt	1	∪——∪—∪∾	4
9.19	nefaria concupiverunt	1	∪—∪∪—∪—∪∾	4
9.20	aes alienum inciderunt ut, si	1	—∪∪—∾	3^{tr}
	rapinarum veterum impulerunt	d3	— ∪∪—∪∪∾	1^{tr+3}
10.23	spargere venena didicerunt	1²	∪∪∪—∪∪∪∪∾	3^{tr+2}
	saltare didicerunt	1²	——∪∪∪∪∾	3^{tr+2}

⏑⏑ – ⏑ ⏑ – –
12.27 qui͜in urbe remanserunt   3^{tr} ⏑⏑ –⏑⏑–⏑∾   4^{tr}

– — ⏑ ⏑⏑⏝
    nostri͜esse voluerunt   1^2 ––⏑⏑⏑⏑∾   m3^{tr+2}

– — ⏑ ⏑⏑⏝
13.29 potentissimamque͜esse voluerunt.   1^2 ––⏑⏑⏑⏑∾   m3^{tr+2}

The addition of 22 instances is helpful: in 19 cases the clausula with
–
-erunt is definitely to be preferred, in two cases there is little to choose,
in one case there is a prosodic difficulty. But, perhaps most important,
in 5 cases Cicero's famed clausula of the *esse videatur* type is spoiled
⏑
if -erunt is read. The resulting clausula does not get a listing in
Primmer's final table and in any case its closing strength would be
rather small (cf. e.g. Cicero, *Orator* 215 and 217).

II. On certain occasions it is hard to describe the clausula in terms of
the system chosen.

– –´⏑ ⏑
    1.36 *et vilissima sunt* has been treated as 11^3, yet other instances
of this clausula have –––´⏑∾ (26,79; 26,123; 80,101; 100,114; 100.149;
100.162), and the accent on the first short is equally a feature of the
closely related and much more common 1^3. Zander, however, notes
– –´⏑ ⏑
natura tristissima sunt (*De ira* 3.19.1). The basic problem is that we do
not know much about accentuation under the influence of enclitics.
See Sommer p. 297 *Musáque, limináque*. Others disagree. We really
need *vilissíma sunt* which appears to be without supporters. See also
the discussion with literature in Soubiran p. 464 ff.

– – –⏑⏑⏑ ⏑ ⏑ —
    41.107 *consummatur itaque bonum͜eius*. If we accept *itáque* there is no
trouble and the clausula is of type 3^1. However, *itáque* is not the
wordgroup we expect; we expect *itaque* (cf. Leumann-Hofmann 1928
p. 181). We are then faced with a clausula ⏑⏑⏑⏑´∾ of which there
are no further instances in our sample; nor are they to be found in
Müller's Curtius or Primmer's Cicero samples. Zander, however, notes
– ⏑⏑ ⏝–   ⏝⏑ ⏑ –
quis nisi Catilina from *De ira* 3.18.2; *ibidem* 28.5 *alius amicum* is a
⏑⏑ ⏑⏑–
separate colon, just as *ep.* 100.70 *lege Ciceronem* (cf. above p. 113.
under v).
    75.60 and 61 both show type 1^3, but otherwise they are as different

as accent can make them. Once again our trouble is that we are imperfectly informed. We do not really know *how* different accent can make these clausulae, we *do not* know whether for a sensitive Roman ear a tension developed between the pitches and stresses of rhythm and word accent, and we do not *know* that in prose they sought coincidence of word accent and clausula ictus, thought it is generally assumed.

75.151 *intentione studii*; it is hard to decide whether we should scan as in the text *intentione studii* or rather *intentione studii* (3^2 ε). See K. Müller, Curtius p. 770 (Kurzer Endvokal vor sp-, st-, scr- wird in der Senkung als Kürze gebraucht). If 2ε, as scanned above, we have a "Hebung" and must equate ii with ī, if 3^2ε we must accept ii. For the latter question see Müller p. 771 (Curtius appears always to have ī, metrically speaking). These genitives are not particularly frequent in the position required. There are no examples in letters 1, 26 (cf. however 26.55), 41, 80, 100. Letter 122 has (colon 182) *Sexti Papini*, which offers little help since the clausula there is troublesome. See also ep. 2.4 *aliquid adversus mortem auxili compara*, where Reynolds rightly prefers 2δ to 2^{tr}; the mss. have *auxilii*. Ep. 66.32 *sola ratio immutabilis et iudicii tenax est* the placement in the grey area preceding the ditrochee is not very helpful; cf. 67.10 *ex consilii sententia*. See also Drexler, Einf. p. 139, Neue-Wagener 1. 149 ff. Cf. 67.15 *in delicis habeat* (Reynolds against *deliciis* ω).

75.167-168 *honesta colimus quantum vacat*. At first sight one thinks of a single colon. The clausula —́‐∪∿, however, proves troublesome since the notation 44βδ offends against the rule that an accentuated long may not occur *in thesi*. Nor is it easy to find any parallels. The accentuation is reasonably certain. We might still accept the colon if Seneca made it his practice to underline unusual content by unusual stylistic means. He does not. The suspicion then arises that *quantum vacat* is a commation of type m.

80.89 An impossible clausula if *ait* is correct: the accentuated syllable túmidus would then occur *in thesi* (type 4^2). If, however, we read

$\widehat{ait}$ (cf. Sommer, p. 545) matters are reasonably simple even if 2^3 is
an exceedingly rare clausula.

80.111 *quid de aliis loquor*. The analysis 4^{tr} as given in the text
offends against the rule that no accentuated syllable of an anapaestic
word may occur *in thesi*. One may think of contraction. Contracted
forms occur on several occasions both in inscriptions and in manuscripts.
See Neue-Wagener II p. 537 who quote i.a. Cic. *De re p.* 1.34.52
(twice : *cum is qui imperat alis / servit ipse nulli cupiditati* and *alis permisso
otio suo*. Ziegler prints *aliis*). OLD quotes CIL 2.5181.50, 8.403, Festus
241 M. Cf. also Lucretius IV 637 *ut quod aliis cibus est aliis fuat acre
venenum*: the first *aliis* (O, *alius* Q) is the metrical equivalent of *alis*
This possibility would equally establish a frequent clausula in colon 115.
Cf. next note.

122.86 *quae in vacuum venit*. The same problem as above 80.111, but
here no convenient *uacFom* turns up to solve our problem: Neue-
Wagener 1.111 produce *vaquom* as the reading of V in Cic. Phil. 7.7.19
(according to Clark OCT *ut tuaquom* V), see, however, Leumann-
Hofmann 215.

BIBLIOGRAPHY

(Major handbooks of classical studies, editions and dictionaries have been omitted. Reviews have been mentioned only if they were helpful in some way; the same applies to textbooks on metre and rhythm).

Abbott, K. M., W. A. Oldfather, H. V. Canter, *Index verborum in Ciceronis Rhetorica, necnon incerti auctoris libros ad Herennium*. Urbana, University of Illinois Press, 1964.

Abel, K., *Bauformen in Senecas Dialogen*, Heidelberg, Winter, 1967.

——, Review of M. Coccia, *I problemi del 'de ira' di Seneca alla luce dell' analisi stilistica* (Roma, Ateneo, 1957) in *Gnomon* 33, 1961 pp. 162-167.

Albertini, E., *La Composition dans les Ouvrages Philosophiques de Sénèque*, Paris, Boccard, 1923.

Albrecht, M. von, *Meister römischer Prosa von Cato bis Apuleius*. Heidelberg, Lothar Stiehm, 1971.

——, "Horazens Brief an Albius, Versuch einer metrischen Analyse und Interpretation", *Rh. M.* 114, 1971, pp. 193-209.

Alexander, W. H., "Seneca's Epistulae Morales, The Text Emended and Explained (I-LXV)", *University of California Publications*, Vol. 12, No. 5, pp. 57-88; (LXVI-XCII), Vol. 12, No. 8, pp. 135-164.

Axelson, Bertil, "Senecastudien, Kritische Bemerkungen zu Senecas Naturales Quaestiones", *Lunds Universitets Årsskrift*, N. F. Avd. 1. Bd 29. Nr. 3 Lund, 1933.

——, "Neue Senecastudien, Textkritische Beiträge zu Senecas Epistulae Morales", *Lunds Universitets Årsskrift*, N. F. Avd. 1 Bd 36. Nr. 1 Lund, Gleerup, 1939.

Ballou, Susan H., "The Clausula and the Higher Criticism", *TAPA* 46, 1915, p. 157-171.

Bernhard, M., *Der Stil des Apuleius von Madaura, Ein Beitrag zur Stilistik des Spätlateins*, Stuttgart, Kohlhammer, 1927 (repr. Amsterdam, Hakkert, 1965).

Blass, Friedrich, *Die Rhythmen der asianischen und römischen Kunstprosa*, Leipzig, 1905.

Bourgery, A., "Sur la prose métrique de Sénèque le philosophe", *Revue de Philologie* 34, 1910, 167-172.

——, *Sénèque Prosateur, Études Littéraires et Grammaticales sur le prose de Sénèque le Philosophe*. Paris, Les Belles Lettres, 1922.

Canter, H. V., "Rhetorical Elements in the Tragedies of Seneca", *University of Illinois Studies in Language and Literature*, Vol. X, 1 Febr. 1925. Urbana, University of Illinois Press.

Capua, F. Di, "L'evoluzione della prosa metrica nei primi tre secoli d. C. e la data dell' Ottavio di Minucio", *Didaskaleion* 2 1913, pp. 1-41.

Cousin, Jean, *Études sur Quintilien I-II*. Paris, Boivin, 1936.

Crusius, F., *Römische Metrik, Eine Einführung* 2. Aufl. neu bearbeitet von H. Rubenbauer. München, Hueber, 1955.

Curtius Rufus, Q., *Geschichte Alexanders des Grossen*. München, 1954. (In particular K. Müller's chapter 'Klauseln, Prosodie, rhythmische Analyse', pp. 755-782).

Drexler, H., *Einführung in die Römische Metrik*, Darmstadt, Wiss. Buchges. 1967.

——, "'Lizenzen' am Versanfang bei Plautus". *Zetemata* 38, München, 1965.

Enk, P. J., "The Latin Accent", *Mnemosyne* Ser. IV, VI 1953, pp. 93-109.

Fehling, Detlev, *Die Wiederholungsfiguren und ihr Gebrauch bei den Griechen vor Gorgias*. W. de Gruyter & Co., Berlin, 1969.

Fraenkel, E., *Iktus und Akzent im Lateinischen Sprechvers*, Berlin, Weidmann, 1928.

——, "Kolon und Satz I", *Nachr. Gött. Ges., Phil.-hist. Klasse*, 1932, 197-213. Kleine Beiträge I, 73-92.

——, "Kolon und Satz II", *Nachr. Gött. Ges., Phil.-hist. Klasse*, 1933, 319-354. Kleine Beiträge I, 93-130, Nachträge, 131-139.

——, "Noch einmal Kolon und Satz.", *Sitzungsberichte der Bayerischen Akad. d. Wiss.*, Phil.-hist. Klasse, 1965, Heft 2.

——, *Leseproben aus Reden Ciceros und Catos*. Roma, Edizioni di Storia e Letteratura, 1968.

Fridh, Åke, "Le problème de la passion des Saintes Perpetué et Félicité", *Acta Univ. Gothoburg. Studia Gr. et Lat. Gothob.* XXVI (pp. 12-45 on prose rhythm).

Gemoll, G., *Adnotationes criticae in L. Annaei Senecae epistulas morales*, Gymnasialprogramm Kreuzburg, 1886.

Gercke, A., *Seneca-studien*, Leipzig, Teubner, 1895.

Grimal, P., "La Composition dans les 'Dialogues' de Sénèque, I. - Le *De constantia sapientis*", *REA* 51, 1949, 246-261.

Groningen, B.A.v., "La composition littéraire archaïque grecque". *Verh. Kon. Ned. Ak. v. Wet., afd. Lett.* LXV 2, 1958.

Groot, A.W. de, *De Numero Oratorio Latino*, Groningen, Wolters, 1919.

——, *A Handbook of Antique Prose-rhythm, I, History of Greek Prose-metre*, Groningen, Wolters, 1918.

——, *Der Antike Prosa-rhythmus*, I, Groningen, Wolters, 1921.

——, *La prose métrique des anciens*. (Collection d'études latines publiées par la Société des Études Latines 2). Paris, 1926.

Grube, G.M.A., "A Greek Critic: Demetrius on Style", *Phoenix*, Suppl. Vol. IV, University of Toronto Press, 1961.

Haffter, H., review of E. Lindholm, *Stilistische Studien. Gnomon*, 1934, pp. 199-203.

Hagendahl, H., "La prose métrique d'Arnobe, Contributions à la connaissance de la prose littéraire de l'Empire", *Acta Universitatis Gotoburgensis*, XLII, 1, 1936.

Hammelrath, O., *Grammatisch-stilistische Beiträge zu den prosaischen Schriften des L. Annäus Seneca*. Beilage zum Programm des Gymnasiums zu Emmerich, 1895.

Hess, Georg, *Curae Annaeanae*, Beilage zum Programm des Königlichen Christianeums zu Altona. Altona, 1887.

Hijmans Jr., B.L., "Drama in Senecas Stoicism", *TAPA* 97, 1966, pp. 237-251.

——, "Two such opposed kings...", *Theta-Pi* II, 1973, pp. 40-59.

Hilgenfeld, H., "L. Annaei Senecae Epistulae Morales Quo Ordine et Quo Tempore Sint Scriptae Collectae Editae". Diss. Phil. Ienensium Ordine, Lipsiae, Teubner, 1890.

Johnson, W.R., *Luxuriance and Economy. Cicero and the Alien Style*. Univ. of Calif. Publ. Cl. St., Vol. 6, Berkeley, 1971.

Kent, R.G., *The Forms of Latin*. Baltimore, Linguistic Society of America, 1946.

Klammer, H., "Animadversiones Annaeanae Grammaticae". Diss. in Univ. Frider. Guil. Rhenana, Bonn, 1878. ·

Knook, P.C., "De overgang van metrisch tot rythmisch proza bij Cyprianus en Hieronymus". Diss. Amsterdam, Purmerend, 1932.

Kolár, A., "De orationum Liviano operi insertarum numerositate", *Mnemosyne* Ser. IV, VI, (1953) pp. 116-139.

Korzeniewski, D., review of Primmer, *Cicero Numerosus. Gymnasium* 77, 1970, pp. 249-252.

Koskenniemi, Heikki, "Studien zur Idee und Phraseologie des Griechischen Briefes Bis 400 n. Chr.", *Ann. Acad. Scient. Fenn.* Ser. B 102,2, Helsinki, 1956.

Koster, W.J.W., *Traité de métrique Grecque suivi d'un précis de métrique latine*. Leyde, Sijthoff, ⁴1966.

Laughton, Eric, Review of Fraenkel, *Leseproben* (as well as the Kolon u. Satz Series). *Journal of Roman Studies* 60, 1970, pp. 188-194.

Lausberg, H., *Handbuch der Literarischen Rhetorik, Eine Grundlegung der Literaturwissenschaft.* 2 vols., München, Hueber, 1960.

Lebek, W. D., "Verba Prisca, Die Anfänge des Archaisierens In der lateinischen Beredsamkeit und Geschichtsschreibung", *Hypomnemata* 25, Göttingen, 1970.

Leeman, A. D., *Orationis Ratio, The stylistic theories and practice of the roman orators, historians and philosophers.* 2 vols., Amsterdam, Hakkert, 1963.

Lindholm, E., *Stilistische Studien zur Erweiterung der Satzglieder im Lateinischen,* Lund, Gleerup, 1931.

Lindsay, W. M., *Early Latin Verse.* Oxford, Clarendon, 1922.

Löfstedt, Einar, "Zu Senecas Briefen", *Eranos,* Vol. 14, 1915, pp. 142-164.

Marouzeau, J., *Traité de stylistique latine,* 2e ed. Paris, 1946.

Maurach, G., *Der Bau von Senecas Epistulae Morales,* Heidelberg, Winter, 1970.

Mazzoli, Giancaro, *Seneca e la poesia,* Milano (Geschina) 1970.

Merchant, F. I., "Seneca the Philosopher and his theory of Style", *A.J.Ph.* 26, 1905, pp. 44-59.

Mewis, F., "De Senecae Philosophi Studiis Litterarum", Diss. Regimont (Königsberg), 1908.

Motto, A. L., *Seneca sourcebook: Guide to the Thought of Lucius Annaeus Seneca in the Extant Prose Works – Epistulae Morales, the Dialogi, De Beneficiis, De Clementia, and Quaestiones Naturales.* Amsterdam, Hakkert, 1970.

Müller, G. H., "Animadversions ad L. Annaei Senecae Epistulas quae sunt de oratione spectantes", Diss. Lips., 1910.

Müller, K., see Q. Curtius Rufus.

Müller, L., *De re metrica poetarum latinorum praeter Plautum et Terentium libri septem.* Editio altera, Petropoli et Lipsiae, 1894.

Muller J. fil., F., "Ad Senecae Naturales Quaestiones Observatiunculas", *Mnemosyne* 45, 1917, pp. 319-337.

Norden, Eduard, *Die antike Kunstprosa vom VI. Jahrhundert v. Chr. bis in die Zeit der Renaissance.* Fünfte Aufl., Stuttgart, Teubner, 1958, 2 vols.

Nougaret, L., *Traité de Métrique Latine Classique.* 3ᵉ édition, Paris, Klicksieck, 1963.

——, "Les problèmes d'édition", *REL* 44, 1966, pp. 122-131.

——, "Analyse Verbale Comparée du *"De Signis"* et des *"Bucoliques".* Collection d'études Latines, Série Scientifique XXX, Paris, Les Belles Lettres, 1966.

Opitz, E., *De latinitate Senecae,* Gymnasialprogramm, Naumburg, 1871.

Otterlo, W.A.A. van, "Untersuchungen über Begriff, Anwendung und Enstehung der griechischen Ringkomposition", *Meded. Ned. Ac.* 7, 3 (1944).

——, "Eine merkwürdige Kompositionsform der älteren griechischen Literatur", *Mnemosyne* 12 (1945) pp. 192-207.

——, "De ringcompositie als opbouwprincipe in de epische gedichten van Homerus", *Verhand. Ned. Kon. Ac.* N.R. 51, 1 (1948).

Otto, A., *Die Sprichwörter und sprichwörtlichen Redensarten der Römer.* Leipzig, 1890. Nachträge zu A. Otto, ——, Eingeleitet ... v. R. Häussler, Hildesheim, 1968.

Parker, L. P. E., *Greek Metric 1957-1970,* Lustrum 15, 1970, pp. 37-98.

Parrish, W.M., *The rhythm of oratorical prose. Studies in Rhetoric and Public Speaking in Honor of James Albert Winans.* New York, Russell & Russell, 1962, pp. 217-231.

Perini, G. Bernardi, *l'Accento Latino. Cenni teoretici e norme pratiche.* Bologna, 1964.

Primmer, Adolf, *Cicero Numerosus, Studien zum antiken Prosarhythmus.* Wien, 1968. (Österreichische Akademie der Wissenschaften, Philosophisch - historische Klasse, Sitzungsberichte, 257. Band).

Rauschning, O., "De Latinitate L. Annaei Senecae Philosophi", Diss. Philol. in Acad. Ienensi Ord., Regimonti Prussorum, 1876.

Raven, D. S., *Latin Metre, An Introduction.* London, Faber & Faber, 1965.

Richards, W.J., "Gebed By Seneca, Die Stoisyn, 'n Godsdienshistoriese studie met verwysing na aanrakingspunte in die Voorsocratici". Diss. Utrecht, 1964.

Rieger, H., "Observationes Annaeanae". Diss. Freiburg in Br., 1889.

Rolland, E., "De l'Influence de Sénèque le Père et des Rhéteurs sur Sénèque le Philosophe", *Rec. de Trav. publ. par la fac. de philos. et lettres*, 32ᵉ fasc., Université de Gand, Gand, Van Goethem, 1906.

Schenkeveld, D. M., *Studies in Demetrius On Style*, Amsterdam, Hakkert, 1964 (and Chicago, Argonaut, 1967).

Schmid, Walter, "Über die klassische Theorie und Praxis des antiken Prosarhythmus", *Hermes, Zeitschr. f. klass. Philologie*, Einzelschr. 12, Wiesbaden, Steiner 1959.

Schrijvers, P. H., "Horror ac divina voluptas, Études sur la poétique et la poésie de Lucrèce". Diss. Amsterdam, Hakkert, 1970.

Sidney Allen, W., *Vox Latina, a Guide to the pronunciation of Classical Latin*. Cambridge, UP, 1965.

——, *Accent and Rhythm, prosodic features of Latin and Greek : a study in theory and reconstruction*. Cambridge, UP, 1973.

Skutsch, F., *Plautinisches und Romanisches, Studien zur plautinischen Prosodie*. 2. unveränderte Aufl., Stuttgart, 1970. (Repr. of Leipzig, 1892).

Sommer, F., *Handbuch der lateinischen Laut- und Formenlehre*. 2. u. 3. Aufl., Heidelberg, Winter, 1914.

Stella-Maranca, F., *Seneca Giureconsulto*, Lanciano, Fratelli Mancini, 1926.

Steyns, D., "Étude sur les Métaphores et les Comparaisons dans les œuvres en prose de Sénèque le Philosophe", *Rec. de trav. publ. par la Fac. de Philos. et Lettres*, 33ᵉ fasc., Université de Gand, Gand, 1907.

Sturtevant, E.H. and Kent, R.G., "Elision and Hiatus in Latin Prose and Verse", *TAPA* XLVI (1915), pp. 129-155.

Thraede, Klaus, "Grundzüge griechisch-römischer Brieftopik", *Zetemata*, Monographien zur klassischen Altertumswissenschaft, Heft 48, München, Beck, 1970.

Trillitzsch, W., *Senecas Beweisführung*, Berlin, Akademie Verl., 1962.

Waszink, J. H., "The technique of the clausula in Tertullian's *De anima*", *Vig. Christ.* 4, 1950, pp. 212-245.

Weber, H., "De Senecae Philosophi dicendi genere Bioneo". Diss. inaug., Marpurg., 1895.

Wellek, R., and Warren, A., *Theory of Literature*, Third Edition, Penguin Books, 1968.

Westerman S.J., J.F., "Archaische en Archaistische Woordkunst". Diss. Amsterdam, GU., 1939.

Wilhelm, F., "Curtius und der jüngere Seneca", *Rhetorische Studien*, herausg. von Dr. E. Drerup, 15. Heft, Paderborn, Schöningh, 1928.

Winterbottom, M., "Problems in Quintilian". *Bull. Inst. Class. Stud. U. of London*, Suppl. 25, 1970.

Wirth, H., "De Vergili apud Senecam Philosophum Usu". Dissertatio inaug. (...), Freiburg-i-Br. (1900).

Zander, C., *Eurythmia vel compositio rythmica prosae antiquae*. 3 vols., Leipzig, 1910-1914.

Zielinski, Th., "Das Clauselgesetz in Ciceros Reden. Grundzüge einer oratorischen Rhythmik", *Philologus*, Supplementband IX, Leipzig, 1904, pp. 589-844.

——, "Das Ausleben des Clauselgesetzes in der römischen Kunstprosa", *Philologus*, Supplementband X, Leipzig, 1907, pp. 429-466.

——, "Der Constructive Rhythmus in Ciceros Reden. Der oratorischen Rhythmik Zweiter Teil", *Philologus*, Supplementband XIII, Leipzig, 1920, pp. 1-295.

Zirin, R.A., *The Phonological Basis of Latin Prosody*, The Hague, 1970 (Janua Linguarum, Series Practica 99).

GENERAL INDEX

Abel, K. 3, 134n12
abiectio 151
accent (shifting) 27n1, 108 + n6
Acilius Buta 161, 165, 166
Aeschylus 131, 132n6
agere 140, 142, 163n56
ait 65n1, 74n1, 171f
Albrecht, M. von 2n4
Albertini, E. 145 + n32, 152n45
alliteration 139
allocutio 142
amplification 1
ἀναβολή 133
anacrusis 112
anaphora, see *repetitio*
anceps 106n2
antithesis, see contrast
Apuleius *Met.* 6.18(142.9): 119
Aquila Romanus 18: 98n30, 99, 100n32
Aristides *Techn. Rh.* 167: 99, 100n32
Aristotle
 Met. 1087b36: 83n2
 Rhet. 1409b13: 83n1
arithmetical center 136, 144, 156
Asinius Pollio 157, 159f
askesis 138
assonance 139
Auctor ad Herennium
 4.18: 158
 4.27: 83, 87n11, 92n20, 93n22
Auftakt, see anacrusis

Beltrami, A. 118n12, 140n27
bonae artes 152
bona mens 142
brevity, see colon

Caligula 103 + n37
Cancik, H. 2n3, 145n33, 161n52
Catullus 132n6
 68b: 131
chiasm 8n1, 45, 89, 93n22, 139
Chinese Ball 133
Chinese Box 2, 133, 136
Cicero 83, 157, 159f
 synaloephe in — 83, 107n5
 on clausula 107n5

morphological definition of clausula 118
style of letters 103f
Seneca's judgment of Cicero's style 157f
 Ad fam. 10,1-2-3; 12,2-3-23: 103n39
 Ad Att. 15,13-13a; 16.9-11: 103n39
 De rep. 1.52: 172
 Brutus
  33: 116n10
  34: 16n35
  173: 146n35
  244: 146n35
  267: 146n35
  287: 100n33
 de inv. 1.92: 146n35
 de orat.
  2.83: 146n35
  3.104: 151n38
  3.193: 116n10
  3.205: 146n35
 opt.gen. 12: 146n35
 Orator
  149: 100n33
  170: 116n10
  176: 146n35
  193: 116n10
  212: 3n7
  213: 125
  215: 170
  217: 170
  218: 113
  225: 101
 part.or. 81: 146n35
 *Cat.*I, 1.1-3.8-4.8-7.16-7.18-11.28-
  12.31: 169
 *Cat.*II, 3.5-5.10-6.12-9.19-9.20-10.23-
  12.27-13.29: 169f
 De signis 167
  2.3-4.7-5.9-8.18-10.22-10.23-14.32-
  16.35-20.42-20.44: 168
 Manil. 30: 85n8
 Phil. 7.19: 172
 Quinct. 56: 86
 Rosc.
  30: 87f
  138: 87
CIL 2.5181.50; 8.403: 172
circular composition 133, 137, **144**